> "Nolo's home page is worth bookmarking."
> —WALL STREET JOURNAL

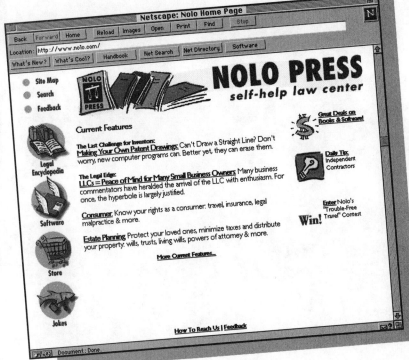

LEGAL INFORMATION ONLINE

www.nolo.com

24 hours a day

AT THE NOLO PRESS SELF-HELP LAW CENTER ON THE WEB, YOU'LL FIND

- Nolo's comprehensive Legal Encyclopedia, with links to other online resources
- Downloadable demos of Nolo software and sample chapters of many Nolo books
- An online law store with a secure online ordering system
- Our ever-popular lawyer jokes
- Discounts and other good deals, our hilarious Shark Talk game

THE NOLO NEWS

Stay on top of important legal changes with Nolo's quarterly magazine, *The Nolo News.*
Start your free one-year subscription by filling out and mailing the response card in the back
of this book. With each issue, you'll get legal news about topics that affect you every day, reviews
of legal books by other publishers, the latest Nolo catalog, scintillating advice from Auntie Nolo
and a fresh batch of our famous lawyer jokes.

FIRST EDITION

Contractors' and Homeowners' Guide to

MECHANICS' LIENS

by Attorney Stephen R. Elias

NOLO PRESS ☆ BERKELEY

Your Responsibility When Using a Self-Help Law Book

We've done our best to give you useful and accurate information in this book. But laws and procedures change frequently and are subject to differing interpretations. If you want legal advice backed by a guarantee, see a lawyer. If you use this book, it's your responsibility to make sure that the facts and general advice contained in it are applicable to your situation.

Keeping Up-to-Date

To keep its books up-to-date, Nolo Press issues new printings and new editions periodically. New printings reflect minor legal changes and technical corrections. New editions contain major legal changes, major text additions or major reorganizations. To find out if a later printing or edition of any Nolo book is available, call Nolo Press at 510-549-1976 or check the catalog in the *Nolo News,* our quarterly newspaper. You can also contact us on the Internet at www.nolo.com.

To stay current, follow the "Update" service in the *Nolo News.* You can get a free one-year subscription by sending us the registration card in the back of the book. In another effort to help you use Nolo's latest materials, we offer a 25% discount off the purchase of the new edition of your Nolo book when you turn in the cover of an earlier edition. (See the "Special Upgrade Offer" in the back of the book.)

First Edition	November 1998
Editor	Stephen Fishman
Illustrations	IMSI (in San Rafael) The Learning Company (© 1996 The Learning Company Inc. and its licensors.)
Cover Design	Terri Hearsh
Book Design	Stephanie Harolde
Proofreading	Joe Sadusky
Index	Patricia Deminna
Printing	Custom Printing Company

Elias, Stephen
   Contractors' and homeowners' guide to mechanics' liens: get paid if you're a contractor don't pay twice if you're a homeowner / by Stephen Elias.
   p. cm.
   Includes index.
   ISBN 0-87337-467-3
   1. Mechanics' liens--California--Popular works.   I. Title.
KFC229.Z9E43   1998
346.79402'4--DC21

          98-23648
          CIP

ACKNOWLEDGMENTS

I wish to express my deepest gratitude to:

Steve Fishman, my editor, whose ability to find the devil in the details is truly remarkable.

Ron Kelly, a Berkeley arbitrator and mediator who specializes in owner/contractor disputes. Ron, who is also a licensed contractor, gave the manuscript a careful going over and added real-world relevance. Ron also made substantial creative contributions to the book's chapter on dispute resolution. Ron can be reached at 510-843-6074.

Gary Ransome Esq., author of *The Contractor's Legal Kit*. Gary also gave the manuscript a careful review from his perspective as a construction lawyer and operator of the Construction Law Hotline. (Details are in Chapter 8.) Gary can be reached at 831-476-8784.

Stephanie Harolde, my longtime Nolo friend, who somehow managed to wrestle the manuscript into a book.

Terri Hearsh, another valued Nolo friend, for her cover design.

Howard and Patti Harvey, who were kind enough to give up some of their sacred Brannan Mountain time to give me a reality check.

Nolo book publisher Mary Randolph, Nolo online publisher Ralph Warner, and the rest of the marvelous folks at Nolo who will be there to keep the Nolo faith, get the book into the libraries and bookstores, sell the book over the phone and world wide.

ABOUT THE AUTHOR

Stephen R. Elias received a law degree from Hastings College of Law in 1969. He practiced in California, New York and Vermont until 1980, when he decided to make a full-time career of helping non-lawyers understand and use the law. Steve has authored and edited a number of other Nolo books. At present, Steve is Associate Publisher of Nolo Press and is involved in a variety of book, software and online projects, as well as minding the many tasks that make Nolo Press a reality— and that make it possible for a book such as this to be born.

TABLE OF CONTENTS

INTRODUCTION

Start Here

CHAPTER 1

How Mechanics' Lien Laws Work

CHAPTER 2

Preparing and Serving the Preliminary Notice

CHAPTER 3

Record Your Mechanics' Lien

CHAPTER 4

The Stop Notice Remedy Against the Owner

CHAPTER 5

The Stop Notice Remedy Against the Lender

CHAPTER 6

Understanding Your Contract Remedy

CHAPTER 7

Recovery Under a Payment Bond

CHAPTER 8

Going to Court

CHAPTER 9

Mechanics' Liens: An Owner's Perspective

CHAPTER 10

Do You Have a Defense?

CHAPTER 11

Removing a Mechanics' Lien From Your Property Record

CHAPTER 12

Negotiating a Settlement

APPENDIX A

Statutes: California Codes

APPENDIX B

Tear-Out Forms

APPENDIX C

Using the Forms Disk

Start Here

To begin at the beginning, mechanics' liens have nothing to do with automobile mechanics. Rather they are used to collect debts owed for work or materials contributed to construction and real estate improvement. However, if an auto mechanic contributes to the improvement of real estate, the mechanic can use this remedy as well as a carpenter, plumber or electrician—if, for instance, an auto mechanic repairs an earth mover or dump truck being used on a construction project.

The first eight chapters of this book are for those of you who provide labor, services or equipment to a private work of improvement, and those of you who supply materials that are actually used or consumed in a private work of improvement.

A "private work of improvement" includes virtually anything that contributes to the construction, modification, improvement or demolition of buildings—and the grading and landscaping of lots and tracts—that is paid for out of private rather than government funds.

Virtually all home-improvement work comes within this category—no matter how small the job—as does the construction of most residential housing (HUD projects excepted) and commercial office space, factories, shopping malls and factories.

Chapters 9 though 11 are for those of you who are owners of real estate that is being improved. This includes anyone—other than a government contractor—who hires someone to remodel their house, install a swimming pool, construct an office building, develop a shopping mall or build a factory.

Finally, Chapter 12 is for everybody who is involved with a private work of improvement and has a mechanics' lien problem. It helps you to negotiate a settlement without going to court.

Who this book won't help

This book will not help cities, counties, school districts or other public property owners. Nor is it written for people who contribute their labor, services and materials to publicly funded works of improvement—that is, projects contracted for by a public entity—such as the State of California, cities and counties and public schools. If your work or ownership involves public funds or property, stop reading here and return the book for a refund. If you are providing materials for a construction project and aren't sure whose money is being used to fund it, find out before you proceed further with this book.

A. IF YOU'RE IN THE CONSTRUCTION BUSINESS

This section is for those who make contributions to works of improvement. Skip to Section B if you are the owner of property being improved and are being affected by a mechanics' lien or other construction-related legal remedy.

This book—and the remedies it addresses—arises from the way the construction business works. The money for construction projects flows downhill from the bank all the way down to the flooring company—typically the last in a long chain of materials suppliers. If everyone gets paid for their labor and materials, there are no problems. But in the construction business non-payment is both frequent and painful.

If you are facing a non-payment problem, the mechanics' lien remedy offers a marvelous solution. If you record a mechanics' lien against the real estate being improved, the owner can't easily sell or refinance the property without first paying off the debt secured by your lien. This means that sooner or later you must be paid, assuming that you take the necessary steps to enforce the lien.

But, marvelous as this remedy is, it is also somewhat complex and involves some picky paperwork. Rest assured, however, that you and any other contractor are perfectly capable of getting it right as long as you proceed in an organized manner. But get it right you must. This book takes you step by step through this process. It also takes you step by step through stop notice procedures—another powerful collection remedy available to those in the construction trades.

B. IF YOU'RE AN OWNER

This section is for those who own real estate that is being improved. Skip to Section C if you are a contractor, subcontractor, materials supplier or other contributor to a work of improvement.

Chapters 9 through 11 provide you, the owner of property being improved, with some tools for dealing with mechanics' liens and stop notices—the two most common special remedies invoked by contributors to works of improvement. We tell you step by step how to obtain a court order that removes a mechanics' lien from your property, and how to respond to a stop notice. We also tell you how to assess whether a mechanics' lien or stop notice claimant has taken the correct legal procedures—without which their claim is no good.

Preventive measures

There are many steps you can take before work ever begins to avoid being on the receiving end of a mechanics' lien or stop notice. Although Chapter 9 suggests how you can minimize the risks of having a mechanics' lien recorded against your property, we don't systematically cover these steps in this book. If you are a homeowner planning a repair or remodeling job and are interested in preventive measures,

consider reading *How to Hire a Home Improvement Contractor Without Getting Chiseled,* by Tom Philbin (St. Martin's Press), or *Renovating with a Contractor,* by Brenner and Kelly (Taylor Publishing Co.).

C. STATUTORY AUTHORITY

The remedies in this book are driven by specific statutes primarily found in the California Civil Code but also in the California Code of Civil Procedure and the California Business and Professions Code. At the end of most chapters we provide a section called Legal Authority in which we briefly identify the various statutes that underlie the discussion in that chapter. This will prevent the text from being cluttered up with statutory references while at the same time providing you with a starting point for doing more research.

For your convenience, Appendix A in the back of the book contains the full text of all of the applicable statutes.

ABOUT THE DISK

Included at the back of this book is a 3-1/2" PC/MS DOS computer disk containing files with word processing (rich text format or RTF) and text-only versions of all tear-out forms included in Appendix B. For specific instructions for using the forms on the disk, see the Disk User's Guide contained in Appendix C.

Macintosh Users: Most newer Macintosh computers (with a 3-1/2" SuperDrive) can also read the enclosed disk. Microsoft Word and WordPerfect for the Macintosh can open and convert the rich text format (RTF) versions of each file.

NOTES AND ICONS

Throughout the text, we have included special notations and icons to help organize the material and underscore particular points:

 A legal or common sense tip helps you understand or comply with legal requirements.

 "Fast track" lets you know that you may be able to skip some material that doesn't apply to your situation.

 A caution to slow down and consider potential problems.

 A reminder.

 Instructions or notes about using the files on the mechanics' lien disk.

 A suggestion to consult another book or resource. ■

CHAPTER 1

How Mechanics' Lien Laws Work

CHAPTER 1

How Mechanics' Lien Laws Work

As you well know, instead of payment in advance for work done and materials provided, you usually get paid after the fact. This, of course, is because in most construction projects money flows downhill—from the bank to the owner to the prime (general) contractor, to the subcontractor, to the supplier of materials and services.

Where you are in the money flow will usually dictate how soon you get paid and how likely it is that you will experience payment problems. Stated differently, the more opportunities there are for diversion of the money flow upstream, the more likely there will be payment problems down below.

For example, in a typical new home construction project, the construction money must pass through three or four levels before it finally reaches the typical provider of construction materials:

- banker to owner (1)
- owner to general contractor (2)
- general contractor to subcontractor (3), and
- subcontractor to the subcontractor's materials suppliers (4)

Clearly a lot can happen to come between a materials supplier and the money due for materials supplied to a work of improvement.

Payment problems arise for many reasons. Sometimes it is a straightforward fiscal issue—not enough money to go around. Other times, someone upstream isn't paid and so can't pay the downstream people.

Probably the most common reason why payment disputes arise is because of disputes over the quality or quantity of the goods and services delivered. Similarly, a general contractor can withhold payment from a subcontractor because of shoddy performance (at least from the general contractor's viewpoint). And a subcontractor, of course, can refuse to pay for shoddy materials.

Other reasons for nonpayment may be an unexpected cost or delay, or a substantial and unauthorized deviation from the original plans.

All this decision making after the goods and services have already been delivered frequently leads to disputes that can easily interfere with people getting paid.

If possession is 9/10ths of the law—and remember the owner of the work of improvement already has received the goods or services in dispute—you would expect there to be very little law left for anyone else. Ordinarily you would be right, but in construction-related disputes you are not. As it turns out, the legal remedy known as a mechanics' lien can be a great equalizer.

The mechanics' lien remedy comes from the California Constitution (Art XIV, §3), which states:

"Mechanics', persons furnishing materials, artisans, and laborers of every class, shall have a lien upon the property upon which they have bestowed labor or furnished material for the value of such labor done and material furnished; and the Legislature shall provide, by law, for the speedy and efficient enforcement of such liens."

Without going into detail here (but we do in later chapters), the mechanics' lien in essence gives the contractor enough leverage to bargain with the owner on an equal basis. Under the legislation enacted in accord with the constitutional provision's mandate [Title 15 of the Civil Code starting at §3082] a person asserting his or her mechanics' lien remedy can, if payment is not forthcoming:

- tie up the underlying property (that is, the property can't easily be sold or refinanced with clear title), and,
- if necessary, go to court to have the property sold at auction.

What this means, of course, is that the owner will have to pay a price—a lien on his or her property—if someone working on, or contributing materials to, the work of improvement doesn't get paid. The result? Most owners bend over backwards to avoid payment disputes. They also do what they can to make sure that the general contractor is making sure that everybody else gets paid because if someone isn't paid, it may well be the owner's property that will be at risk.

In effect, the mechanics' lien remedy is best thought of as:

- a strong motivation for the owner to make sure you get paid

- powerful bargaining leverage for you in case of a payment dispute, and

- a prerequisite to filing a foreclosure action on the property subject to the work of improvement.

And, for reasons explained in Chapter 3, if payment is not forthcoming, it puts you in the strongest possible position as a creditor.

There are other remedies available to you if you suffer payment problems. These remedies are separate from and independent of the mechanics' lien. You can also:

- freeze and then collect payment from any construction funds that are still in the hands of the lender or owner (except that the prime (general) contractor can't go after the owner's funds), and

- file a breach of contract action against whoever it was who was responsible for paying you.

An important reminder

Even if you don't qualify for the mechanics' lien or stop notice remedies, perhaps because you didn't follow the correct procedures, you still have the right to sue the party you contracted with. We discuss contractual remedies in Chapter 6.

Section B, below, introduces you to each nonpayment remedy and explains how it may apply to your particular situation. Subsequent chapters provide step-by-step guidance for using these remedies if and when they become appropriate.

THE QUICK AND LEGAL ROUTE FOR CLAIMS UNDER $5,000

For those readers familiar with courts and lawsuits, being able to sue may not seem like much of a remedy. However, if your claim is in the neighborhood of $5,000 or less (or it is for more but you are willing to settle for less), you can use the Small Claims Court to obtain a judgment for breach of contract against whoever hired you. Small Claims Court has proven to be a quick and inexpensive remedy for these types of disputes.

If you do obtain a judgment (in any court, including Small Claims Court), the law gives you a very powerful collection device against any judgment debtor who is required to hold a license issued by the Contractors' State Licensing Board. This includes general contractors, subcontractors, architects, engineers and surveyors. All you have to do is send the judgment to the Contractors' State Licensing Board. If you are not paid within 90 days, the judgment debtor's license may be suspended and remain suspended until you are paid— including costs and interest.

In Chapter 8 we tell you more about how to enforce a money judgment against a judgment debtor licensed by the Contractors' State Licensing Board.

A. WHO CAN BENEFIT FROM CHAPTERS 1-8 OF THIS BOOK?

If you are contributing services or supplying materials for any project involving the privately funded improvement of privately owned real estate—or supplying machines or other equipment for such a purpose—you necessarily must be concerned about payment. Chances are you are providing your goods or services under a loose sort of credit arrangement: You'll do the work or deliver the materials today and get paid next week (or next month, or next quarter or when the person hiring your services or purchasing your materials gets paid). If you do business under these conditions, you will benefit from at least some of the first eight chapters—even if you don't have a non-payment problem.

1. Home Improvement Projects

Payment arrangements for many home improvement construction projects may be exceedingly simple:

- A licensed contractor to a Home Depot supply agent: "Deliver a load of Grade A redwood 2 by 8's later this week and put it on my bill."

- A homeowner to an electrician: "I need a separate 220v line on my deck for my new spa. Bill me for labor and materials."

- A general contractor (hired to add a bathroom to a single family residence) to a tile layer: "I'll need you to start installing the tile on (a specific date) and to finish by (specific date). Bill me at your normal rate for labor, plus materials."

Home improvements are defined by statute as "the repairing, remodeling, altering, converting or modernizing of, or adding to, residential property and shall include, but not be limited to, the construction, erection, replacement or improvement of driveways, swimming pools, including spas and hot tubs, terraces, patios, awnings, storm windows, landscaping, fences, porches, garages, fallout shelters, basements and other improvements of the structures or land which is adjacent to a dwelling house."

Any person involved in any of these activities will benefit from some or all of the remedies covered in these beginning eight chapters.

Also benefiting from these chapters will be:

- anyone involved in the installation of home improvement goods or furnishing improvement services, such as carpeting, texture coating, fencing, air conditioning or heating equipment and termite extermination, and

- anyone who supplies any goods that are to be attached to real property, even if they could later

be disconnected, such as light fixtures, doors and temporary buildings.

2. Commercial and New Home Construction Projects—and Site Improvements

Especially for large projects, there may be literally hundreds of separate contractual arrangements. The owner-developer may contract with an architect. Once the plans are approved, the owner-developer hires a prime contractor, who typically will enter into separate contracts with a full list of subcontractors—graders, ditch diggers, steel and concrete workers, carpenters, masons, electricians, plumbers, painters and roofers, dry wallers, haulers and equipment and machine lessors—and many of these subcontractors will be using subcontractors of their own. The contractors, subcontractors and sub-subcontractors—if any—will be getting their supplies from many different suppliers, which in many cases will be delivered to the work site by many different haulers.

All of these contributors to projects involving the improvement of real estate—from architecture to site improvement to finish labor—will benefit from one or more of the remedies in this part of the book.

B. AN OVERVIEW OF YOUR REMEDIES

Here we set out the basic steps you need to take to maximize your chances of getting paid. Section C discusses these steps in more detail.

Do you have a license?

If you are required to have a license, failure to have one during the time you supplied your materials or contributed your services probably will prevent you from enforcing any of these remedies in court. An exception to this rule can be made if the non-licensure was accidental. However, this exception is rarely successfully invoked. The courts have no patience with unlicensed contractors.

1. Subcontractors, Materials Providers and Lessors of Equipment

Even if you don't anticipate a payment problem, if you are a subcontractor, general contractor working as a subcontractor for another general contractor, materials provider or lessor of equipment, you should serve a preliminary notice on the owner, prime (general) contractor and lender within 20 days of the day you start providing materials or labor to the project site. (Chapter 2 covers the preliminary notice in detail.)

Always serve the preliminary notice

Although serving the preliminary notice may seem like a hostile act, this requirement is a strict one—no preliminary notice, no mechanics' lien for goods and services contributed earlier than the 20-day period just prior to when you do finally serve the notice. Since service of the preliminary notice is required by law (if you wish to preserve your mechanics' lien, stop notice and payment bond rights), you have no need to apologize for it.

If there is even a small hint of a payment problem, you should consider recording a Claim of Mechanics' Lien—against the property being improved—with the county recorder's office (Chapter 3). Thankfully, there is not quite the same urgency about this deadline as there is with the preliminary notice. You can record your

Claim of Mechanics' Lien any time within 30 days after all work on the project (yours and everyone else's) has been completed or halted (and sometimes up to 60 or 90 days after work stops). This subject is covered in Chapter 3, Section E.

If the lender or owner are in possession of construction funds loaned for the work of improvement in question, you can serve what's known as a stop notice on either or both of them in order to secure the payment you expect to receive for your labor or materials. To be effective, the stop notice on the lender must be accompanied by a payment bond. (See Chapter 5 for more on bonded stop notices.)

Always negotiate if possible

If it appears that payment will likely be a problem, you should immediately start thinking about negotiating a solution. The longer a payment dispute festers, the harder it becomes to resolve it. See Chapter 12 for some negotiating tips and information about how to get a mediator to help you if outside help is needed.

If recording the mechanics' lien doesn't produce payment, you can file a lawsuit to enforce the mechanic's lien and stop notice. (See Chapter 8.) You must accomplish the filing within 90 days of the date you record your Claim of Mechanics' Lien. You may also file a lawsuit for breach of contract (which usually is part of the lawsuit to enforce the mechanics' lien). (See Chapters 6 and 8.)

2. Prime (Original, General) Contractors and On-Site Wage Laborers

If you are the prime contractor (also commonly referred to as the general contractor and original contractor) who reports directly to the owner, or you worked on site for wages, you should serve a preliminary notice on the lender within 20 days of the day you start providing materials or labor to the site (optional by statute but still a good idea).

If there is even a small hint of a payment problem, you should record a Claim of Mechanics' Lien—against the property being improved—with the county recorder's office. (See Chapter 3.) Thankfully, there is not quite the same urgency about this deadline as there is with the preliminary notice. You can record your Claim of Mechanics' Lien any time within 30 days after work on the project has been completed or halted (and sometimes up to 60 or 90 days after work stops).

Employees who haven't been paid need not sue

While an employee of a licensed contractor technically has the right to sue the owner under the mechanics' lien laws, in practice such suits are rarely brought because it's much easier to obtain redress for unpaid wages from the California Labor Commissioner's Office. This state agency helps resolve wage disputes between employees and employers.

If the lender is in possession of construction funds loaned for the work of improvement in question, you can and should serve what's known as a stop notice on it to secure payment of the funds you expect to receive for your labor or materials. To be effective, the stop notice on the lender must be accompanied by a payment bond. (See Chapter 5 for more on bonded stop notices.)

Always negotiate if possible

If it appears that payment will likely be a problem, you should immediately start thinking about negotiating a solution. The longer a payment dispute festers, the harder it becomes to resolve. See Chapter 12 for some negotiating tips and information about how to get a mediator to help you if outside help is needed.

If recording the mechanics' lien doesn't produce payment, you can file a lawsuit to enforce the mechanic's lien and stop notice. (See Chapter 8.) You must accomplish the filing within 90 days of the date you record your Claim of Mechanics' Lien. You may also file a lawsuit for breach of contract (which usually is part of the lawsuit to enforce the mechanics' lien). (See Chapters 6 and 8.)

3. If You Contracted Directly With Owner Other Than the Prime Contractor and On-Site Wage Laborers

If you contracted directly with the owner to perform your services or supply materials to the work of improvement, you should serve a preliminary notice on the lender—assuming there is one—within 20 days of the day you start providing materials or labor to the site. (See Chapter 2.) You aren't required to serve a preliminary notice on the owner or the prime (general) contractor. However, serving a preliminary notice won't hurt and is a good idea, just to be safe.

Always serve preliminary notice on lender

Although serving the preliminary notice may seem like a hostile act, the 20-day deadline is a strict one—no timely preliminary notice, no mechanics' lien for goods or services contributed prior to the time that you do ultimately serve the preliminary notice.

If there is even a small hint of a payment problem, you should record a Claim of Mechanics' Lien against the property being improved with the county recorder's office. (See Chapter 3.) Thankfully, there is not quite the same urgency about this deadline as there is with the preliminary notice. You can record your Claim of Mechanics' Lien any time within 30 days after work on the project has been completed or halted (and sometimes up to 60 or 90 days after work stops).

If the lender or owner is in possession of construction funds loaned for the work of improvement in question, you can and should serve what's known as a stop notice on either or both of them in order to secure payment of the funds you expect to receive for your labor or materials. To be effective, the stop notice on the lender must be accompanied by a payment bond. (See Chapter 5 for more on bonded stop notices.)

Always negotiate if possible

If it appears that payment will likely be a problem, you should immediately start thinking about negotiating a solution. The longer a payment dispute festers, the harder it becomes to resolve. See Chapter 12 for some negotiating tips and information about how to get a mediator to help you if outside help is needed.

If recording the mechanics' lien doesn't produce payment, you can file a lawsuit to enforce the mechanic's lien and stop notice. (See Chapter 8.) You must accomplish the filing within 90 days of the date you record your Claim of Mechanics' Lien. You may also file a lawsuit for breach of contract (which usually is part of the lawsuit to enforce the mechanics' lien). (See Chapters 6 and 8.)

4. Design Professionals' Lien for Services Before Work of Improvement Begins

A special lien remedy exists for design professionals—certificated architects, registered professional engineers and licensed land surveyors. If a building permit or other government approval has been issued for the project, you may record a lien for the services you render before the actual work of improvement is commenced. This lien is in addition to mechanics' lien rights that apply once the work of improvement has commenced. To take advantage of this lien, you will need to:

- serve a written demand for payment
- record your lien with the county recorder, and
- file a court action to enforce the lien no later than 90 days after you record it and before the work of improvement begins.

Once the work of improvement begins, you may take advantage of the regular mechanics' lien remedy in the same way as others who contract directly with the owner. (See Section B3, above.) We tell you how to use the Design Professionals' Lien in Chapter 3, Section H.

C. A Closer Look at the Remedies and the Steps Necessary to Use Them

Here we describe in more detail the main steps and remedies outlined in Section B.

1. The Preliminary Notice

The function of the preliminary notice is to let all interested parties know that labor, services, equipment or materials are being contributed to the work of improvement and that the contributor reserves the right, if he or she isn't paid, to:

- record a Claim of Mechanics' lien against the property
- serve a stop notice against available construction funds loaned for the work of improvement in question, and
- proceed against a payment bond, if there is one.

With three exceptions, to take advantage of the mechanics' lien, stop notice and payment bond remedies a contributor to a work of improvement must serve a preliminary notice on:

- each owner of record (whoever is on the deed)
- the prime (general) contractor (if there is one), and
- the lender (this can include an insurance company doling out funds to repair covered real estate).

The people who must serve a preliminary notice on all three of these parties are contributors who customarily do not contract directly with the owner—typically subcontractors and materials suppliers.

The three exceptions are:

1. The prime (general) contractor need not serve a preliminary notice on the owner, but must serve a preliminary notice on the lender if there is one.

2. Anyone paid wages for on-site work need not serve a preliminary notice on the owner or lender.

3. Any other contributor to the work of improvement or supplier of materials who contracts directly with the owner need not serve a preliminary notice on the owner, but must serve the lender.

If you have already started working on a project but blew the 20-day deadline, you may still serve a notice and pursue your mechanics' lien remedy, but the mechanics' lien will only apply to work or materials you contribute during the 20-day period prior to your notice and all work and materials furnished after the preliminary notice is served.

Be safe and serve the preliminary notice

Even if you are exempt from some or all of the preliminary notice requirements, we strongly recommend that you serve a preliminary notice on all three parties—as we later instruct in Chapter 2. It's easy to do and serves as a hedge against a later argument by a clever lawyer that for some reason you were not exempted from the filing requirement after all.

When and how to serve the preliminary notice is discussed in Chapter 2.

2. The Claim of Mechanics' Lien

A mechanics' lien is a right that the law gives anyone who provides labor or materials to a privately owned "work of improvement" to claim payment out of the property that has been improved.

Under this law, your right to claim payment arises retroactively from the date the work of improvement commenced, which was when some overt activity first occurred at the work of improvement site, such as the demolition of existing structures or installation of a power pole.

If you aren't paid, you will have the same rights as a mortgage company, which means you can foreclose on the property and, if necessary, have it sold at auction. And just like a mortgage company, your right to payment precedes all liens and encumbrances recorded against the property after the date the project commenced.

Assuming you earlier complied with your duty to serve a timely preliminary notice, you can secure your mechanics' lien rights by recording a document called a Claim of Mechanics' Lien with the county recorder's office no later than:

- for all contributors except the prime (general) contractor, 30 days from the date the owner recorded a document showing that work on the project was finished, or
- for the prime (general) contractor, 60 days from the date the owner recorded a document showing that work on the project was finished, or
- if the owner did not record a document showing that work on the project was finished, 90 days after work on the project stopped or was in all important respects completed.

Once you record your Claim of Mechanics' Lien, and as long as the lien remains valid, you are entitled to payment ahead of any other creditor of the owner except:

- other mechanics' lien claimants, and

- any creditor who recorded a security interest in the property before the work of improvement began (most often the mortgage and construction lenders).

This means that if the property is to be sold or refinanced while the lien claim is on record, you, the mechanics' lien claimant, will have to be paid if the owner is to pass clear title—unless the owner goes to the time and expense of obtaining a bond to cover the amount in dispute (called bonding around the lien). Obviously, the owner has a very strong motivation to pay up quick.

Chapter 3 provides step-by-step instructions for recording a Claim of Mechanics' Lien.

THE DESIGN PROFESSIONALS' LIEN

As described earlier in Section B4, the Design Professionals' Lien is very similar to the mechanics' lien, but is tailored for those professionals who typically do their work before construction begins. Step-by-step instructions for using the Design Professionals' Lien remedy are in Chapter 3, Section H.

3. The Stop Notice: Withholding Construction Funds

The mechanics' lien remedy described in Section 2, above, ultimately depends upon the ability of the owner—or the property being improved—to produce enough money to pay off the lien claim. Unfortunately,

many construction projects are abandoned well short of completion. Not only is the owner bankrupt, but the property itself, if sold at auction, would produce less than is owed to the original lender—which means there would be nothing left to pay off the mechanics' lien.

With this possibility in mind, the law allows a contributor to a work of improvement, upon learning that he or she is not being paid, to lay early claim to construction loan or insurance funds that haven't yet been disbursed.

Example 1: Paul Hernandez takes out a $75,000 home equity loan from his credit union to pay for remodeling his kitchen. He hires Firesign Kitchen Designers to do the job. Firesign, acting as the general contractor, lines up Pete's Plumbing, Ron's Woodwork, now the carpenter, Peri's Painting Service and Joan the tile layer as subcontractors. Under the contract Paul signs with Firesign, the work is to proceed in four stages, payment to be made to Firesign at the completion of each stage. At the completion of the second stage, Paul decides that Firesign isn't right for the job and fires them—after paying in full for the work done during the second phase.

The unexpected change puts Firesign in a financial bind and they decide to hold off paying Pete's Plumbing and Ron the carpenter, the two subcontractors who did most of the work during the second phase. Pete's and Ron in turn put off paying their materials suppliers.

Pete's, Ron and the materials suppliers all serve a stop notice on both Paul and the credit union demanding that they withhold any authorized but undisbursed loan funds. If, for example, the credit union is disbursing the funds to Paul by phase of completion, it will withhold the amount of the funds specified in the stop notice, provided that the stop notice is accompanied by an appropriate bond. (See sidebar, below.) If the entire loan was disbursed to Paul, and Paul still has some of the loan proceeds left, the stop notice can direct Paul to withhold the funds from the general contractor in favor of the those who served the stop notices. The stop notice to the owner doesn't require a bond.

Example 2: Assume the same facts as Example 1, above, except that Paul is repairing his kitchen because it suffered from fire damage and the funds come from his homeowner's insurance policy. The bonded stop notice would be served on the insurer and the insurer would be required to withhold the funds.

Payment bond may preclude use of stop notice

On occasion the prime (general) contractor may have posted a payment bond. If so, the lender or insurer will not be under any obligation to withhold under a stop notice. Payment bonds are not common in private projects.

The same people who qualify for a mechanics' lien qualify to use a stop notice, except that an original or prime contractor (Firesign in the example above) cannot use this remedy against the owner. So in the previous example, had Paul not paid Firesign for the second phase of the project, Firesign could not use the stop notice to make Paul hold on to any proceeds of the loan that he had in his possession. However, if the credit union still had some of the loan funds, Firesign could use the stop notice against them, again provided the stop notice was accompanied by a bond.

THE BONDED STOP NOTICE

There are two types of stop notice: bonded and unbonded. A stop notice directed to construction funds held by the owner may, but doesn't have to be, accompanied by a bond. It is also possible to serve an unbonded stop notice on a lender who is holding construction funds. But without a bond, the lender is not required to withhold the funds (and rarely will). Which means it's not much of a remedy. If, on the other hand, you accompany the stop notice with proof that you've obtained a bond for 125% of the value of the stop notice demand, the lender will have to withhold the funds.

The downside of the bonded stop notice remedy is that you have to obtain the bond—which for many people may be difficult due to the stringent criteria that sureties use to qualify people for bonding. Also, of course, the non-refundable bond premium may be an expensive outlay at a difficult time (typically 10% of the bond), even though you may be able to recover its cost later in a settlement or a lawsuit. Chapter 5 explains bonded stop notices in more detail.

Whether or not you ever proceed to enforce your stop notice, you at least can initiate the process by serving a stop notice demand on the owner and/or lender within specified time limits and then, if no payment is forthcoming, sue in court to enforce the stop notice.

---

4. Filing a Lawsuit to Enforce Your Remedies

So far, all the steps described do not involve the courts. Rather, they involve:

- serving a preliminary notice to put the appropriate parties on notice that you reserve the right to invoke your mechanics' lien and stop notice remedies, and

- actually initiating these remedies by recording the Claim of Mechanics' Lien and serving the stop notice.

Most often, simply taking these initial steps will be enough to secure payment, especially if you are willing to negotiate a compromise. But, if you can't settle, the next step requires going to court. In fact, if you don't file a timely court action to enforce your mechanics' lien or stop notice, both remedies go away. The mechanics' lien lasts only for 90 days from the date you record it—unless you file an enforcement action. Similarly, your stop notice remedy lapses unless you file an enforcement lawsuit within 120-180 days from the date the project is completed or work stops.

COURT CONSOLIDATION

Throughout this book we treat Municipal Courts and Superior Courts as being separate entities. However, in the Spring of 1998, an initiative passed that allowed these courts to be consolidated. As of September 1998, most counties have taken this step. However, Los Angeles and a few other counties have not. If your county has consolidated its courts, then you needn't worry about the Superior Court-Municipal Court distinction. This issue is explained in more detail in Chapter 8.

Here is what you can file in court:

• a breach of contract action against the person who hired or purchased materials from you (in Small Claims, Municipal or Superior Court, depending on the amount in dispute)

• an action to enforce your mechanics' lien, which in essence is a suit to foreclose on the property because of the non-payment (either in Municipal or Superior Court, depending on the amount in dispute)

• an action to recover the withheld loan funds from the person or entity who you served with the stop notice (either in Municipal or Superior Court, depending on the amount in dispute)

• if there is a payment bond in the picture (which usually is the case only for larger construction projects), an action against the bond issuer,

known as the surety (see Chapter 7 for more on payment bonds), and

• an action against the subcontractor's or contractor's state license bond (currently $7,500 for contractors and $10,000 for swimming pool contractors).

You can bring all of these actions in one lawsuit, or you can bring them in different lawsuits. However, the courts will most often "consolidate" all your claims into one action. Most people voluntarily choose to do it all at once, but there may be good reasons not to.

Lawsuits to enforce a mechanics' lien or a stop notice must be filed in Municipal or Superior Court (depending on the size of the claim), whereas the lawsuit for breach of contract (and recovery on a payment bond, if any) can optionally be filed in Small Claims Court if the amount in issue fits within the Small Claims Court limit of $5,000 (or you are willing to reduce your claim to that amount). So, assuming your claim is in the neighborhood of $5,000 or less, you may decide to file in Municipal Court to enforce your mechanics' lien and stop notice remedies, but save your breach of contract action for Small Claims Court where you can more easily represent yourself and avoid attorney fees.

Example: Andrenae Buckley inherits a single family residence in Hayward worth $200,000. She decides to remodel the home and swings a $100,000 line of credit with her local bank for the expected costs. She hires Mike Leeds, a general contractor, to go over her wish list, and they come up with a plan for how her $100,000 will be spent, in four phases. When Mike invoices Andrenae for the third phase, Andrenae notes that the amount just about finishes off her $100,000 loan. Although Mike offers a justification for the cost overrun, Andrenae doesn't buy it and tells Mike to cut the bill back to its originally estimated amount. Mike refuses to do this and Andrenae tells him to get lost.

Because he hasn't been paid for the third phase, Mike doesn't pay his subcontractors for their contributions to the third phase, and they in turn don't pay their materials suppliers for supplies used in that phase. Mike and the non-paid parties immediately record mechanics' liens. The subcontractors and materials suppliers serve stop notices on Andrenae (the owner) for whatever is left of the $100,000. Mike cannot use the stop notice remedy against Andrenae because he is the prime contractor and she is the owner. Since there is no lender that is holding construction funds, Mike has no stop notice remedy at all.

The subcontractors and materials suppliers decide to enforce their mechanics' lien and stop notice remedies and file timely actions in Municipal Court, since each of their respective claims is less than $25,000. Of the four subcontractors and two materials providers involved in the third phase, all but one of subcontractors have individual claims of less than $5,000. All of these parties decide to use the Small Claims Court to sue Mike for breach of contract. They can't sue Andrenae, since they didn't contract directly with her. The subcontractor with the claim of well over $5,000 brings his breach of contract action as part of the Municipal Court enforcement action.

Fortunately, as mentioned several times previously, mechanics' lien enforcement lawsuits are seldom necessary. After all, no property owner wants to defend such a lawsuit—which may ultimately result in sale of the property at auction at far less than its actual value, and likely will cost the owner more in attorney fees or bonding premiums (if the owner decides to bond around the lien) than the amount of the mechanics' lien claim.

However, if the owner does decide to defend your suit, your task will suddenly become much more complex. And it is not uncommon for owners who decide to fight to also countersue the mechanics' lien claimant—often for much more than the claimant is seeking in the enforcement lawsuit. See Chapter 8 for how to file an mechanics' lien enforcement lawsuit and, if necessary, find someone to help you push it through the courts and deal with any countersuit.

ARBITRATION NOTE

If you are working under a contract calling for binding arbitration, you must still file the lawsuit to save your mechanics' lien and stop notice. However, if you want the arbitration, you must, at the same time you file the lawsuit, also file a motion requesting the court to stay (stop) all further court proceedings while you proceed with your arbitration. If you win the arbitration, you must then file the arbitration decision in the court to enforce your judgment. (See Chapter 12, Section G, where we explain more about arbitration.)

If, on the other hand, you don't care to arbitrate the dispute, you can proceed with the lawsuit without filing a motion for a stay. This has the legal effect of giving up (waiving) your right to arbitration. If the owner responds to your lawsuit, but also doesn't ask for a stay, there will be no arbitration. Both of you will have given up or waived your rights to arbitrate under the contract. On the other hand, if the owner insists on arbitration and opposes your court action, the court may order you to arbitrate.

D. WHAT TO DO NEXT

What you do next will depend on what stage you are in the construction process.

If you are a design professional contributing services before the work of improvement commences, see Chapter 3, Section H.

If you haven't yet begun contributing to a work of improvement, but plan to in the near future, carefully read Chapter 2 and, if required, be prepared to serve a preliminary notice on the necessary people described in that chapter. Remember that you must serve the notice within 20 days of the first day you start your work or deliver materials.

If you missed the 20-day deadline

If you have already started working on a project, but blew the 20-day deadline, you may still serve a notice and pursue your mechanics' lien remedy. However, the mechanics' lien will only apply to work or materials you contribute during the 20-day period prior to your notice and all work and materials furnished after the preliminary notice was served.

If you haven't been paid according to your agreement with the person who hired you or purchased materials from you, but you have properly served your preliminary notices, you may want to record a Claim of Mechanics' Lien as soon as possible (don't wait for the deadline). (See Chapter 3.)

If you have any reason to believe that there may be construction funds in the hands of a lender or the owner, serve a stop notice or bonded stop notice on the owner (unless you are the prime contractor) and a bonded stop notice on the lender. If you can't afford a bond, then at the very least serve a regular stop notice on the lender and owner and hope for the best. (See Chapters 4 and 5.)

At any time after it is clear that you won't receive what you are entitled to receive under your contract, you should try to negotiate a settlement with or without the help of mediation. (See Chapter 12.) But if that doesn't work, you can file a breach of contract action in the appropriate court. (See Chapter 8.)

If you recorded a Claim of Mechanics' Lien (and/or served a stop notice) and you still haven't been paid, continue with your attempt to negotiate or mediate a settlement. (See Chapter 12.) If that doesn't work after about 60 days, consider filing an enforcement action in the appropriate court. (See Chapter 8.)

If you haven't yet filed a breach of contract lawsuit, consider bringing these lawsuits in the same case in the same court.

E. TIMING OF MECHANICS' LIEN PROCEDURES

The table below concisely summarizes when you have to take certain steps to successfully pursue your mechanics' lien and stop notice remedies.

TIMELINE CHART	
From Time Work Began or Materials Supplied	
20 days	Serve preliminary notice
From Time Project Finished or Completed	
30 days	Subcontractors and suppliers must record mechanics' lien and serve stop notice if completion or cessation notice recorded
60 days	Contractors must record mechanics' lien and serve stop notice if completion or cessation notice recorded
90 days	All potential claimants must record mechanics' lien and serve stop notice if no notice of completion or cessation recorded
120 days	Subcontractors and suppliers must file stop notice enforcement suit if notice of completion or cessation recorded
150 days	General contractor must file stop notice enforcement suit if notice of completion or cessation recorded
180 days	All stop notice claimants must file stop notice enforcement suit if no notice of completion or cessation recorded
six months	Lawsuit against payment bond must be filed
From Actual Date Claim of Mechanics' Lien Recorded	
90 days	Mechanics's lien enforcement lawsuit must be filed by all claimants

F. LEGAL AUTHORITY

Here we set out the citations to the California statutes that support the major points covered in this chapter. All citations are to California Civil Code sections except as noted. The statutes themselves are reproduced in Appendix A.

Definition of home improvements	§7151
Definition of site improvement	§3102
Definition of work of improvement	§3106
Who can use lien	§3110
License requirement for using mechanics' lien remedy [Business and Professions Code]	§7031
Statutes governing design professionals' lien	§§3081.1-3081.10
Requirements for who must get preliminary notice	§3097 (a) and (b)
Definition of lender (including insurers)	§3087
What interests the mechanics' lien attaches to	§3128
When lien takes effect	§3134
When 90-day period for recording mechanics' lien begins to run	§§3115, 3116
No bond required for stop notice on owner	§3158
Requirement for bonded stop notice to lender	§3159
Time limits to serve stop notice	§3160
Enforcement of stop notice	§3172
Enforcement of mechanics' lien	§3144 ■

Preparing and Serving the Preliminary Notice

In Chapter 1, we introduced you to a variety of remedies available to you if you have not been paid for your contributions to a privately financed California real estate improvement project. With certain exceptions, to get maximum use of the mechanics' lien, stop notice and payment bond remedies, you must first—very early on—let the owner, prime (general) contractor and lender (if any) know what work you're doing or what materials you're providing.

The law calls this requirement a "20-day preliminary notice," because to fully preserve your mechanics lien remedy you must give it within 20 days after beginning work or supplying materials to the work of improvement. This normally is long before you know whether there will in fact be any payment problems.

Since you never know whether payment problems will occur down the line, or what remedies you may wish to pursue, you should always serve a timely preliminary notice for work or materials you contribute or plan to contribute to a work of improvement.

A. THE PURPOSE OF THE PRELIMINARY NOTICE

The reason for the preliminary notice requirement is to let the owner of the property being improved (and general contractor and lender) know about possible mechanics' liens, stop notice and payment bond claims. This knowledge will enable those parties to take what steps they can to make sure potential lien claimants get paid.

Although you may think that serving a preliminary notice would lead these folks to stop doing business with you in the future, serving the preliminary notice is standard operating procedure in the construction trades and should not be a cause for concern.

B. WHO MUST PROVIDE THE PRELIMINARY NOTICE

If you are a subcontractor, equipment lessor or materials supplier, you must provide the preliminary notice to the owner, prime (general) contractor and lender (if there is one)—unless you contracted directly with the owner.

If you contracted directly with the owner but are not the prime (general) contractor or someone who worked on site for wages, you need only provide a preliminary notice to the lender (if any).

If you are a materials supplier who supplied materials to two or more subcontractors for the same project, you should also provide each subcontractor with a preliminary notice.

If you are the prime (general) contractor or someone who worked on site for wages, you have no legal obligation to provide a preliminary notice.

Design professionals (architects, engineers and surveyors) whose work is typically carried out before the work of improvement is commenced must also provide a preliminary notice to the appropriate parties if they later want to use the mechanics' lien remedy. In addition, for work done under a written contract after a building permit has been obtained, but before the work of improvement has begun, they have an independent lien right called a Design Professionals' Lien. (See Chapter 3, Section H.)

Example 1: Tixton Construction Co. owns and develops a 10-acre condominium project in Kelseyville, California with funds loaned by Merchant's Saving and Trust. Tixton contracts with Jonas Foulks, a Kelseyville general contractor, to handle the project. Foulks lines up the necessary subcontractors who in turn hire laborers, order supplies from Kelseyville Lumber Co. and lease equipment from a local equipment lessor. Under this scenario, everyone but Foulks would have to provide at least one preliminary notice to Tixton, Foulks and Merchant's Savings and Trust to preserve their mechanics' lien, stop notice and payment bond remedies.

In addition, because Kelseyville Lumber is providing materials for different subcontractors, it would have to serve a separate preliminary notice on the owner for each such subcontractor.

Example 2: After winning the lottery, Gifford Cloud buys some land in northern Humboldt County for the purpose of building his dream house. He works with an architect to develop some plans and hires Isaac McKinnon to put in the foundation, framing and roof. McKinnon brings in several laborers to help with the work. Gifford does the rest of the work himself (such as the sheet rock, stucco and painting) except that he hires Ely Electrician to install the wiring and Pricilla Plumber to install the plumbing. Gifford purchases all the materials himself. Because there is no lender in the picture, and because everyone either contracted directly with the owner or performed on-site labor for wages, none of the contributors to the work of improvement needs to serve a preliminary notice.

Example 3: Assume the same facts as Example 2, above, except that Gifford hired McKinnon to handle the whole job. McKinnon, who has a general contractor's license, contracted with Chris Carpenter, a licensed contractor, to construct the house, Pricilla Plumber and Ely Electrician to install the plumbing and electricity and A-1 Painters to paint the interior and exterior, and used his own employees for the remaining tasks. McKinnon also purchased the materials.

Under these facts, everyone except the architect and McKinnon would have to serve a preliminary notice on Gifford and McKinnon to preserve their mechanics' lien rights. Since there is still no lender in the picture, neither McKinnon nor the architect would have to serve a preliminary notice to preserve their mechanics' lien, stop notice or payment bond rights.

Example 4: Taking the facts from Example 3, assume that instead of using his lottery proceeds, Gifford borrowed the money for the house from the bank and put up the property as collateral. Since there is now a lender in the picture, the architect (who contracted directly with the owner) would have to serve a preliminary notice on the lender. In addition, all the other contributors would also have to serve the lender as well as Gifford (owner) and McKinnon (general contractor). McKinnon, however, is not obliged to provide a preliminary notice to anyone.

Go overboard on serving the preliminary notice

On occasion we suggest some overkill. This is one such time. Even if you are excused from providing a preliminary notice to one or more parties, we recommend that you do it anyway. This means you should always provide a notice to the owner, prime (general) contractor (unless this is you) and the lender, if any. The reason? If you are required to provide a preliminary notice, but fail to do so, you cannot use the mechanics' lien, stop payment or payment bond remedies for any work done or materials supplied prior to the 20-day period proceeding the date you do get around to serving it. This may be far too late. If down the line a court rules that you were wrong about which category you fit in, your mechanics' lien remedy will evaporate. Anyway, as you'll see in Section F, below, giving notice is not difficult.

If you don't know the identity of the owner, prime (general) contractor or lender, Section C, below, provides some suggestions for how to find out.

INSURANCE COMPANIES CAN BE LENDERS

The legal definition of "lender" includes any person or business who is holding funds destined to pay for construction. If the cost of the construction in your case is being met by an insurance company under an insurance policy—for instance, rebuilding due to fire or flood that qualifies as an insurable loss—the insurance company should be considered the lender and be served a preliminary notice. This will not only preserve your mechanics' lien remedies against the improved property, but also preserve your right to file a stop notice against the insurer in its "lender" capacity. To find out whether insurance proceeds are funding the construction, ask the owner or general contractor.

C. DETERMINING THE IDENTITY OF THE OWNER, GENERAL CONTRACTOR AND LENDER

It's easy enough to say you must serve a preliminary notice on the owner, general contractor and lender. But what if you don't know who these people are? On home improvement projects, the owner is easily identified, as is the general contractor. But you may not have a clue as to whether there is a lender in the picture and, if so, who it might be.

On most large construction or other property improvement projects, the owner, contractor and lender are all prominently identified on construction fencing or special signs put up for marketing purposes. But not always. You may have to go searching for all three—owner, lender and general contractor—if the signs and documents in your possession don't identify these people.

For example, if you were hired as a subcontractor by another subcontractor to deliver and operate certain equipment on site, the only name you may be familiar with is the subcontractor who hired you. You wouldn't necessarily know who owns the project, who is operating as the general contractor or whether there is a

construction lender in the picture. But if you don't serve a preliminary notice on all three of these players, you may be forfeiting your mechanics' lien rights.

There are five possible sources of information about owners, general contractors and lenders:

- a title insurance company (for the owner and lender)
- your county recorder's office (for the owner and lender)
- your local issuer of building permits (for the owner, lender and general contractor)
- the owner (for the lender and the general contractor), and
- the general contractor or subcontractor's office (for the owner, lender and general contractor).

1. Title Insurance Companies

Most title insurance companies maintain a customer service department that will be willing to provide you all the information they have on a particular property. Typically, this information includes the identity of the current owner, the existence of any liens on the property and who owns the liens (which in turn will identify the construction lender).

Because the title insurance business is highly competitive, this service is most often free. Before traveling to the recorder's office or building permit issuer (see items 2 and 3, below), it would be wise to curl up with the Yellow Pages and see what your fingers can find. Look under Title Insurance.

2. County Recorder's Office

Your county recorder's office will tell you who owns property located at a particular address. So as long as you know the address of the project, you can find the owner. Also, when a lender provides property improvement funds, it often will require the owner to execute and record a deed of trust. Under the law, the deed of trust is supposed to be labeled Construction Deed of Trust at the top. When recording this type of document, the Recorder is supposed to enter that title in its index.

This means that when you check the status of the property being improved, you should easily be able to find out whether there is a lender in the picture, and if so, who it is.

If you want to be extra thorough, you can check the actual records rather than just the index to see whether a deed of trust has been recorded against the property.

For more information on using the recorder's office, see Chapter 3, Section E.

3. Building Permit Issuer

All building permit applications should identify both the owner and the lender (if there is one). So, you can visit the city hall or other municipal agency that is in charge of issuing building permits for your area and check for the owner and lender's name. Usually, you will also find the general contractor's name on the application, if there is a general contractor in the picture (other than the owner).

Get the building permit in advance

Although we tell you here to obtain a copy of the building permit application from the issuing agency, you would be wise to obtain a copy of the permit itself in advance of doing the work involved. Building permit issuers can be difficult to deal with, and you may be much better served by obtaining a permit as a condition of doing the work.

4. Owner

The owner will usually be willing to tell you the name of the general contractor and/or the identity of any lender in the picture.

5. Contractor or Subcontractor's Office

If you are a materials supplier, you often can get the information you need directly from the contractor who has purchased the materials. Similarly, a subcontractor can often get the necessary information about the lender or owner from the prime (general) contractor.

D. WHEN YOU MUST SERVE THE PRELIMINARY NOTICE

Timely service of your preliminary notice is vital to preserve your legal remedies. Here are three rules to keep in mind:

Rule 1: If you are a design professional (architect, engineer, surveyor) and want to fully preserve your mechanics' lien rights for services rendered prior to the start of the work of improvement, you must provide the preliminary notice *no later than 20 days after the work of improvement begins.* (CC §3097(c)(6).)

However, you don't have to wait that long. You can serve your notice the instant you get the job. Because it is sometimes hard to tell when a project begins, the best practice is for you to send your notice as soon as you get the job—assuming, of course, that you haven't yet been paid in full for your efforts. Since your design work usually will be carried out before the project begins, this rule should assure promptness.

If you have contracted directly with the owner, as is often the case with architects, then notice to the owner or general contractor is not technically required. But, as we mention above, it is a good idea to serve them anyway. Even if you contracted directly with the owner, however, you must serve a preliminary notice on the owner's lender, if any.

Other remedies for design professionals

Before the work of improvement commences, design professionals may also obtain a "design professionals' lien." This remedy is separate from the mechanics' lien remedy. Both can be used. See Chapter 3, Section H, for more on how to obtain a design professionals' lien and how that lien relates to the mechanics' lien.

Rule 2: If you are anyone other than a design professional contributing work, materials or equipment to a work of improvement, and you are required to provide a preliminary notice, you will maximally preserve your remedies by serving the notice *no later than 20 days of the date you make your first contribution.*

However, you don't have to wait that long. You can give the notice as soon as you've gotten the job. It may seem strange to be sending off a notice when you have no reason to think there will be a problem, but that's what the law requires if you later want to use the mechanics' lien, stop notice and payment bond remedies. The best practice is for you to provide the notice as soon as possible.

Rule 3: If you failed to provide your notice by the end of the initial 20-day period, you may still serve a preliminary notice on the necessary parties. However, if you later wish to take advantage of your mechanics' lien, stop notice or payment bond remedies, the mechanics' lien will only cover your claim for work or materials that you contribute during the 20-day period prior to the date you serve your notice, and during the period following your notice.

Example 1: Egyptian Tile Shop is hired to provide tile for the kitchen and two bathrooms in a new residential dwelling. The work on one of the bathrooms is promptly completed within 20 days, but the other work is delayed for a month because of tile shortages. Egyptian forgets to serve a preliminary notice on the appropriate parties within the 20-day period following the beginning of the tile work. Although it will now be too late to bring the work on the first bathroom under the protection of the mechanics' lien, stop notice or payment bond remedies, Egyptian can still serve a preliminary notice that lets them take advantage of those remedies for the work on the second bathroom and kitchen.

Example 2: Assume instead that Egyptian Tile in Example 1, above, takes 30 days to complete the first bathroom. On the 31st day, Egyptian serves its preliminary notices on the necessary parties. Egyptian will not be able to use the mechanics' lien, stop notice and payment bond remedies for the work done during the first 11 days, but it will be able to use these remedies for the work done during the last 19 days of the project (since the late notice applies to work done during the 20-day period preceding service of the notice).

E. PREPARING THE PRELIMINARY NOTICE

As forms go, the preliminary notice is a simple one. A filled-in sample is set out below. A blank copy is included on the forms disk in the back of the book under the file name PRELIM. If you don't have access to a computer, you may use the tear-out form in Appendix B.

As an alternative, you may wish to purchase and use a quadruplicate form available in most stationary stores. It will save you copying costs and remind you that you should always serve the notice on at least three parties—the lender, the owner and the general contractor—and in some cases on the subcontractor.

California Preliminary Notice

NOTICE TO PROPERTY OWNER

IF BILLS ARE NOT PAID IN FULL FOR THE LABOR, SERVICES, EQUIPMENT OR MATERIALS FURNISHED OR TO BE FURNISHED, A MECHANICS' LIEN LEADING TO THE LOSS, THROUGH COURT FORECLOSURE PROCEEDINGS, OF ALL OR PART OF YOUR PROPERTY BEING SO IMPROVED MAY BE PLACED AGAINST THE PROPERTY EVEN THOUGH YOU HAVE PAID YOUR CONTRACTOR IN FULL. YOU MAY WISH TO PROTECT YOURSELF AGAINST THIS CONSEQUENCE BY (1) REQUIRING YOUR CONTRACTOR TO FURNISH A SIGNED RELEASE BY THE PERSON OR FIRM GIVING YOU THIS NOTICE BEFORE MAKING PAYMENT TO YOUR CONTRACTOR OR (2) ANY OTHER METHOD OR DEVICE THAT IS APPROPRIATE UNDER THE CIRCUMSTANCES. (THIS STATEMENT IS APPLICABLE TO PRIVATE WORKS ONLY.)

Please take notice that _James Torville_ ,whose address is at _7745 East 27th St., Woodland Hills, CA 91356_,

has furnished or will furnish labor, services, equipment or material to the work of improvement located at _306 Valley Vista Road, Encino, CA 91237_

as follows: _Contracted to lay tile floor in kitchen and both bathrooms_

James Torville   Contractor   March 2, _____

Signature   Title   Date

The name and address of the person or business who contracted for the labor, services, equipment or supplies described earlier is _Kenneth Moon, Owner of property,_ 306 Valley Vista Road, Encino, CA 91237.

This preliminary notice is being served on the following persons and businesses at the indicated addresses:

☒ Owner

Kenneth Moon

306 Valley Vista Road, Encino, CA 91237.

☒ Original Contractor

Orville Patch

525 C. St., Woodland Hills, CA 91356.

[X]   Construction Lender

        Driscoll Financing
_____

        5212 Wawona Drive, Studio City, CA 91221
_____ .

☐   Insurer

_____

_____ .

☐   Trust

_____

_____ .

☐   Subcontractor

_____

_____ .

Estimated price of the labor, services, equipment or materials described above is

$ ___ $7,780.00 ___ .

---

1. The Mandatory Notice

This language is required by law to be on your preliminary notice and is included in our notice form:

NOTICE TO PROPERTY OWNER

IF BILLS ARE NOT PAID IN FULL FOR THE LABOR, SERVICES, EQUIPMENT OR MATERIALS FURNISHED OR TO BE FURNISHED, A MECHANICS' LIEN LEADING TO THE LOSS, THROUGH COURT FORECLOSURE PROCEEDINGS, OF ALL OR PART OF YOUR PROPERTY BEING SO IMPROVED MAY BE PLACED AGAINST THE PROPERTY EVEN THOUGH YOU HAVE PAID YOUR CONTRACTOR IN FULL. YOU MAY WISH TO PROTECT YOURSELF AGAINST THIS CONSEQUENCE BY (1) REQUIRING YOUR CONTRACTOR TO FURNISH A SIGNED RELEASE BY THE PERSON OR FIRM GIVING YOU THIS NOTICE BEFORE MAKING PAYMENT TO YOUR CONTRACTOR OR (2) ANY OTHER METHOD OR DEVICE THAT IS APPROPRIATE UNDER THE CIRCUMSTANCES. (THIS STATEMENT IS APPLICABLE TO PRIVATE WORKS ONLY.)

2. Your Name and Address

If you are operating your own business, enter your business name and address. Then sign the form in the indicated space and enter your title. If you are a sole proprietor, enter "Owner." If you are a partner in your business, enter "Partner." If your business is a corporation or limited liability company, enter your actual title, whatever it is. You don't have to be an officer to sign the notice, but you should have authority to sign documents on behalf of the corporation or company.

3. Description of What You've Furnished or Will Furnish Owner

This is to give notice of how you fit into the general scheme of the work of improvement. If you have contracted to do all the plumbing, simply put "plumbing for entire project." If you are doing a very specific task, such as installing sheetrock, put "installing sheetrock." If you use an invoice, what you put on your invoice should suffice.

4. Name and Address of Person You Contracted With

Who this is will depend on your role in the work of improvement. For most providers of equipment and materials, it will be a subcontractor who ordered them. For most subcontractors, it will be the general contractor. If you are a materials supplier and are supplying materials to more than one subcontractor, you will want to provide a separate notice to the owner, general contractor and lender for each subcontractor who you deal with—as well as a notice to the subcontractors themselves.

5. Names and Addresses of Owner, Original Contractor, Lender and Subcontractor

If you don't know these names, see Section C, above, for some suggestions on how to find them. If those suggestions don't work and after giving it an honest effort you still can't find out the name and address of one of these parties, you have an alternative: Simply address your notice to "Lender and General Contractor" and serve these C/O the owner in the same manner as you serve the owner his or her copy.

If you use this method of service, make sure you keep track of your efforts to locate the parties in question. You may later be called on to prove that you made these efforts.

When to include the subcontractor's name

You only need to include the subcontractor's name and address if you have supplied materials to two or more subcontractors for the same project and are therefore serving separate preliminary notices on all parties—that is, the owner, general contractor and lender—for each subcontract. For instance, a building supply yard supplying lumber to a framing subcontractor and decorative rock to a landscaping subcontractor for a new apartment complex would need to serve separate preliminary notices on the owner, general contractor and lender for each type of material, and identify and serve each of the subcontractors as well.

If there is more than one owner

Property often has more than one owner of record, especially when it is a single family residence and for a variety of reasons is held as community property or joint tenancy. It is important that you provide a notice to each owner. While this may seem like a waste of paper, it prevents you from later being blindsided by one of the owners who claims he or she never received notice in his or her own right.

6. Estimated Cost of Your Labor, Services, Equipment or Materials

This refers to the work described in Section 3, above. This figure should be easy for you to provide.

7. Name and Address of Express Trust

This provision is to assure that the trust knows of your work and will be alerted to claim its share of any proceeds you recover as a result of your mechanics' lien or stop notice remedies, if either become necessary. Only fill this in if your work is subject to a trust under a labor agreement.

F. SERVING THE PRELIMINARY NOTICE

When we occasionally say "provide a preliminary notice," what we really mean is to serve the preliminary notice—"serve" being the more technically correct term. If the person or business being served resides in California (lives or has a place of business here), you can use any of these methods for serving the notice:

- if the party is an individual person, personally hand the notice to the person (this method will

usually take care of the general (prime) contractor)

• personally deliver the notice to the person's residence or place of business and leave it with some
person in charge

• send the notice registered or certified first class
mail to the person's residence or place of business (this method will usually take care of the
owner and lender and costs about $3), or

• send the notice registered or certified first class
mail to the address for the person that you found
on the building permit or in the recorder's office.
(See Section C, above.)

If the person or place of business is outside of
California, you can use any of the methods just described for in-state residents. Or, if none of these
methods works (they can't be found and mailings are
returned undelivered), you can send the notice to the
owner by registered or certified mail care of the construction lender or original (general) contractor.

Ordinary mail won't work

If you use ordinary first class mail to send the
preliminary notice, you haven't complied with the
law and the notice will be invalid. You must use one
of the methods of service described here to make
your preliminary notice effective.

When personally serving the preliminary notice on
an entity—including a corporation, a partnership or a

limited liability company—you will want to find out, if
possible, who it is who is authorized to accept such
service. Usually, if you show up at the entity's main
office, someone there will be happy to assume responsibility or at least tell you who will. If not, you can always
use one of the other methods of service listed above.
Certified, first class mail with return receipt is ordinarily
the best method.

G. PROVING THAT YOU SERVED THE PRELIMINARY NOTICE

If payment later becomes a problem and you need to
rely on your mechanics' lien, stop notice or payment
bond remedies, you will need to prove that you properly served the 20-day preliminary notice. You do this
by preparing a document called "Proof of Service."

A blank Proof of Service form is on the forms disk
at the back of the book under the file name PRFPREL. If
you don't have access to a computer, you can use the
tear-out form in Appendix B.

To fill in the Proof of Service form:

• Enter your name.

• Check the appropriate box to indicate how you
served the notice.

• Enter the date you served the notice (the date
you either personally delivered the notice or the
date you deposited the certified or registered envelope with the post office).

• Enter the date you are signing the Proof of Service (ideally, the same day you served the notice)
and the city or town where you are signing it.

• Sign the Proof of Service.

If you are using certified or registered mail, make
sure you attach the receipts you get back from the post
office to your Proof of Service. Also make sure that you
keep your Proof of Service in a safe place. A lot is riding
on this document.

H. RECORDING YOUR PRELIMINARY NOTICE (OPTIONAL)

Although not required by law, it is a very good idea to record your preliminary notice with the county recorder for the county where the work of improvement is located. We tell you in Chapter 3, Section E, how to record documents by mail or in person.

By law, each recorder's office is supposed to maintain a separate file for all preliminary notices, indexed by the property address, and to use their "best efforts" to notify you if the project's owner files a Notice of Completion or Notice of Cessation. Getting this information can be critical to your mechanics' lien claim.

As a general rule, the deadline for recording your Claim of Mechanics' Lien or serving a stop notice is 90 days after the date a project is completed (or work on it finished). However, this period can be shortened to 60 days for the general contractor and 30 days for everyone else if the owner records (with the county recorder) a Certificate of Completion within 10 days after the project is complete, or a Notice of Cessation (after no work is expended on the project for 30 continuous days).

Clearly, getting notice that one of these documents has been recorded by the owner can be valuable information. Chapters 3 and 4 explain these timelines in detail for mechanics' liens and stop notices and provide step-by-step instructions on how to initiate these remedies. (Also, see Chapter 5 for information on bonded stop notices.)

I. WHAT'S NEXT

Once you've served and (optional) recorded your preliminary notice, put your copies of the preliminary notice and proof of service in a place where you will be able to find them if there are problems down the road. If you get paid, you will have no further use for these documents. If, however, you don't get paid, your mechanics' lien and stop notice remedies will be entirely frustrated if you can't produce them.

J. LEGAL AUTHORITY

Here we set out the citations to the California statutes that support the major points covered in this chapter. All citations are to the California Civil Code. The statutes themselves are included verbatim in Appendix A.

Legal authority governing preliminary notices	§3097
Proof of Service required for the preliminary notice is covered	§3097.1
Rules governing preliminary notice	§3097
Rule governing preliminary notice by general contract or wage work	§3097(b)
Rule governing late preliminary notice	§3097(d)
Rule governing how preliminary notice must be served	§3097(f)
Rule governing how preliminary notice can be recorded ■	§3097(o)

Record Your Mechanics' Lien

In Chapter 1 we introduced you to mechanics' liens. We explained that most anyone who contributes labor, services or materials to a real estate improvement project can use the mechanics' lien remedy to exact payment out of the real estate itself—provided that all necessary steps are taken. The first step—serving a timely preliminary notice—was covered in Chapter 2. In this chapter we review the preliminary notice requirement and then explain what additional steps are necessary.

If you are a design professional (architect, engineer or surveyor), you have two lien remedies: the design professional's lien and the mechanics' lien. The design professional's lien only applies to work done before the work of improvement commences. In Sections A-G of this chapter, we deal only with the mechanics' lien. If

you are interested in the design professional's lien, skip to Section H.

A. HAVE YOU SERVED THE PRELIMINARY NOTICE ON THE APPROPRIATE PEOPLE?

The mechanics' lien process starts when you serve your preliminary notice on the necessary parties. If you don't serve your preliminary notice on the necessary parties, you will not be able to use your mechanics' lien, stop notice or payment bond remedies. To summarize the basic points we discussed in Chapter 2:

• You must serve a preliminary notice on the owner, general contractor and lender unless you are the prime (general) contractor, or someone who worked on-site for wages, or someone who contracted directly with the owner.

- If you are the prime (general) contractor or performed on-site labor for wages, you don't have to serve a preliminary notice on anyone (although it is a good idea to do so).

- If you are anyone else who contracted directly with the owner and there is a construction loan in the picture (there usually is), you must serve the lender.

- If you are a materials supplier who has supplied two or more subcontractors for the same project, you must provide a separate preliminary notice for each subcontractor, and serve each on the subcontractor as well as on the other required parties.

- To take full advantage of your mechanics' lien remedy, you must serve the preliminary notice no later than 20 days after the first day you begin your work or provide materials (or within 20 days after the work of improvement itself begins if your contribution was made before it began—for instance, if you are an architect).

- If you are over the 20-day limit, you can still serve the preliminary notice, but your mechanics' lien will only be for work or materials you contribute during the 20 days directly preceding the date you serve the preliminary notice, and for any work or materials contributed during the period that follows.

- You must serve the preliminary notice in the manner outlined in Chapter 2. Service by regular first class mail is like no service at all.

B. PREPARE A DEMAND FOR PAYMENT LETTER

The law does not require you to make a separate demand for payment. Rather, you are only required to include a demand for payment in your Claim of Mechanics' Lien document. (See Section D, below.) Nevertheless, the better practice is to first demand payment and only record your Claim of Mechanics' Lien if your demand doesn't work. The reason for taking this extra step is simple. On many projects, property owners

would rather settle with you than have you record a Claim of Mechanics' Lien against their property. It would ordinarily be a mistake not to first try and negotiate a settlement with either the owner or the party you contracted with.

1. How Much Should You Demand?

Your demand should be as close as possible to what the law allows you to include in your Claim of Mechanics' Lien. This is the amount specified in your contract (plus any additional amount for authorized work that was actually performed), or the value of the services or materials you actually provided, whichever is less.

In Chapter 6 we explain that all labor, materials, equipment or services you contribute to a work of improvement are contributed under a contract—whether the contract is written or oral, or whether the terms of the contract are implied from the circumstances and past relationships. Whatever you are entitled to under that contract provides the basis for your lien. However, while the contract provides a starting point, there clearly may be more to the picture.

If you completely performed your obligations under the contract, then the contract amount and the value of your goods or services are the same. But if you delivered less, then your mechanics' lien claim is for the lesser amount. For instance, assume that you were only able to complete 85% of the tile work you were hired to do. Your mechanics' lien is for 85% of the original contract price. Or, assume that some of your work was judged by the owner, general contractor or AIA (architect) to be substandard, and that you don't wish to contest the point. Again, the value of your services would be less than the contract amount, and your mechanics' lien would be appropriately reduced.

The amount you are owed under the initial contract can be increased if your contract was amended in writing to include such extra amount. For instance, assume you are a lumber yard and you originally quoted one price for a particular grade of lumber, but the price of lumber went up unexpectedly. You may charge an extra amount if, before you deliver the lumber, the person buying the lumber from you agrees to the increase in price.

Also, because many projects are carried out in phases, you may have already been paid a portion of what you're entitled to for the entire job. For instance, if you were paid for phase one and phase two, but did not get paid for phase three, your demand should only be for what you are owed for phase three.

2. Items That Shouldn't Be Included in Your Demand

Because the mechanics' lien remedy is tied to the contributions made to the work of improvement, the Claim of Mechanics' Lien cannot include items that didn't actually go into improving the property in question. Two such items have been held to be:

- contractually based damages for delays caused by the owner or general contractor, and
- attorney fees for an arbitration or a lawsuit brought to enforce the mechanics' lien (but you can recover attorney fees in a suit to enforce a bonded stop notice—see Chapter 5).

3. Claims Involving Two or More Structures on Land Owned by the Same Owner

When two or more separate structures are being constructed on the same land owned by the same owner, any money owed for work or materials contributed to these structures can be combined in one demand (and one Claim of Mechanics' Lien). However, each of the structures is considered to be a separate work of improvement. If your contract specifies a lump sum for the entire job, you can allocate your claim among the units on a proportionate basis. But if you

were hired on a per unit or hourly basis, then you must allocate the payments due to specific units.

Example 1: You are hired to do the tile work for a development involving 10 structurally separate residential units. Your contract specifies a lump sum payment for the whole project. If you are making your demand after you have completed your work on all 10 units, and you haven't been paid for any of it, your demand would specify that 1/10 of your claim is allocated to each unit. If you have been paid for the first half of your work but not the second half, you would allocate 20% to each of the five units that you worked on but weren't paid for. If you were hired on a per unit basis, then you must specify what units your demand covers. See the Mechanics' Lien Claim Worksheet in Appendix B. It will help you articulate your demand.

Example 2: You are a materials supplier. You contract with a framing contractor to supply the framing hardware for the entire 10-unit project on an as-needed basis. You fill orders from time to time. At some point the carpenter stops paying you and, having dutifully served your 20-day notice, you want to start the process to record a mechanics' lien. How do you know where your hardware has actually been used? After an on-site inspection you determine that four houses have gone up, presumably using your materials. Assuming that of the total materials ordered you have been paid for 75% and not paid for 25%, you can reasonably make a demand against the most recently completed unit.

Clearly, if you are providing work or materials to a multi-unit development, you will be ahead of the curve if your invoices are able to itemize which units the work and materials are intended for, and the precise unit at which they were dropped off.

Materials suppliers may have to prove use of materials

If you are a materials supplier, you may ultimately have to prove that your materials were actually used or consumed as part of the work of improvement. The fact that the party who ordered the materials picked them up from your site, or that you delivered the materials to the site, may not be enough. The closer track you keep of what happens to your materials, the better position you'll be in if you have to go to court to enforce your mechanics' lien. The best way to do this is to make advance arrangements with the contractor or subcontractor purchasing your materials for keeping track of how they are used.

Appendix B includes a Mechanics' Lien Claim Worksheet that will help you arrive at your demand amount. The worksheet is also on the forms disk under the file name MLCWRKSHT. It is this figure that also will be part of your Claim of Mechanics' Lien that you record with the county recorder if your payment demand doesn't work. Here is a sample filled-in Mechanics' Lien Claim Worksheet:

Mechanics' Lien Claim Worksheet

	Unit 1	Unit 2	Unit 3	Unit 4	Unit 5	Unit 6	Unit 7
Materials	$ 2,075	$ 3,450	$	$	$	$	$
Labor	$ 1,525	$ 2,725	$	$	$	$	$
Services	$	$	$	$	$	$	$
Equipment	$	$	$	$	$	$	$
Less credits	$	$ 1,000	$	$	$	$	$
Less offsets	$	$	$	$	$	$	$
Total Due	$ 3,600	$ 5,175	$	$	$	$	$

Also in Appendix B is a fill-in-the-blanks demand letter. The letter is also on the forms disk under the file name DEMLTR. Here is a sample:

SAMPLE DEMAND LETTER

Steve Greenberg
Greenberg Construction
243 Elm St.
Fresno, CA 90006

April 29, 1999

Re: Upgrade of kitchen at 3372 Estates Drive

Dear Owner:

On February 28 I served you with a preliminary notice explaining that I had or would be furnishing ☒ labor ☐ services ☐ equipment ☒ materials towards the work of improvement located at 3372 Estates Drive and owned by you. I have in fact furnished such items but have not yet received payment for them. I am currently entitled to receive $4,989.00.

As you know, under the California mechanics' lien law, the property being improved is ultimately responsible for payment of those who contribute to the improvement. I am therefore requesting that you, the owner of the improved property, pay me the amount stated above or agree to meet with me to explore other ways to resolve this issue.

Unfortunately, if I am to preserve my mechanics' lien remedy, time is of the essence. I therefore request that you get back to me within five days of receiving this letter. Otherwise, I will be forced to record a Claim of Mechanics' Lien in the Fresno County Recorder's Office against your property. Please understand that even if I have to take that step, I will still be open to settlement discussions.

Sincerely,

Steve Greenberg

Steve Greenberg

ACCURACY IS REQUIRED, NOT PERFECTION

Although you should try your best to be accurate in your demand, you should know that the law will not consider your mechanics' lien invalid if you make a mistake in your demand so long as you didn't intend to mislead or defraud anyone. So, don't be scared of going forward even if you are uncertain about the exact dollar amount. Use your best judgment and be fair in your calculations.

C. IF YOU HAVE BEEN PAID: SIGNING A WAIVER AND RELEASE FORM

Owners of construction and real estate improvement projects—and their lenders—naturally fear having the improved property being tied up by mechanics' liens. For this reason, if you are paid as a result of your demand, the owner will want you to sign a document giving up your mechanics' lien rights for that project (which you no longer need because you've been paid).

1. Waivers

Even if there is no payment issue, it is customary for owners to withhold payments to the prime contractor until the prime contractor obtains mechanics' lien waivers from all subcontractors and materials providers, especially those who have served a preliminary notice. It is these people who must sign valid lien waivers if the owner is to feel secure that no liens will be filed on his or her property. Sometimes the withholding-payment approach is used for each phase of the project. Other times, only the final payment is withheld. Sometimes an owner or lender issues joint checks to the original (prime) contractor and the subcontractor (or materials supplier). (See Section C2, below.)

Example 1: Jones Construction Company is serving as the prime contractor for a custom-built new home in rural Santa Barbara County.

Under the construction agreement, the home is to be built in four phases: 1) site grading and improvement; 2) foundation, roofing and framing, doors, windows and siding; 3) plumbing and electrical; and 4) finish (tile, sheetrock, painting, appliance installation). Incremental 25% payments are to be made after completion of each phase. Before making each payment, the owner—Jermaine Cateraine—requires Jones Construction to secure mechanics' lien waivers from each subcontractor, equipment lessor and materials provider who has served a preliminary notice on the owner (see Chapter 2) or who has performed labor for wages at the site.

Example 2: Assume the same facts as in Example 1, except that the owner withholds only the final 25% payment to Jones as a condition of Jones securing mechanics' lien waivers for all work and materials contributed to the project in all of its phases.

You may be wondering what to do if a general contractor, owner or lender asks you to sign a waiver giving up your mechanics' lien rights. For your protection, mechanics' lien waivers are heavily regulated. Under California law there are four types of waivers. The law mandates the specific language that each type of waiver must contain. The four types of waivers are:

- Conditional Waiver and Release Upon Progress Payment
- Unconditional Waiver and Release Upon Progress Payment
- Conditional Waiver and Release Upon Final Payment
- Unconditional Waiver and Release Upon Final Payment.

These different types of waivers are intended to take into account the different contexts in which the waivers are typically sought. We have already covered the difference between a waiver in the progress context and a waiver in the final payment context. An unconditional

waiver is one that is signed after payment has been made (that is, the check has been cashed and the funds are in the payee's account). A conditional waiver is one that is signed when the payment hasn't yet been made. Until the payment is actually made and the money shows up in your account, a conditional waiver has no legal effect.

For your purposes (assuming you are not the prime contractor), if you are asked to sign either type of unconditional waiver, make sure you have been paid what is coming to you *and the check has already cleared your bank.* A bounced check doesn't invalidate an unconditional release of your lien rights.

If you are asked to sign a conditional waiver, you don't need to worry, since the waiver will have no effect without your being paid. But don't sit on your rights. If you have signed a conditional waiver but haven't been paid, make sure you record your Claim of Mechanics' Lien on time (see Section E, below) and, if necessary, file a lawsuit to enforce it. (See Chapter 8.)

2. Joint Checks

Another way for owners to protect against mechanics' liens is to make out each check to the original (prime) contractor and the subcontractor (or materials supplier) jointly (meaning they contain the original (prime) contractor's name and the name of each contributor who has served a preliminary notice). By this means, the owner tries to assure that the contractor pays the subcontractor.

D. PREPARING YOUR CLAIM OF MECHANICS' LIEN

If your efforts to negotiate a solution and your demand don't result in payment, your next step is to prepare the simple document we've been referring to as a Claim of Mechanics' Lien. The Claim of Mechanics' Lien is very similar to the preliminary notice you prepared in Chapter 2. Here is a filled-in sample. A blank form is in Appendix B and on the forms disk under the file name MECHCLM.

Recording requested by

and when recorded mail
this document to 2074 Apple Valley Road,
Sonoma, CA 95476

For recorder's use

Claim of Mechanics' Lien

Name of Claimant: ___Gloria Sexton_____

Legal Description of Property Where Work of Improvement Occurred:

___4345 Pear Valley Rd. Sonoma, CA 95476_____

_____.

Claimant hereby claims a lien in the real property described above in the following amounts:

    ☒ Total claim after offsets and credits $__4,350_____

    ☐ Total claim of $_____, allocated after credits and offsets
    among two or more units as follows: Unit 1 _____ Unit 2 _____ Unit
    3 _____ Unit 4 _____.

This claim includes the principal due from _____11/2/98_____ , plus interest at the
rate of %_____10___ per annum.

Description of ☐ labor ☐ services ☐ equipment ☒ supplies furnished to be used
and actually used in the Work of Improvement:

___Custom draperies for the living room and two bedrooms_____

_____

_____.

General Description of Work of Improvement:

___A new single family dwelling_____

_____

_____.

Name of Party Who Contracted for or Requested Claimant's Labor, Services
Equipment or Materials: ___Kerry Jones, General Contractor___.

Name and Address of Owner of Work of Improvement:

Jacob Dershowitz

444 Alamo Road West

Petaluma, CA 95472

Gloria Sexton
Signature

VERIFICATION

I, ___Gloria Sexton___, the undersigned, say I am the
___N/A___ of the claimant of the foregoing Claim of Mechanics' Lien. I have read said Claim
of Mechanics' Lien and know the contents thereof; the same is true of my own knowledge.

I declare under penalty of perjury that the foregoing is true and correct. Executed on
___2/5/99___, at ___Sonoma___, California.

Gloria Sexton
Signature

Here is how to fill it in:

1. Recording Information

In the upper left-hand corner, enter your name and
address.

2. Mechanics' Lien Claimant

Here you insert your name. This should be the same
name as you included on your preliminary notice. If you
didn't serve a preliminary notice because you are the
prime contractor, the name you put here should be the
same as that on your contractor's license. If you didn't

serve a preliminary notice because you were a laborer
for wages or because you contracted directly with the
owner, enter your full name. But remember, if the work
you were doing requires a license and you didn't have
one, you will probably not qualify for the mechanics'
lien remedy.

3. Property Description

Here you identify the property that your labor, services,
equipment or materials helped to improve. If the
property has a definite address, the address is sufficient.
However, if there is no address—for example, because
the project was never completed and assigned a specific

address by the locality in question—you should include a legal description of the property. This description can be obtained from the county recorder's office by searching under the owner's name. You may also be able to obtain the legal description from a title insurance company.

4. Demand

Here you insert the amount included in your demand letter, less any payments received after you served your demand letter, plus any interest due. If a short period of time has elapsed since you discovered you weren't being paid, it probably isn't worth your while to claim interest. However, if a significant period of time has elapsed, it probably is worthwhile.

Unless your contract specifies a different rate, you should charge simple interest at 10% per year for

unpaid amounts. If there have been no payments, credits or offsets from the time the payment first became due until the present, compute the interest this way: Multiply the amount due by the applicable interest rate (for instance, $5,000 due by 10% interest rate) and then multiply the product ($500) by the ratio of the number of days the payment has been due over the approximate number of days in a year (for simplicity purposes, 360 days). Assuming the payment has been due for 120 days, you would multiply $500 by 120/360, or 1/3, for a total interest due of $166.66.

If there have been payments, credits or offsets during the period of time that you have been owed money, you will need to compute your interest on the basis of the changing balance. We provide a worksheet for this purpose in Appendix B. The form is also on the forms disk under the file name INTCALC.

Here is a filled-in sample:

KEEPING TRACK OF INTEREST (CALCULATION SHEET)

A Starting Date	B Ending Date	C No. of Days	D Balance (F from line above)	E Payment	F New Balance (D – E)	G Interest Due (D x 10% x C/360)
1/10/96	3/28/96	78	$6,000.00	$621.00	$5,379.00	$130.00
3/29/96	7/15/96	106	$5,379.00	$420.00	$4,959.00	$158.38
7/16/96	8/18/96	32	$4,959.00	$420.00	$4,539.00	$44.08
8/19/96	9/21/96	32	$4,539.00	$250.00	$4,289.00	$40.35
					(Sub)total	$372.81

5. Description of Labor and Materials

Here you insert a general description of the work, labor or materials that you actually contributed to the project. This description may be the same as that included in your preliminary notice (if you served one), or it may be different if the nature of the work or materials changed after you served the preliminary notice.

6. General Description of Project

Here you enter a general description of the project—for example: kitchen remodel, swimming pool or construction of a single family residence.

7. Who Contracted for Work or Materials

Here you enter the person or company you contracted with to provide the work or materials. This information should be the same as you entered on the preliminary notice.

8. Names and Addresses of Owners

Here you enter the names and addresses of the owners of the property being improved. These should be the same as those you entered in your preliminary notice unless you've later learned that your earlier information was wrong.

9. Signing

Here you enter the name of the firm who provided the work or materials, and sign where indicated.

10. Verification

In this clause you declare under penalty of perjury that the information in your Claim of Mechanics' Lien is true. In the first blank put your position in the firm identified on the signature line. After the declaration language, enter the date you're signing the Claim of Mechanics' Lien and the city where you are signing it. Then sign the verification. The person signing the verification should be the same person you identify in the first blank of the verification.

11. Proof of Service

Attach a Proof of Service of your preliminary notice (see Chapter 2, Section G), which also should have the appropriate post office receipts attached if you served it by certified or registered mail.

12. Copies

Make two copies of all the documents.

E. RECORD YOUR CLAIM OF MECHANICS' LIEN

To be valid, your Claim of Mechanics' Lien must be recorded in the correct county recorder's office.

1. How to Record Your Claim of Mechanics' Lien

A document is recorded the moment it is received in the county recorder's office. The document is stamped as received for recording at the hour and minute received and given a document or instrument number (sometimes a book and page number are used). A photocopy is then made for the recorder's records and bound with other similar documents in books of "Official Records" in the recorder's office, which are available for the public to inspect. Using an alphabetical grantor-grantee index (by name of owner or buyer), or the county assessor's records (by address), you can find the proper page of these records to consult a particular document.

To record your Claim of Mechanics' Lien, take or mail the original Claim of Mechanics' Lien you prepared in Section D to the county recorder's office for the county where the work of improvement is taking place. If you use the mail, remember to include a self-addressed, stamped envelope and the required recording fee. Call the recorder's office to find out how much this is. Fees vary from county to county, but plan on spending between $10 and $20.

The county recorder will stamp the original with the recording information that you may need to use later, and return it in the self-addressed, stamped envelope (if you are using the mail).

Hand deliver Claim if deadline approaching

If you are approaching the expiration of the period in which you must record your Claim of Mechanics' Lien, do not mail the Claim. Hand deliver it to the recorder's office so that if it is rejected for some reason by the recorder, you can quickly amend the Claim and not lose days waiting for the mail to go back and forth.

Calendar crucial dates

After recording your Claim of Mechanics' Lien, enter the following dates on your calendar: First, make note of the date that is 89 calendar days from the date you record your claim. This date is crucial: If you still haven't been paid, you will have to file a foreclosure action in court by this time to preserve your Claim of Mechanics' Lien. See Chapter 8 for more on this foreclosure action. Also note a date 70 days after recording your Claim. If you intend to file a lawsuit on the lien, you'll need to start by this date so you will have enough time to prepare the complaint or contact a lawyer to do so for you.

2. When to Record Your Claim of Mechanics' Lien

You may record your Claim of Mechanics' Lien as soon as it becomes reasonably clear you won't be paid for your work or materials. This is so even if the legal deadline for recording hasn't yet begun to run. Just when you should assume there is a payment problem will depend on:

- customary payment arrangements, if any
- what your contract says about payment, and
- information you learn from the grapevine (for instance, other contractors that submitted invoices before you aren't getting paid).

Although not required by law, it is always a good idea to fire off a demand letter before turning to the county recorder's office. (See Section B, above, for information about writing a demand letter.) Also, see Chapter 12 for suggestions on how to conduct effective negotiations.

Example: Upon completion of the roof on Sarah's summer cottage, Frank Foster submits his invoice for a final payment of $8,000, payable in 20 days. After 30 days Frank assumes he won't be paid and records his Claim of Mechanics' Lien. Although Frank technically is within his rights to do this, his assumption that Sarah won't pay may be mistaken, since the invoice isn't the same thing as a demand. Frank should have first tried to negotiate a payment with Sarah and, if that didn't work, send her a demand letter for payment within 10 days. Then, if Sarah still doesn't pay or make other arrangements with Frank, Frank can feel comfortable about going ahead with his mechanics' liens remedy.

a. The deadline for recording your Claim of Mechanics' Lien

The law sets an outside deadline for recording your Claim of Mechanics' Lien that you must meet or lose your mechanics' lien rights. This deadline depends, in your particular case, on one or more of these factors:

- when the project reached completion
- whether or not you were the prime (general) contractor
- whether your work or materials were being contributed to two or more units on one piece of property, and

- what documents (if any) the owner recorded to declare the project completed.

b. Determining when the project reached completion

To get a clear fix on your deadline, you first need to know when the work of improvement project reached completion. This is not as straightforward as you may think. The law provides five possible dates of completion:

- The date the work of improvement is actually completed.

    Example: Jonas hires Franco Construction Co. to add a bathroom to his house. After Franco is finished, no further work is done on the bathroom. The bathroom will be deemed completed.

- The date the owner accepts the work of improvement.

    Example: Jonas hires Franco Construction Co. to add a bathroom to his house. Payments are to be made in three phases: a down payment, a progress payment and a final payment. When Franco is done, Jonas makes the final payment. The bathroom will be deemed completed.

- The date the owner occupies the work of improvement.

    Example: Jonas hires Franco Construction Co. to add a bathroom to his house. When Franco is done, Jonas is pleased with the result and starts using the bathroom. The bathroom will be deemed completed.

- The date upon which no labor has been performed on the project for 60 continuous days and no notice of completion or cessation has been recorded by the owner (see sidebar, below).

    Example: Jonas hires Franco Construction Co. to add a bathroom to his house. Payments are to be made in three phases: a down payment, a progress payment and a final payment. Although

Franco thinks he's done with the project, Jonas doesn't agree, but doesn't file a notice of completion or cessation. Sixty continuous days pass without any labor being done on the project. The bathroom will be deemed completed.

- The date upon which no labor has been performed on the project for 30 continuous days, and the owner has recorded a notice of completion or cessation (see sidebar, below).

    Example: Jonas hires Franco Construction Co. to add a bathroom to his house. Payments are to be made in three phases: a down payment, a progress payment and a final payment. Although Franco thinks he's done with the project, Jonas doesn't agree. Thirty continuous days pass without any labor being done on the project, and Jonas records a notice of cessation. Franco records a Claim of Mechanics' Lien. The project will be deemed completed on the thirtieth day.

c. Computing your recording deadline

Now that you have an idea of the different ways a project will be deemed completed, the next step is to understand how much time you have from that date to record a Claim of Mechanics' Lien.

If the owner fails to record any completion documents, you have 90 days from the date of completion.

Example: You were hired as a subcontractor by a mechanical contractor for a lump sum to install heaters in 20 units of a new home development. The mechanical company runs into financial difficulties and is unable to pay you. As long as work has not stopped on the units where you installed the heaters, you may record a Claim of Mechanics' Lien against the development. Once one or more of the units is completed, however, the period of time for you to record your mechanics' lien starts to run as to those units. Assuming that the owner doesn't record a completion document, you have 90 days to record your mechanics' lien after each unit is completed.

If the unit completion rate is slow

If the unit completion rate for the overall project is extremely slow, you may have to record more than one Claim of Mechanics' Lien. For instance, if there is a three-month delay between the date you complete units #1 through #4 and the date you begin work on units #5 through #8, you should think of the two phases as two entirely different projects. You'll likely have to record an additional Claim of Mechanics' Lien on the later completed units. However, your original preliminary notice will still be effective for the entire project.

COMPLETION DOCUMENTS: WHAT THEY ARE AND WHAT EFFECT THEY HAVE ON THE CLAIM OF MECHANICS' LIEN

When a work of improvement is finished, the owner can shorten the deadline for recording mechanics' liens and serving stop notices. This can be done in two ways:

- If labor has ceased on the project for a continuous 30 days, the owner can record what's called a notice of cessation.

- If the project is completed (see Section E2, above), the owner can record what's called a notice of completion within 10 days after the date of completion.

If either of these "completion" documents was timely recorded by the owner, you have 30 days from the date the completion document was recorded to record your Claim of Mechanics' Lien if you are a subcontractor, materials provider or equipment lessor, and 60 days from the date the completion document was recorded to record your Claim of Mechanics' Lien if you are the general (prime) contractor.

THE MECHANICS' LIEN TIMELINE

For subcontractors, design professionals, materials providers, equipment providers, haulers and laborers:

Serve preliminary notice: On owner, general contractor and vendor, within 20 days of when your work first begins.

Record Mechanics' Lien: No later than 90 days after completion or cessation if no notice of completion or cessation filed. Within 30 days of recording date of completion or cessation notice, if one is filed.

Enforce Mechanics' Lien in Court (file lawsuit on mechanics' lien): Within 90 days of recording mechanics' lien.

For prime (general) contractors:

Serve preliminary notice: On lender within 20 days of when your work first begins.

Record Mechanics' Lien: No later than 90 days after completion or cessation if no notice of completion or cessation filed. Within 60 days of the recording date of a completion or cessation notice, if one is filed.

Enforce Mechanics' Lien in Court (file lawsuit on mechanics' lien): Within 90 days of recording mechanics' lien.

Bankruptcy Note: When a person or business files for bankruptcy, all attempts to collect on a debt are supposed to cease. However, bankruptcy laws allow you to record your Claim of Mechanics' Lien. (11 USC §546 (b)). See Chapter 8, Section N, for more on the effect of bankruptcy on a mechanics' lien enforcement action.

3. When Your Recorded Claim of Mechanics' Lien Becomes Effective

Recording your Claim of Mechanics' Lien will produce a dramatic result. Your claim against the property will be deemed to have arisen at the very moment the work of improvement began. It makes no difference that your work or materials may have been contributed long after that date. For example, assume you are a glazier and in July 1999 you install the glass for a large office building project originally started in January 1997. When properly recorded, your mechanics' lien claim will be retroactive back to January 1997.

4. Why the Mechanics' Lien Effectiveness Date Is Important

The effectiveness date of your Claim of Mechanics' Lien is important because that date determines its priority vis a vis other liens. Only those creditors whose liens on the property predate the beginning of the construction project will have priority over your lien. Typically, the only creditors whose liens will predate yours will be the original lender that funded the purchase of the real estate and the lender of the funds that are earmarked for the construction.

This means that all creditors who come along after the original construction loan is obtained have to stand in line behind you to collect what is owed them. And if the creditor files for bankruptcy, your Claim of Mechanics' Lien will give you a preferred standing as a secured creditor. (For more on what this means, see *Collect Your Court Judgment,* by Scott, Elias and Goldoftas (Nolo Press).)

What about other mechanics' lien claimants? All other Claims of Mechanics' liens that are enforced in court (see Chapter 8) will have a priority equal to yours. For instance, suppose 100 subcontractors and 50 materials providers record Claims of Mechanics' Liens because the prime contractor refuses to pay them the agreed-upon price. All of these mechanics' lien claimants will compete against each other as lienholders—

assuming they follow up their claims by filing enforcement actions in court. How much money each mechanics' lien claimant will get will depend on how much money is left after the property is auctioned off and the top-priority lienholders paid. As a general rule, payment will be made on a pro-rata basis—that is, each claimant gets an equal percentage of the whole.

F. ENFORCING YOUR CLAIM OF MECHANICS' LIEN

Once you've recorded your Claim of Mechanics' Lien, you have 90 days before you have to take the next step. Hopefully, the owner will pay you within that 90-day period but, if not, you will need to file a lawsuit in court to keep your Claim of Mechanics' Lien alive. Filing a lawsuit to enforce your mechanics' lien is a relatively simple task. It involves:

- preparing a document called a complaint that briefly describes the facts giving rise to your mechanics' lien and asks the court to award you a judgment on your lien and order the property sold to satisfy the judgment

- filing the complaint in the appropriate court (usually for a fee between $100 and $200), and

- serving (personally delivering) the complaint on the owners and other people who have an economic interest in the property.

We include a sample complaint in Appendix B and on the forms disk under the file name COMPLAINT that you can adapt for your own purposes. In Chapter 8 we tell you how to prepare and file the complaint.

Combining all remedies in one action

In Chapter 1 we explained that the mechanics' lien foreclosure action can be combined with an action to enforce a stop notice (Chapter 4), to recover damages for breach of contract (Chapter 6) and to recover under a payment bond (Chapter 7). Because combining these actions is usually the most efficient way to proceed, make sure you carefully read Chapter 8 to fully understand all your options and remedies before you file any lawsuits.

G. IF YOU CAN'T FILE YOUR CASE WITHIN 90 DAYS

If you can't make the 90-day deadline, the law provides a basis for extending the time you have to file your enforcement lawsuit. If the owner is willing to agree to what's called a "Notice of Credit," you can extend the 90-day period up to one year after the date the Claim of Mechanics' Lien was recorded. There are several good reasons why the owner would agree to this:

- you and the owner are involved in negotiations and you need more time

- the owner is working on a way to pay you, but can't get it done before the 90-day period expires, or

- the owner would rather not push you into filing your suit just because of the 90-day deadline.

As a general rule, getting the owner to sign off on a Notice of Credit is a bad idea for you. Most importantly, it prevents you from taking any action to enforce your lien before the extension period expires. For instance, if the Notice of Credit extends the filing date for three months, you can't sue to enforce the lien during that three-month period. Even if other mechanics' lien creditors go after the property during this period, you will not be able to act on your lien during the extension period.

If you feel compelled by circumstances to obtain a Notice of Credit, obtain it for the briefest amount of time feasible. (See Chapter 12 for more on the Notice of Credit, including how to prepare and record one.)

Bankruptcy Note: If the owner files for bankruptcy before you get around to filing your enforcement lawsuit, you may be told to not worry about the 90-day deadline, that it will be extended while the person is in bankruptcy. This is not necessarily true. This issue is discussed in more detail in Chapter 8, Section N.

H. DESIGN PROFESSIONALS' LIEN

The design professionals' lien is intended to protect a specific group of people—certificated architects, registered professional engineers and licensed surveyors—who from time to time provide services in connection with works of improvement that never get off the ground. Because mechanics' liens are only available for works of improvement that *do* get off the ground, the Legislature felt that these particular groups needed some additional pre-project protection.

1. When to Use Both Lien Remedies

The design professionals' lien does not confer any priority advantage over mechanics' liens. So, if you are pretty sure that the work of improvement is going to go forward, you might well wait until it does, and then take the steps outlined in Chapter 2 and in the previous provisions of this chapter. However, if you want to take maximum advantage of all remedies available to you, follow these steps and, when the work of improvement does happen, serve the necessary preliminary notices (Chapter 2) and use the mechanics' lien remedy. (See Sections A-G, above.)

2. When to Use the Design Professionals' Lien Remedy Alone

If you contribute your services to a work of improvement for which a building permit is issued, but for which work is never begun, you cannot obtain a mechanics' lien. The only lien remedy you have is your design professionals' lien.

3. Building Permit Required

A design professionals' lien cannot be recorded unless a building permit (or other governmental approval) is obtained for the project to which your services are contributed. No permit, no design professionals' lien.

4. Written Contract for Services Required

To use the design professionals' lien, your services must be provided under a written contract. This is unlike the mechanics' lien remedy, where the contract may be written or oral. So if you didn't use a written contract, this remedy isn't available for you.

5. Design Professional Must Make a Written Demand

To use the design professionals' lien, you must first serve a written demand for payment for services rendered prior to the actual commencement of the work of improvement. The demand must be sent by certified or registered mail. If your services were delivered after the work of improvement commenced, you should use the mechanics' lien remedy described in earlier sections of this chapter. Here is a sample demand letter. A blank copy is in Appendix B and included on the forms disk under the file name DEPLTR.

DESIGN PROFESSIONAL'S DEMAND LETTER

Jerrry Costanza
4938 Sycamore Drive
Sacramento, CA 91992

January 18, 2000

Re: Architectural services rendered

Dear Owner,

As you may know, I have contributed ☒ architectural ☐ surveying ☐ engineering services for a planned work of improvement located at 18700 Rosita Street, Sacramento, under a written contract dated October 10, 1999. My services were contributed between the dates of October 15 and November 1. I have not been paid for these services as required by the contract, and you are therefore in default. I hereby demand that you pay me this amount within 10 days, plus interest at 10% per annum. Otherwise I will be forced to record a design professionals' lien against your property.

Sincerely,

Jerry Costanza

Jerry Costanza

6. Preparing and Recording the Design Professionals' Lien

To use the design professionals' lien, you must record a Notice of Lien more than 10 days after you mailed the written demand, but less than 90 days after you know or have reason to know that the landowner will not be commencing the work of improvement.

You must record the Notice of Lien in the county where the property listed on the building permit is located.

Here is what the Notice of Lien for Design Professionals looks like:

A blank Notice of Lien for Design Professionals is in Appendix B and on the forms disk under the file name PROLIEN. It is self-explanatory. For more information regarding the owner and the legal description of the real estate, see Section D, above.

Recording requested by

and when recorded mail

this document to

For recorders use

Notice of Design Professionals' Lien

_____Roark Architectural Services_____, Claimant, hereby records a Design

Professionals' Lien against the following property in regard to which Claimant contributed

professional services:

4215 Beachview Terrace

Laguna Niguel, CA 90017

_____.

Amount of claim and lien: $___$10,500___, including the principal due from

___5/10/99___, plus interest at the rate of ___10___% per annum.

Description of Services:

Architectural plans for a four-unit condominium project

_____.

Building Permit Information:

Permit #7C449458 issued by the city of Laguna Niguel

_____.

Name and Address of Owner of Property:

_____ Robert Renfro _____

_____ 25 Breeze Way _____

_____ Newport Beach, CA 90012 _____.

Stephen Roark
_____
Signature

VERIFICATION

I, _____ Stephen Roark _____, the undersigned, say I am the

_____ President _____ of the claimant of the foregoing Notice of

Design Professionals' Lien. I have read said Notice of Design Professionals' Lien and

know the contents thereof; the same is true of my own knowledge.

I declare under penalty of perjury that the foregoing is true and correct. Executed on

____ 8/23/99 ____ at _____ Costa Mesa _____,

California.

Stephen Roark
_____
Signature

7. When the Lien Expires

The design professionals' lien expires upon the happening of either of the following events:

- Upon commencement of the work of improvement.

- 90 days after the date the lien is recorded (unless an enforcement lawsuit is filed).

8. Enforcement of Design Professionals' Lien

The design professionals' lien is enforced in the same manner as the mechanics' lien. The enforcement suit must be filed no later than 90 days after the lien is recorded. See Chapter 8 for more information about bringing an enforcement suit. The sample complaint in Chapter 8 won't work for this particular type of lien, but it will give you an idea of what's involved.

9. Lien Unavailable for Some Single Family Homes

The design professionals' lien doesn't apply to a single family owner-occupied residence where the construction costs are less than one hundred thousand dollars.

I. WHAT HAPPENS IF THE LIEN IS PAID IN FULL OR IN PART

If you receive full or part payment on your lien claim, you are required to prepare and record a document that sets out the payment and releases the lien to that extent. A Partial Release of Lien and a Full Release of Lien are in Appendix B and on the forms disk under the file names PARTREL and FULLREL. Here is what these forms look like:

Partial Release of Lien

The Claim of Mechanics' Lien recorded on __3/15/99_____ , in Book __165__ of Official Records, page __27__ , records of _____Colusa_____ County, California, against _____John Fitzgerald_____ is hereby partially satisfied and is therefore partially released and discharged as follows:

_____ Payment of $2,000 against the recorded claim of mechanics' lien in the _____

_____ amount of $4,500, leaving a balance of $2,500, plus interest _____

_____ .

State of _____California_____

County of _____Colusa_____

On _____ , before me, a notary public in and for said state, personally appeared _____ , personally known to me (or proved to me on the basis of satisfactory evidence) to be the person(s) whose name(s) is/are subscribed to the within instrument, and acknowledged to me that he/she/they executed the same in his/her/their authorized capacity(ies) and that by his/her/their signature(s) on the instrument the person(s), or the entity upon behalf of which the person(s) acted, executed the instrument.

_____

Signature of Notary

Full Release of Lien

The Claim of Mechanics' Lien recorded on ___3/15/99___ , in Book _165_ of Official Records, page _27_, records of _Colusa_ County, California, against _____John Fitzgerald_____ is hereby fully satisfied and is therefore fully released and discharged.

The property affected by this release is described as follows:

Property located at:

4545 Huntington Beach Lane

Huntington Beach, California 94452 .

State of _____California_____

County of _____Orange_____

On _____ , before me, a notary public in and for said state, personally appeared _____, personally known to me (or proved to me on the basis of satisfactory evidence) to be the person(s) whose name(s) is/are subscribed to the within instrument, and acknowledged to me that he/she/they executed the same in his/her/their authorized capacity(ies) and that by his/her/their signature(s) on the instrument the person(s), or the entity upon behalf of which the person(s) acted, executed the instrument.

_____

Signature of Notary

J. LEGAL AUTHORITY

Here we set out the citations to the California statutes that support the major points covered in this chapter. All citations are to the California Civil Code unless otherwise stated. The text of the statutes themselves is included in Appendix A.

Rule governing the content of the Claim of Mechanics' Lien	§3084
Rule governing the amount of the mechanics' lien	§3123(a)

Your mechanics' lien may be for more than the contract amount if written amendments support the increase   §3123(b)

Claim of Mechanics' Lien must allocate among separate units if you were hired on a per unit or hourly basis   §§ 3130,3131

The law will not consider your mechanics' lien invalid if you make a mistake in your demand but didn't intend to mislead or defraud   §3261

The statute regulating waivers of mechanics' liens   §3262

Statute governing extension of time to file enforcement lawsuit   §3144

Claim of Mechanics' Lien arises from time work of improvement begins   §3134

Statute governing when work is completed   §3086

When Claim of Mechanics' Lien must be recorded ■   §3115,3116

The Stop Notice Remedy Against the Owner

This chapter tells you how to go after construction funds that are still in the owner's possession. This is accomplished by serving a stop notice on the owner.

If there is a lender that also has undistributed construction funds, you can also go after those if you are willing and able to post a bond. This remedy is discussed in Chapter 5.

This remedy is unavailable for prime contractors

If you are the prime (general) contractor in charge of the work of improvement, you can't use the stop notice remedy against the owner. You can, however, serve a bonded stop notice against the lender. (See Chapter 5.)

A. HOW THE STOP NOTICE REMEDY WORKS

When you use the stop notice remedy, the owner becomes directly responsible for paying you out of remaining construction funds under the owner's control.

If the owner doesn't pay you after being served with your stop notice, you have the right to sue the owner in court for the funds, provided that you file your suit in a timely manner. As we point out in Chapter 1, this lawsuit can—and ordinarily should—be combined with a lawsuit to enforce a mechanics' lien and to recover damages for breach of contract.

What does the stop notice remedy against the owner accomplish that you can't also accomplish through the mechanics' lien? The mechanics' lien is directed at the owner's property itself, whereas the stop notice attaches to the owner's undisbursed construction funds. Attaching or freezing all or a portion of the owner's undisbursed construction funds will certainly get the owner's attention if the mechanics' lien has not,

and often will result in a payment directly from the owner to you (if you are a subcontractor or materials supplier, the owner then deducts the amount from future payments to the general contractor).

Of course, this remedy won't be effective unless construction funds are available for you to proceed against. If construction activities are still going on, it's probably safe to assume that at least some money is left. But if construction is over, the funds may be depleted. What to do? Our recommendation is that you simply assume there are funds and proceed with your stop notice remedy. Let the owner or lender raise lack of funds as a defense.

You don't have to choose remedies

If you had to choose between a stop notice and a Claim of Mechanics' Lien, we would suggest the stop notice as the simpler and more comprehensive remedy. Fortunately, there is no need to choose. You can and should use both. Each has its advantages and disadvantages. And, also fortunately, each is easy to enforce in its early stages. Remember, all construction payment remedies are separate and cumulative, which means you don't have to choose between them.

That being said, here is an exception. If you are a subcontractor or materials supplier and the general contractor has recorded a payment bond, then the owner need not withhold the construction funds and instead can require you to proceed against the payment bond. See Chapter 7 for more on going after payment bonds. As a general rule, payment bonds are rarely used in home improvement and other small construction projects in California. They are much more common in larger projects.

The stop notice remedy involves five steps:

- Serving a preliminary notice on the proper parties (see Chapter 2)

- Preparing the "stop notice" document to be served on the owner (Section C, below)

- Serving the stop notice document on the owner (Section D, below)

- Preparing a Proof of Service of Stop Notice (Section E, below)

- If necessary, filing a lawsuit against the owner to enforce the stop notice (see Chapter 8).

You don't have to post a bond to use the stop notice remedy against the owner—however, you have the option of doing so. The advantage of doing so is that if you have to go to court to enforce the stop notice, you may be able to recover your attorney fees—which may be necessary to make the enforcement lawsuit feasible in the first place. The disadvantage is that you will have to obtain the bond, which may be both difficult and expensive (although you may be able to recover the cost of the bond if you win).

If you are comfortable shopping for a bond and have the money to pay the premium, the bonded stop notice may well be your best choice, even though a bond is not required for a stop notice on the owner. (See Chapter 5 for more on bonded stop notices, which are required for lenders.)

B. THE PRELIMINARY NOTICE

The stop notice process starts when you serve your preliminary notice on the necessary parties. To summarize the basic points we discuss in Chapter 2:

- You must serve a preliminary notice on the owner, general contractor and lender (which in-

cludes an insurer) unless you are the prime (general) contractor or a laborer who worked on-site for wages, or you contracted directly with the owner.

- If you are the prime (general) contractor or performed on-site labor for wages, you don't have to serve the owner or lender (but you should at least serve the lender).

- If you are anyone else who contracted directly with the owner and there is a construction loan in the picture (which there often is), you need not serve the owner or prime contractor, but you must serve the lender.

- If you are a materials supplier who has supplied materials to two or more subcontractors for the same project, you must provide separate notices for each subcontractor and should serve the subcontractors as well as the owner, general contractor and lender.

- You should serve the preliminary notice no more than 20 days after the first day you began your work or provided materials (or within 20 days after the work of improvement begins if your contribution was made before it began—for instance, if you are an architect).

- If you are late, you can still serve the preliminary notice, but any mechanics' lien claim will only be for work or materials you contribute during the 20 days directly preceding the date you serve the preliminary notice and during the period that follows.

The rest of this chapter is for people who are only serving a stop notice on the owner. If you are also serving a bonded stop notice on the lender, skip to Chapter 5 and complete the stop notice and Proof of Service as described in that chapter.

C. PREPARE THE STOP NOTICE

A blank stop notice form is in Appendix B and on the
forms disk under the file name STOPNOT. Almost all of
the information in this document is the same as that
provided in the preliminary notice (Chapter 2) and the
Claim of Mechanics' Lien (Chapter 3).

Here is a filled-in sample:

Stop Notice for Private Works

☐ To Owner: _____ Vera Cruz _____

☐ To Lending Institution: ___ First National Bank and Trust _____

YOU ARE HEREBY NOTIFIED that:

Claimant: _____ Joe Morgan _____, who is located at: ___ 237 Maple St. ___

_____ ,

has contributed ☐ labor ☒ services ☐ equipment ☐ materials

in the amount of $_____ $2,400 _____

under contract with _____ Fred Smith Contracting _____

for the contract price of $___ $2,400 _____

to be used and actually used in the work improvement consisting of:

_____ Site preparation _____

_____

_____

located on the property described as

_____ 1076 Marina Drive _____

_____ Shelter Cove, CA 97752 _____

_____

owned by _____ Vera Cruz _____ .

Claimant hereby demands that, under Section ☒ 3158 ☐ 3159 of the California Civil Code, you withhold from construction funds under your possession or control the amount of $_____2,400_____, which amount is due and owning Claimant as of the date of this stop notice.

Dated: ___1/13/99___   Signed: ___*Joe Morgan*___

VERIFICATION [CCP § 446]

I declare under penalty of perjury under the laws of the State of California that the foregoing is true and correct, this _____ day of _____ at _____

_____, California.

_____
Signature

D. SERVE THE STOP NOTICE ON THE OWNER

To be valid, the stop notice must be properly served on the owner. Technically, it doesn't make any difference whether you are not yet owed anything for your contribution, as long as you are under contract and have made at least some contribution to the work of improvement. However, the far better practice is to wait until a payment problem rears its ugly head.

You must serve the stop notice prior to the deadline for recording a mechanics' lien. This is between 30-60 days after the project is completed if the owner records a document of completion or cessation of work, and 90 days after work on the project has ceased if no such document is recorded. (See Chapter 3, Section E2, for more on this deadline.) However, the stop notice can be served much earlier than this deadline. It can and should be served as soon as a payment problem arises.

The stop notice is served in the same manner as the preliminary notice. (See Chapter 2, Section F.) As with the preliminary notice, you cannot use regular first class mail to serve the stop notice. You must either personally serve it or use one of the other methods approved by statute. The best is certified mail, return receipt requested.

1. Effect of Serving Stop Notice

Once you serve the stop notice on the owner, the owner is under a duty to withhold the funds claimed in the stop notice unless the general contractor has recorded a payment bond. As we cautioned you earlier, a recorded payment bond takes the owner off the hook. Your stop notice is a type of attachment or garnishment on construction funds that the owner controls but has not yet disbursed.

Since most construction projects are paid for out of funds that have been loaned especially for that purpose, the owner may have opened a separate savings or checking account for funds received from the lender. But homeowners who hire you to work on home improvement projects may not have a separate account. Rather, they may be drawing from their general bank account in which they have previously deposited the proceeds of a home equity loan.

Regardless of where or how the funds are kept, if the funds originated from a construction loan, your stop notice obligates the owner to withhold enough money to meet your payment demand, should this prove necessary.

E. PREPARE PROOF OF SERVICE

The statutes governing stop notices don't require you to prepare a Proof of Service. However, we think it's a good idea, just in case the owner ever claims that he or she was not properly served. A blank Proof of Service of Stop Notice form is in Appendix B and on the forms disk under the file name PRSTOP. Here is a filled-in sample:

Proof of Service of Stop Notice

I, _____Joe Morgan_____, declare that I served copies of the above stop notice on:

☒ (Owner)

John Roundtree

_____

☒ (Lender)

First American Savings & Trust

_____

☐ by personally delivering a copy to ☐ Owner at _____

_____

☐ Lender at _____

_____

☒ by First Class Certified or Registered Mail service, postage prepaid, addressed to

☒ Owner at _100 Shadow Lane, Fortuna, CA_ on
_1/14/99_ .

☒ Lender at _50 Main St., Eureka, CA_ on
_1/14/99_ .

VERIFICATION [CCP § 446]

I declare under penalty of perjury under the laws of the State of California that the foregoing is true and correct, this _____ day of _____ at _____

_____ , California.

_____
Signature

F. ENFORCING THE STOP NOTICE

As with the mechanics' lien, the stop notice is only valid for a specific period of time unless you file a lawsuit to enforce it. The deadline for filing an enforcement lawsuit is between 10 days after serving the stop notice on the owner and 90 days from the date the right to record a Claim of Mechanics' Lien would expire (which is roughly between 30 and 90 days from the date the project is completed). In other words, your deadline for enforcing a stop notice is between 120 and 180 days after the project is completed or work ceases.

Because this deadline is dependent upon whether the owner recorded a document of completion, you are best served by the conservative approach: File your enforcement lawsuit as soon as possible after the 10-day period following the date you served the stop notice expires. Keep in mind that you may want to combine your enforcement lawsuit with the other actions available to you.

We tell you how to prepare and file a stop notice enforcement lawsuit in Chapter 8.

Bankruptcy Note: If the owner files for bankruptcy before you get around to filing your enforcement lawsuit, you may be told to not worry about the deadline, that it will be extended while the person is in bankruptcy. This is not necessarily true. This issue is discussed in more detail in Chapter 8, Section N.

G. WHAT IF THE OWNER FAILS TO WITHHOLD

The stop notice enforcement lawsuit is designed to recover from funds that the owner was supposed to have preserved just for this purpose. Unfortunately, it's quite possible that the owner will fail to withhold the money despite having been served with your stop notice. If this happens, the owner will be held personally liable for the payment. So, in terms of your right to obtain a money judgment, it is basically irrelevant whether the money is still there or has been spent. Of course, if the money is still there, collecting your judgment will be a lot easier.

H. LEGAL AUTHORITY

Here we set out the citations to the California statutes that support the major points covered in this chpater. All citations are to the California Civil Code. The text of the statutes themselves is included in Appendix A.

Stop notice remedy against the owner	§3158
Bonded stop notice remedy against the lender (or insurer)	§3159
Recovery of attorneys fees for bonded stop notice	§3176
Deadline for serving the stop notice	§3160 (b)
Deadline for enforcing stop notice	§3172 ■

The Stop Notice Remedy Against the Lender

Most works of improvement are paid for by funds borrowed from a commercial lender—typically a bank, savings and loan or credit union. For larger projects, the borrowed money may be a construction loan doled out by the bank in accordance with phased completion dates. For smaller homeowner-financed projects, the borrowed money may be in the form of a home equity loan from which the homeowner can draw down funds as needed. Money may also be available in the form of insurance proceeds earmarked to pay for repairs to insured real estate, but not yet disbursed.

Whatever the type of loan or insurance coverage, if there are funds committed to the work of improvement in the hands of a lender or insurance company, by serving a "bonded" stop notice you can require the lender or insurance company to withhold the undisbursed loan funds in an amount equal to what is owed you for your contribution to the project. Then, if there is a payment problem, you can file an enforcement action to recover the funds from the lender or insurance company.

This remedy is called a bonded stop notice. It works in much the same way as the stop notice against the owner. (See Chapter 4.) However, there are some important differences, particularly the requirement that your stop notice be accompanied by a bond. (See Section D, below.)

A. WHY USE THE BONDED STOP NOTICE REMEDY?

The bonded stop notice is superior to the mechanics' lien remedy in one very important way: The loan granted by the construction lender typically is secured by a deed of trust on the property being improved. Under the law, this construction loan deed of trust has first priority over liens that come later—including mechanics' liens (assuming the work of improvement wasn't physically commenced on site prior to the recording of the construction loan).

If the property owner defaults on the loan and the lender forecloses on the property, there may be little or no equity left in the property after the lender is paid off. Since all mechanics' liens have equal priority with each other, the mechanics' lien claimants all must scramble for a piece of a pie that ordinarily has already been eaten up by the construction lender.

However, if you have legally required the lender to withhold from the loan funds an amount sufficient to pay you, your claim against the lender will not be affected by any foreclosure that happens later. This puts you in a much better position than if you relied on your mechanics' lien remedy alone.

Example: Chris Carpenter, a licensed contractor specializing in rough framing, is hired by the prime contractor to do $10,000 worth of framing for a new commercial office building. A dispute over payment arises, and Chris is only paid $6,000 even though he completed the task. Chris immediately records both a mechanics' lien for $4,000 and serves a bonded stop notice for this amount on First Mutual Bank, the construction lender.

After the project is completed and prior to any litigation, the building's vacancy rate is unacceptably high, and the owner is forced to sell the building at a price that is just barely enough to repay the construction loan and the original loan the owner used to purchase the property. Because there is nothing left after these two large lenders are paid, Chris's mechanics' lien is worthless. However, Chris can recover the amount specified in the *bonded* stop notice from the lender. If for some reason the lender refuses to turn over to Chris the funds it was supposed to withhold, Chris can file a lawsuit against the construction lender to enforce the bonded stop notice and recover the cost of the bond premium.

There is another good reason to use the bonded stop notice. If you are the prevailing party—that is, win your lawsuit—you may be able to get the judge to order the other side to pay your attorney fees in an action to enforce a bonded stop notice (CC §3176), but not in an action to enforce a mechanics' lien or unbonded stop notice.

The availability of attorney fees often makes the difference between being able to find an attorney to take your case and having to handle it yourself. If you combine all your enforcement actions in one lawsuit, it is likely that you will be able to pay an attorney to handle everything, even though the attorney fees are technically recoverable only from the stop notice portion.

B. WHO QUALIFIES TO USE THE BONDED STOP NOTICE REMEDY?

Anyone who qualifies for the mechanics' lien remedy also qualifies for the bonded stop notice remedy, except the prime (general) contractor can't use it against the owner. This includes:

- all people who contribute labor, services, materials or equipment to a work of improvement

- those who contribute to improvement of the site where the work of improvement will occur, and

- design professionals who contribute services in preparation for the work of improvement.

See Chapter 3 for more on who qualifies for the mechanics' lien (and therefore the bonded stop notice) remedy.

C. THE PRELIMINARY NOTICE REQUIREMENT

As with mechanics' liens and stop notices against the owner, it is necessary to first have served a preliminary notice on the proper parties to take advantage of the bonded stop notice remedy. To remind you:

- You must serve a preliminary notice on the owner, general contractor and lender (or insurance company) unless you are the prime (general) contractor or a laborer who worked on site for wages, or you contracted directly with the owner.

- If you are the prime (general) contractor or performed on-site labor for wages, you don't have to serve anyone (although it is a good idea to do so anyway).

- If you are anyone else who contracted directly with the owner and there is a construction loan in the picture (which there often is), you must serve the lender or insurance company.

- If you are a materials supplier who supplied materials to two or more subcontractors for use in a single project, you'll need to serve a separate preliminary notice for each subcontractor and serve each subcontractor as well as the owner, general contractor and lender.

- You should serve the preliminary notice no more than 20 days after the first day you began your work or provided materials, or within 20 days after the work of improvement begins if your contribution was made before it began (for instance, if you are an architect).

- If you are late, you can still serve the preliminary notice, but any mechanics' lien claim will only be for work or materials you contribute during the 20 days directly preceding the date you serve the preliminary notice and during the period that follows.

D. THE BONDING REQUIREMENT

Unlike the stop notice against the owner, to be fully effective the stop notice against the lender or insurance company must be accompanied by a bond for 125% of your demand—that is, the value of your contribution which has not been paid for (your claim amount). (CC §3083) The purpose of the bond is to recompense the lender or insurance company if your stop notice claim turns out to be invalid.

While there is nothing to prevent you from serving an unbonded stop notice against a lender or insurance company, the lender or insurance company is under no obligation to withhold, absent a bond. This, of course, makes the bond pretty much mandatory.

Readers who are required to have a license to ply their trade are already familiar with bonds, since they must have a bond to obtain a license. But laborers, truckers and materials providers may have never had to obtain a bond. Basically, a bond is simply a promise by a bonding company to pay the amount of the bond under certain specified circumstances. The person who is covered by the bond must pay the bonding company a nonrefundable fee—called a premium—to have the bond issued.

If it turns out that the bond wasn't needed, the person purchasing the bond is only out the premium. If, however, some or all of the bond's face value is paid out by the bonding company to qualified claimants, the bonding company is entitled to come after the purchaser for recompense.

This seems straightforward enough. If you have the money to pay the premium, you get the bond and proceed with your stop notice remedy. If you win, you may recover the premium as well as what you are owed. If you lose, you'll have to answer to the bonding company for any damages that it is forced to pay out to the lender.

Alas, it's not quite that simple. Most bonding companies want you either to have good credit or to post collateral as security for the bond in case they need you to reimburse them for a claim against the bond. If you are already dealing with a bonding company because of a license requirement (or for any other reason), you can probably just go ahead and purchase your stop notice bond from the same company.

However, if you are new to bonding, you may have to spend considerable effort shopping around to find a bond. Probably the best approach is to look in the Yellow Pages for larger cities under Bonding Companies. Also, larger insurance brokerage firms or local builders' exchanges may provide referrals.

E. LENDER OPTIONS

Especially in large commercial projects, the developer or owner may require the prime contractor to record a pay-

ment bond guaranteeing payment of all qualified contributors to the work of improvement. If the payment bond has been recorded before you have made your contribution to the work of improvement, the lender has a choice: It can proceed to withhold the funds as required in the stop notice, or it can choose to disburse the funds to the owner, requiring you to go after the payment bond to get what you're owed. (See Chapter 7 for more on payment bonds.) If the bond was recorded after you make your contribution to the work of improvement, it won't interfere with your stop notice remedy.

Example: You contracted to deliver 500 tropical plants to be used in landscaping a 200-unit tropical-motif hotel being constructed. After you deliver the plants but before they are transplanted into the soil, a freak storm destroys half of them. The landscape contractor who purchased the plants from you informs you that he can only afford to pay for the half that survived. You record a mechanics' lien against the project owner, serve an unbonded stop notice on the owner and serve a bonded stop notice on the construction lender. It turns out the prime contractor has purchased a payment bond. The lender informs you that your remedy lies against the payment bond and that it elects to reject the stop notice and disburse the funds as planned.

F. PREPARING AND SERVING A STOP NOTICE ON THE LENDER

Below is a filled-in sample of a bonded stop notice to be served on the lender. This is the same form that we used in Chapter 4. It is in Appendix B and on the forms disk under the file name STOPNOT. If you have already prepared that form but have decided to use the bonded stop notice remedy against a lender, simply check the box preceding "To Lending Institution," and you can send the same form to both owner and lender. If you are only serving a stop notice on the lender, then fill in this form, checking the "To Lending Institution" box and leaving the "To Owner" box blank.

Stop Notice for Private Works

☐ To Owner: _____

☒ To Lending Institution: __First American Savings and Trust_____

YOU ARE HEREBY NOTIFIED that:

Claimant: ___Joseph Hodge_____, who is located at: _____
_____1419 Apricot Lane, Fresno CA_____,

has contributed ☐ labor ☒ services ☐ equipment ☐ materials

in the amount of $__5,900_____

under contract with _____Modern Kitchen Concepts_____

for the contract price of $___$5,900_____

to be used and actually used in the work improvement consisting of:
_____Kitchen remodel_____

_____

located on the property described as _____1914 Peach Lane, Fresno_____

_____

owned by _____Marcus Ortiz_____.

Claimant hereby demands that, under Section ☒ 3158 ☐ 3159 of the California Civil Code, you withhold from construction funds under your possession or control the amount of $___5,900_____, which amount is due and owing Claimant as of the date of this stop notice.

Dated: ___4/7/99_____   Signed: __*Joseph Hodge*_____

VERIFICATION [CCP § 446]

I declare under penalty of perjury under the laws of the State of California that the foregoing is true and correct, this __7th___ day of __April 1999___ at _____Fresno_____, California.

__*Joseph Hodge*_____
Signature

G. SERVING THE STOP NOTICE

To be valid, the bonded stop notice must be properly served on the lender (and on the owner if you are using the remedy against the owner as well). You may accomplish this service any time prior to the deadline for recording a mechanics' lien. This is either up to 30, 60 or 90 days after work on the project has terminated. (See Chapter 3, Section E2, for more on this deadline.) As a general rule, you should serve the notice as soon as a payment problem becomes evident.

The bonded stop notice can be served on the lender and owner in the same manner as the preliminary notice. It can be personally delivered, or it can be sent by registered or certified mail. Service on the lender should be made to the manager (or other responsible official) of the branch office of the lending institution responsible for administering or holding the construction funds. This person will usually be the real estate loan officer.

Do not serve the bonded stop notice by regular mail. This will not be considered a legal service and will likely forfeit your stop notice rights. Either personally serve the bonded stop notice or send it certified mail, return receipt requested.

For specific instructions on how to accomplish service, see Chapter 2, Section F.

As mentioned, once you serve the bonded stop notice on the lender or insurer, and provided the prime contractor has not recorded a payment bond, the lender or insurer is under a legal duty to withhold the funds claimed in the stop notice. Your stop notice is a type of attachment or garnishment on construction funds that the lender or insurer controls but has not yet disbursed. Since most construction projects are paid for out of funds that have been loaned especially for that purpose, the lender or insurer will most likely have an earmarked fund.

H. PREPARING PROOF OF SERVICE

The statutes governing stop notices don't require you to prepare a Proof of Service. However, we think it's a good idea anyway, just in case the owner ever claims that he or she was not properly served. A blank Proof of Service of Stop Notice form is in Appendix B and on the forms disk under the file name PRSTOP. Here is a filled-in sample:

Proof of Service of Stop Notice

I, _____Joseph Hodge_____, declare that I served copies of the above stop notice on:

☐ (Owner)

_____

_____

☒ (Lender)

First Interstate Savings & Loan
_____

_____

   ☐ by personally delivering a copy to ☐ Owner at _____

_____

   ☐ Lender at _____

_____

   ☒ by First Class Certified or Registered Mail service, postage prepaid, addressed to

      ☐ Owner at _____ on

_____.

      ☒ Lender at _____2319 Blackstone Ave., Fresno_____ on
          4/7/99

VERIFICATION [CCP § 446]

I declare under penalty of perjury under the laws of the State of California that the foregoing is true and correct, this ___7th___ day of _April 1999_ at _____Fresno_____, California.

_____Joseph Hodge_____
Signature

I. REQUESTING NOTICE OF ELECTION

When you serve the bonded stop notice on the lender or insurer you may also serve a written request for notice of election not to withhold, plus a copy of the payment bond. This request should be accompanied by a self-addressed, stamped envelope. Of course, if there is no payment bond, then there is no reason for this request. But since you may not know whether there is a payment bond or not, this is an easy way to find out.

Here is a sample Request Notice of Election. A blank form is in Appendix B and included on the forms disk under the file name REQELECT.

REQUEST NOTICE OF ELECTION

Joseph Hodge
5011 South Maple
Fresno, CA 91117

August 11, 1999

RE: Stop Notice Served by Toni Warner

To Whom It May Concern:

Please notify me within 30 days as to whether you intend to withhold the amount claimed in my stop notice served on you on 4/7/99, or whether you elect instead to not withhold because of a payment bond taken out by the beneficiary of the construction funds. If you do elect not to withhold, please furnish me with a copy of the payment bond.

Sincerely,

Joseph Hodge

Joseph Hodge

J. ENFORCING THE STOP NOTICE

As with the mechanics' lien, the bonded stop notice is only valid for a specific period of time unless you file a lawsuit to enforce it. The deadline for filing an enforcement lawsuit is between 10 days after serving the stop notice on the owner and 90 days from the date the right to record a Claim of Mechanics' Lien would expire (which is between 30 and 90 days from the date the project is completed).

In other words, your deadline for filing a lawsuit to enforce a bonded stop notice is roughly between 120 and 180 days after the project is completed or work ceases. You will be best served by the conservative approach: If it is necessary, file your stop notice enforcement lawsuit as soon after the initial 10-day period expires as possible, keeping in mind that you may want to combine your enforcement lawsuit with the other actions available to you.

We tell you how to prepare and file a bonded stop notice enforcement lawsuit in Chapter 8.

K. WHAT IF THE MONEY IS GONE?

The stop notice enforcement lawsuit is designed to recover from funds that the lender was supposed to have preserved just for this purpose. Unfortunately, it's quite possible that the money will be long gone. If that happens, the lender will be held liable for the payment. So, in terms of your right to obtain a money judgment, it is basically irrelevant whether the money is still there or not. Of course, if the money is still there, collecting your judgment will be a lot easier.

L. LEGAL AUTHORITY

Here we set out the citations to the California Statutes that support the major points covered in this chapter. The statutes themselves are reproduced in Appendix A.

Authorizes the stop notice on the lender	§§3159, 3162
Describes information that must be contained in stop notice ■	§3103

CHAPTER 6

Understanding Your Contract Remedy

In earlier chapters we explained how the mechanics' lien and stop notice remedies can give you a head start as a creditor against:

- the property being improved, and
- the assets of the people and companies responsible for withholding construction funds in response to your stop notice.

However, if push comes to shove, it will be necessary to file a lawsuit to enforce your remedies.

Underlying those remedies and, if necessary, the lawsuit, is your right to be paid for your contribution to the work of improvement. This chapter discusses the starting point for determining how much you are entitled to be paid: the underlying contract between you and the person who hired you or promised to pay for your contribution.

A. UNDERSTANDING YOUR CONTRACT

When a subcontractor orders a load of materials from a supplier or a general contractor hires a subcontractor to perform certain specified services, a contract is created. This contract essentially says: "In exchange for payment of an agreed-upon price by one party, the other party agrees to provide certain labor or materials of a specified type and grade." The contract may be written or oral, but it's still a contract. And when one party performs his or her end of the contract, the other party must do likewise.

Contracts come in three basic flavors: written, oral and implied. Whatever type of contract you have, your agreement is the starting place for determining what you can recover in a breach of contract suit and by way of a mechanics' lien or stop notice.

1. Written Agreements

It's always best to have a written contract that not only describes the work to be done and the method and amount of payment, but also takes Murphy's law fully into account (what can go wrong will go wrong) and sets out ways to address whatever glitches may arise. An excellent resource to help you understand and prepare sound construction contracts is *The Contractor's Legal*

Kit, by Gary Ransone (A Journal of Light Construction Book).

2. Oral and Implied Agreements

Written agreements are not always used. Instead, you may have made your contribution on the basis of a handshake and an oral agreement on the basic terms: what you were to provide, when you were to provide it and how much you were to provide it for.

Or, there may have been no discussion at all. Instead, things may have just happened according to what's happened before. For instance, a homeowner who has successfully used a particular contractor before may hire that contractor without any accompanying negotiations (for example: "When can you come out and fix my roof?"). This arrangement also creates a valid contract. However, the terms of the contract are implied from past practice rather than from a specific agreement. In effect the contract "reads" like this:

"In exchange for a promise by Party I (Owner, Contractor or Subcontractor) to pay Party II its regular charges, Party II (Contractor, Subcontractor or Materials Provider) agrees first to perform the labor requested by Party I (and/or provide materials of a standard type and grade) and to start the work in a timely manner."

Under this type of contract, when Party II performs his or her end of the contract, Party I must do likewise—by making the payment. In this case the payment would be whatever Party II normally charges for this type of job (Party I may or may not already know this).

The virtue of oral or implied contracts is that they're simple and don't involve lawyers. The downside, however, is that they don't address such contingencies as:

- What happens if Party II is late starting the work?
- What happens if Party II doesn't do work that meets Party I's expectations?
- What happens if Party I doesn't pay Party II?
- What happens if Party I wants Party II to change the scope of the work?

Unfortunately, these and other issues always lurk in the background of every construction project. This is why it's always advisable to use a written agreement.

Special rules for swimming pool and home improvement contracts

All swimming pool and home improvement contracts must be in writing if the value of the labor and materials to be furnished by the contractor exceeds $500.

B. RESOLVING PAYMENT DISPUTES UNDER YOUR CONTRACT

Every construction and home improvement contract raises several important issues that will determine what remedies are available to you in the event of non-payment.

1. Breach of Contract Lawsuits

First, when a party to a contract—regardless of the type—doesn't perform as promised, a breach of contract occurs. The typical remedy for breach of contract is to bring a lawsuit in court to recover from the breaching party the monetary value of the damages caused by the breach. In the case of non-payment, the recovery would be for the contractual amount (the amount the contract says will be paid for the work) or the value of the goods or services provided. In most cases, the contractual amount and the value of the goods or services provided are the same. Other times, the services actually performed or the materials actually delivered are less than or different from those specified in the contract.

If there is a payment or performance bond, the company issuing the bond may also be sued or, if the bond calls for it, subjected to arbitration.

You are entitled to file a breach of contract lawsuit even if you also plan to enforce your mechanics' lien and stop notice remedies. Your breach of contract lawsuit is directed at the personal or business assets of the people who are liable for the breach, while the mechanics' lien and stop notice remedies are directed respectively at the property being improved and the owner's funds that have been earmarked for that improvement (often held by a construction lender).

These are all separate and independent remedies and can be used for the same claim of nonpayment. Most often, all remedies are used together, although there are exceptions, such as when a general contractor uses the mechanics' lien and breach of contract remedies but not the stop notice remedy because there is no lender and the mechanics' lien law doesn't let the general contractor serve a stop notice on the owner.

2. Arbitration of Disputes

If your contract—whether written or oral—does not address how disputes such as non-payment should be resolved, you will need to take your dispute to court unless you and the other party can agree on a different method of resolution, such as arbitration or mediation. (See Chapter 12.)

If, however, you are working under a written contract, it may address the process by which you must resolve disputes. Many written construction contracts provide that any dispute will be resolved either by taking the matter to Small Claims Court (if the amount in controversy fits within the Small Claims Court's limit, which is $5,000 in California), or by turning to binding arbitration.

Binding arbitration uses a third-party decision maker to hear both sides and issue a decision. The process is much less formal and often much quicker than court. The term "binding" refers to the fact that the arbitrator's decision is final. You can't have a second hearing before a judge. A typical binding arbitration clause reads this way:

"Any controversy or claim arising out of or relating to this contract, or the breach thereof, shall be settled by arbitration administered by the American Arbitration Association under its Construction Industry Arbitration Rules, and judgment on the award rendered by the arbitrator(s) may be entered in any court having jurisdiction thereof."

As mediation becomes more common in construction disputes, some written contracts include a clause that requires the parties to first try mediation and then go to binding arbitration if the mediation fails to produce a result. Here is a clause that combines mediation and binding arbitration:

VOLUNTARY SETTLEMENTS—
DIRECT AND MEDIATED NEGOTIATIONS

We agree that, should any difference of interpretation, or any other controversy or claim arise out of, or related to, our contract dated _____ , or the breach thereof, we shall immediately make good faith efforts to negotiate our own written voluntary resolution of the matter directly between ourselves. We agree that, if the matter still remains unsettled for [thirty, forty-five, etc.] days after certified mail notification that a dispute exists, we shall immediately jointly retain a mutually agreed-upon neutral mediator with at least ten years' experience in dispute resolution in this field, and conduct and participate in confidential mediation, to continue attempting to work out our own written voluntary settlement. We agree that if any of us files any arbitration claims, or administrative or legal actions, for disputes to which this clause applies, without first having attempted to resolve the dispute ourselves through neutral mediation, then that filing party shall not be entitled to collect attorney fees or procedural costs, even if they would otherwise be entitled to them (subject to the discretion of the arbitrator or court involved).

ARBITRATION OF DISPUTES. We agree that if, and only if, the dispute still remains unsettled for an additional [thirty, forty-five, etc.] days, then we shall submit the dispute to binding neutral arbitration. In this event, we agree that any controversy or claim arising out of, or relating to, our contracts dated _____, or the breach thereof, shall be settled by binding arbitration in accordance with the applicable rules of the American Arbitration Association then in effect as modified below. We agree that a mutually agreed-upon arbitrator with at least ten years' experience in dispute resolution in this field shall serve as our neutral arbitrator. We stipulate and agree not to seek to introduce in evidence, and not to compel the production of, documents prepared for, or statements made in the course of, our settlement discussions including the confidential mediation process, in any subsequent arbitration, litigation or administrative proceeding, except that fully initialed journal entries as described above, and any written change orders and dispute settlement agreements which have been fully signed by all necessary parties, may be introduced in evidence.

We stipulate and agree that no mediator shall submit, and no arbitrator, court or other adjudicative body shall consider, any mediator evaluations, recommendations, declarations or findings, unless all mediation participants specifically later agree in writing. We agree that judgment upon the award rendered by the arbitrator(s) may be entered in any court having jurisdiction thereof.

C. IS YOUR PAYMENT CONDITIONED UPON THE GENERAL CONTRACTOR BEING PAID FIRST?

Because construction funds typically flow from the owner down through the prime contractor to the subcontractors, written contracts between prime contractors and subcontractors typically condition payment of the subcontractor on the prime contractor first being paid by the owner. These are called "pay when paid" clauses. Here is an example of such a clause:

"Receipt of payment from Owner is a condition precedent to paying Subcontractor under this Agreement."

Under this clause, if the prime (general) contractor doesn't get paid, the prime (general) contractor supposedly is under no obligation to pay the subcontractor. However, in 1997 the California Supreme Court ruled that these clauses are invalid. (*Clarke v. Safeco*, 15 Cal.4th 882 (1997).) Therefore, the subcontractor can sue the prime (general) contractor even if the prime (general) contractor is never paid by the owner. And if the prime (general) contractor has taken out a payment or performance bond, the bond issuer can also be sued. (See Chapter 7.)

D. CONTRACT PROVISIONS REGARDING SATISFACTORY PERFORMANCE

The owner or prime contractor will often claim that you haven't been paid the amount you contracted for due to a deficiency in your performance or materials. If you have a written contract, it will typically condition payment on the satisfactory completion of your services. If you don't have a written contract, you are still held to a reasonable standard of quality regarding your goods or services (often referred to as a "workmanlike" standard).

The result is that you may ultimately be called on to convince a judge or arbitrator as to the actual value of your services or materials—whether it be the amount contracted for or something less. If your performance or materials have been deficient, you likely will not be able to recover all you contracted for. Instead, you'll receive the amount your work was worth. The more deficient your work or materials, the less you'll receive.

Example: Tim, an electrician, does $700 worth of electrical work on a spa installation. The owner who hired Tim to do the work accuses Tim of cutting some corners and only pays him $400. If Tim sues the owner, Tim can prove that the contract called for $700, and it will be up to the owner to prove either that Tim didn't provide all the labor and materials called for under the agreement or that Tim's work or materials were defective.

1. Prime Contractors Responsible for Whole Project

Written construction and home improvement contracts between the owner and the prime (general) contractor typically require the prime (general) contractor to satisfactorily perform the job as a condition of getting paid. Under these contracts, the prime contractor becomes responsible for the entire job. If a subcontractor does shoddy work, or materials are substandard, the prime (general) contractor will have to answer to the owner for the problems.

Example: John Miller wins the lottery and sets out to build a country home all by himself. Very early on he changes his mind, deciding that he would rather spend his time building his business. He hires Jack O'Donnell, a general contractor, to complete the job. Under the contract, O'Donnell will get paid in four installments. It will be up to O'Donnell to round up the necessary subcontractors to do the grading, framing, stone work, plumbing, roofing, electrical work, landscaping, flooring and painting. None of these subcontractors will ever meet Miller, since Miller will be devoting full time to his business activities—which involve frequent travel—around the time the house is being built. Before leaving, Miller executes a power of attorney naming his brother Irvin Miller to deal with O'Donnell and disburse the payments as they become due.

When John Miller takes a break from his business and inspects the finished house, he discovers a number of serious problems in the stone work and landscaping. As a matter of convenience, he contacts O'Donnell and requires O'Donnell to fix the problems. O'Donnell is legally bound to do so because under the contract it is O'Donnell rather than the subcontractors who must answer to Miller.

2. Subcontractors Responsible for Their Work

The contracts between the prime contractor and the subcontractors typically make the subcontractor responsible for their portion of the job. If performance isn't up to snuff under the contract, then payment is withheld in whole or in part.

Example: Assume the same facts as the previous example. After fixing the problems, O'Donnell withholds payment from the stone-work and landscaping subcontractors in the amount it cost O'Donnell to fix the problems. O'Donnell is legally entitled to do this because his contracts with the subcontractors provided that they were responsible for performing their jobs satisfactorily.

3. Construction Materials

The situation with construction materials is somewhat different than that for labor. Construction materials usually come under both what's called an implied warranty that the materials will be fit for their intended purpose, and an express warranty, which is whatever the manufacturer and/or supplier explicitly offers. If the warranty is not honored, then the owner can sue for breach of contract—essentially for the cost of replacing the defective materials. Here is an example of a typical warranty provision:

"Contractor provides a limited warranty on all Contractor and Subcontractor supplied labor and materials used in this project for a period of one year following substantial completion of all work. One year after substantial completion of the project, the Owner's sole remedy (for materials and labor) on all materials that are covered by a manufacturer's warranty is strictly with the manufacturer, not with the Contractor.

"Repair of the following items is specifically excluded from Contractor's warranty: damages resulting from lack of Owner maintenance; damages resulting from Owner abuse or ordinary wear and tear; deviations that arise such as the minor cracking of concrete, stucco and plaster; minor stress fractures in drywall due to the curing of lumber; warping and deflection of wood; shrinking/cracking of grouts and caulking; fading of paints and finishes exposed to sunlight.

"THE EXPRESS WARRANTIES CONTAINED HEREIN ARE IN LIEU OF ALL OTHER WARRANTIES, EXPRESS OR IMPLIED, INCLUDING ANY WARRANTIES OF MERCHANTABILITY, HABITABILITY OR FITNESS FOR A PARTICULAR USE OR PURPOSE. THIS LIMITED WARRANTY EXCLUDES CONSEQUENTIAL AND INCIDENTAL DAMAGES AND LIMITS THE DURATION OF IMPLIED WARRANTIES TO THE FULLEST EXTENT PERMISSIBLE UNDER STATE AND FEDERAL LAW."

E. WHAT DOES THE CONTRACT SAY ABOUT ATTORNEY FEES?

Many written construction and home improvement contracts have a clause that addresses attorney fees. Here is a typical clause

> "We agree that in any action, or arbitration claim, brought to interpret or enforce the terms of our contract dated _____, and any written settlement agreements as described above, the prevailing party shall be entitled to reasonable attorneys fees and costs."

This clause makes it a lot easier to get an attorney if you end up in court or arbitration. Some contracts state that attorney fees can only be awarded to one of the parties (typically the party that drafted the contract). However, under California law (CC §1717), if a clause gives attorney fees to one party, the other party may also get them if that party prevails in (wins) the lawsuit.

F. WHERE TO FILE A LAWSUIT FOR BREACH OF CONTRACT

The most common place to file a breach of contract is in the county where the work of improvement is located. But it is also possible to file the suit in the county where the party being sued lives or does business.

There are three levels of courts to consider when filing your lawsuit: Small Claims Court, Municipal Court and Superior Court.

1. Small Claims Court

If you are combining your breach of contract lawsuit with a lawsuit to enforce a mechanics' lien or stop notice, you must file in either Municipal Court or Superior Court. However, if you are bringing a separate breach of contract lawsuit, you can use the Small Claims Court if your claim is $5,000 or less, or you agree to scale back your claim in order to use this court.

As with lawsuits in other courts, there is much you can do to increase your chance of success. If you are headed towards Small Claims Court, we highly recommend that you obtain a copy of *Everybody's Guide to Small Claims Court,* by Ralph Warner (Nolo Press).

2. Municipal Court

If your breach of contract claim is considerably more than $5,000 but less than $25,000, you can file your breach of contract action in Municipal Court. (If your claim is just a little more than the small claims maximum, you may prefer to give up the balance and just go for the $5,000.) We provide more details about Municipal Court lawsuits in Chapter 8.

3. Superior Court

If your claim is well over $25,000, you will have to take your breach of contract case to Superior Court. Fortunately, because of the amount of money involved, it is often easier to find an attorney to take your case, and even worth the cost in attorney fees. In Chapter 8 we help you draft and file the breach of contract complaint.

However, if you decide to handle your own Superior Court lawsuit from that point on, you'll have to do some heavy research into Superior Court rules and procedures. Nolo Press does not have a book for Superior Court breach of contract lawsuits. Nolo Press does, however, publish a book called *Represent Yourself in Court,* by Paul Bergman and Sara Berman-Barrett, which helps you deal with the advocacy aspect of a lawsuit.

Court consolidation note: In many counties, the Municipal and Superior Courts have been merged into one court, the Superior Court. See Chapter 8 for more detail on this court consolidation development.

4. Arbitration

If you are working under a written contract, you may have agreed to use binding arbitration instead of the court to resolve your payment issue. If so, the clause is likely to tell you very little about how to get the arbitration started. If the clause names a service such as the American Arbitration Association, contact them. If not, you will need to agree with the owner as to which service to use. For more on finding an arbitrator, see Chapter 12, Section G.

If you are filing a lawsuit to enforce your mechanics' lien as well as pursuing your other remedies, you or the property owner will have to ask the court to stay the enforcement proceeding pending the arbitration outcome. If neither of you ask for a stay, the arbitration will be deemed waived and all your remedies will be handled in court—including your stop notice enforcement and breach of contract remedies. In Chapter 8 we explain the stay process in more detail but also suggest that you contact an attorney to help you enforce your arbitration rights.

5. Mediation

Mediation is a process in which a skilled and neutral third party helps disputing parties to voluntarily settle their dispute on terms they can both live with. If the reason for the non-payment has to do with a real disagreement over the terms of the contract and the quality of the work, mediation may well be the best answer of all, because you still maintain control of the outcome. However, if the only issue is whether the party contracting for your work or materials can be forced to pay you, mediation won't help. For more on the role of mediation in construction disputes, see Chapter 12, Section F. ■

CHAPTER 7

Recovery Under a Payment Bond

Especially on larger construction projects, the owner may require the general contractor to post what's known alternatively as a "labor and materials" or "payment" bond. This chapter explains what this bond means and the steps you need to take to make sure you can sue to recover under the bond if it becomes necessary (lawsuits are covered in Chapter 8).

Payment bonds usually mean attorneys

Payment bonds are not commonly used in private construction projects. They are even rarer in small works of improvement such as home improvement projects and single residence construction projects. If there is a payment bond in your situation, you'll almost certainly need an attorney to get your money out of the surety, because insurance companies are notoriously unwilling to cough up payment. To know whether a payment bond exists, serve a request for a Notice of Election to Not Withhold on the lender at the same time as you serve your stop notice. (See Chapter 5, Section I.)

A. PURPOSE OF PAYMENT BOND

A payment bond is designed to protect the owner against claims of non-payment by all those other than the general contractor who contribute to the work of improvement. In essence, the payment bond provides an additional source of payment to mechanics' lien and stop notice claimants.

Unlike the mechanics' lien (which goes after the property) and the stop notice (which goes after construction loan funds), the payment bond is a means to assure payment of a judgment that a party obtains in a breach of contract action. In other words, before you are entitled to collect from the payment bond you must establish your right to payment, either through settlement or in court. See Chapter 6 for more on breach of contract suits.

Example: Lakeside Developers is constructing a 500-unit timeshare village on the shore of Lake Elsinore in Southern California. The prime contractor for the project is Jermelian General Contractors, Inc. To qualify for the contract, Jermelian is required to post a payment bond in the amount of $10,000,000, the estimated cost of labor and materials for the project. If any payment problems arise in the course of the project, they most likely will be resolved in a breach of contract suit against Jermelian and a suit against the issuer of the bond to recover on the breach of contract suit.

As mentioned above, payment bonds generally aren't common on small projects. Although any owner of a work of improvement can, in the construction contract, require the general contractor to post a payment bond, most small project owners don't. If they did, the cost of the bond would simply be added to the cost of the project.

Example: Tom and Debbie Timmons are adding a second bathroom to their home. They have hired Bathrooms Deluxe as the general contractor. They initially want Bathrooms Deluxe to secure a payment bond to cover the estimated cost of labor and materials, which is $20,000. The premium for such a bond would be roughly $1,500. When they learn that they will end up paying the premium as part of the cost of the entire job, they decide to put their money into a higher grade bathtub instead.

B. WHO ISSUES THE BOND?

The company issuing the bond is known as a surety. The surety, in essence, guarantees payment of any obligation owed by the general contractor to work or materials providers, even if the general contractor is not paid by the owner.

The surety may then sue the general contractor to recover funds paid out under the bond. In other words, under the payment bond scenario, the general contractor may ultimately get stuck for a major share of the costs of a construction project. Although the owner may technically be liable for these costs, the owner may be judgment proof (that is, have no assets or income out of which a judgment could be collected) or may have filed for bankruptcy, leaving the general contractor high and dry.

> **Example:** In the example of the Timmons' bathroom, assume that they are willing to pay for the bond premium and Bathroom Deluxe proceeds to purchase the bond. The Timmons tender a $500 down payment and make several progress payments along the way. However, when the job is done, the Timmons still owe Bathroom Deluxe $7,500. Because of a job loss and a medical emergency, the Timmons are forced to file for bankruptcy. Bathroom Deluxe, in turn, is unable to pay its subcontractors and materials providers. The surety company issues a check to the subcontractors and materials providers for the money due them and then proceeds to sue Bathroom Deluxe for recompense. Bathroom Deluxe is liable to the surety, since it was Bathroom Deluxe who purchased the bond and breached its contract with the subcontractors and materials providers.

C. PAY WHEN PAID CLAUSES

To avoid the problem described in the previous example, many contractors took to inserting what are known as "pay if paid" clauses in their contracts with subcontractors. In essence, these clauses provided that the contractor only was obliged to pay the subcontractor if the contractor was paid by the owner. Since a surety company only is required to pay under a bond if the principal on the bond (in this case the general contractor) is liable for the amount being claimed, non-liability of the general contractor under a pay if paid clause meant non-liability for the surety company as well.

Unfortunately for the surety companies, in 1997 the California Supreme Court ruled that pay when paid clauses are illegal and will not be enforced. In other words, a surety is liable under a payment bond even in the presence of a pay if paid provision. (*Clarke v. Safeco*, 15 Cal.4th 882 (1997).)

D. THE PRELIMINARY NOTICE

As with the other remedies discussed in this book, a timely preliminary notice is required as a condition of getting paid out of a payment bond. To remind you:

- You must serve a preliminary notice on the owner, general contractor and lender (or insurer) unless you are the prime (general) contractor or a laborer who worked on site for wages, or you contracted directly with the owner.

- If you are the prime (general) contractor or performed on-site labor for wages, you don't have to serve anyone (although it is a good idea to do so anyway).

- If you are anyone else who contracted directly with the owner and there is a construction loan in the picture (which there often is), you must serve the lender (or insurer).

- If you are a materials supplier who supplies materials to two or more subcontractors for the same project, you must serve separate notices for each subcontractor and should serve the subcontractor as well as the other required parties.

- You should serve the preliminary notice no more than 20 days after the first day you began your work or provided materials, or within 20 days after the work of improvement begins if your contribution was made before it began (for instance, if you are an architect).

- If you are late, you can still serve the preliminary notice, but any mechanics' lien claim will only be for work or materials you contribute during the 20 days directly preceding the date you serve the preliminary notice and during the period that follows.

See Chapter 2 for step-by-step instructions on preparing and serving a preliminary notice.

E. RELATIONSHIP BETWEEN PAYMENT BOND AND OTHER REMEDIES

Some surety companies require a claimant against the bond to also pursue his or her mechanics' lien remedy as a condition of qualifying for payment under the bond. In addition, if the surety company records the payment bond before the project is completed, a potential claimant only qualifies for payment if he or she either timely records a Claim of Mechanics' Lien or serves a Notice of Action on the surety within the period required for recording a Claim of Mechanics' Lien. (See Section F for more on the written Notice of Action.)

Preserving your remedies

If you are faced with a situation where a prime (general) contractor has posted a payment bond

and you want to preserve your right to go after the bond proceeds, make sure you either pursue your mechanics' lien remedy described in Chapter 3 or send the required notice described in Section F, below.

F. PREPARING AND SERVING THE WRITTEN NOTICE OF ACTION

This section describes how to prepare and serve the Notice of Action.

1. Preparing the Notice of Action

A sample Notice of Action is set out below. A blank copy of this notice is in Appendix B and on the forms disk under the file name NOTACTN.

Notice to Surety on Payment Bond

To: _____Acme Contractor Bonding Co._____

YOU ARE HEREBY NOTIFIED UNDER CIVIL CODE SECTIONS 3240 AND 3241 that

_____Frank Leung_____ (claimant) furnished ☐ labor ☐

services ☐ equipment or ☒ materials consisting of

_____Sheetrock_____

to _____Humboldt Contractors, Inc._____ , to be used and actually used in

the work of improvement consisting of

_____A new bedroom_____

_____ ,

located at _____4757 5th St., Fortuna, CA_____.

The labor, services equipment or materials described above were to be furnished for the

contractual amount of $__475_____. The value of the labor, services, equipment or

materials actually furnished ☒ is equal to the contractual amount ☐ is

$_____.

Dated: ___4/19/99_____   Signed by Claimant: _____*Frank Leung*_____

2. Serving the Notice of Action

The Notice of Action may be personally served on the surety or sureties or mailed by prepaid certified or registered first class mail to any of the following locations:

- If to an individual surety, at his residence or place of business, if known.

- If to an individual surety and his or her residence is unknown, then in care of the county clerk of the county in which the bond has been recorded.

- If to a corporate surety, at the office or care of the agent designated by the surety in the bond as the address to which such notice should be sent.

- At the office of or care of any officer of the surety in California.

- At the office or care of the statutory agent of the surety in California.

FINDING OUT ABOUT THE SURETY

Clearly, to legally serve the surety you'll need some information. Most often the surety will be a California corporation. The address for the surety will be on the bond, which will have been recorded with the county recorder's office. Ask a title insurance company to get you a copy of the bond, or visit the recorder's office and get your own copy. If the surety is out of state, call the Secretary of State's Office and ask for information about the statutory agent for that surety.

- By service in the manner provided by law for the service of a summons in a civil action. (This provides some alternative forms of service, such as by publication. However, you shouldn't use these alternatives without first speaking with an attorney. One of the other methods of service listed earlier should be sufficient.)

G. ENFORCING A CLAIM AGAINST A PAYMENT BOND

As with the mechanics' lien and stop notice remedies, it is necessary to file a lawsuit against the surety for recovery under the bond. The time limit for doing this is six months after the project is completed. The usual practice is to combine the payment bond enforcement action with all the other enforcement actions.

Because the other enforcement actions have shorter time limits, this enforcement action will usually be brought long before the six month deadline, if it is brought at all. In any event, the payment bond action is almost always combined with the breach of contract action, since the breach of contract must be established before the surety will be held liable.

H. LEGAL AUTHORITY

All references in this section are to California Civil Code sections. These statutes are reproduced in Appendix A.

Requirement of Notice of Action   § 3240

Service Requirements   § 3241 ■

Going to Court

I n Chapter 1 we outlined your possible remedies as a contributor of labor, services, equipment or materials to a work of improvement (including site improvements). We then devoted separate chapters to each remedy. Each of the chapters took you through all the preliminary steps and then explained that to actually get your money you would have to file a lawsuit in court—unless, of course, you were able to negotiate a settlement with the person who owed you.

This chapter is where we tell you how to get into court. The good news is that few lawsuits of this type are actually brought. Most construction payment disputes are settled short of litigation. And when lawsuits are in fact filed, they most often are quickly settled. The bad news is that construction-related lawsuits can get complicated in a hurry and require a level of information that is beyond the scope of this or any other self-help law book.

A. Do You Need an Attorney?

If you have to go to court, you will probably be better off if you can find an attorney to bring the lawsuit for you. An attorney familiar with the construction trades and construction law can bring a lot to the table. If you can't afford representation, or prefer to handle your own case, you should at least try to find a law coach. (See Section O.)

CONSIDER USING THE CONSTRUCTION LAW HELP LINE

Sometimes it helps to talk to a knowledgeable attorney about your case before hunting for a lawyer to actually represent you. The Construction Law Help Line is a telephonic service operated by Gary Ransone, a lawyer, general contractor and author of *The Contractor's Legal Kit*. For a reasonable fee, attorney Ransone will help you assess your case and make the ultimate decision as to whether you should pay an attorney to take it any further. The Construction Law Help Line can be reached at 831-476-8784.

1. Review Your Case

An attorney will be able to review your case before you file it to make sure you've complied with all the prerequisites, such as properly serving the preliminary notice and properly recording the Claim of Mechanics' Lien or serving the stop notice. The attorney will also make sure that your contribution to the work of improvement actually qualifies you for a mechanics' lien or stop notice.

For instance, if you are a materials provider, the attorney can assess whether you'll be able to satisfactorily prove that your materials were used or consumed in the work of improvement.

A good attorney familiar with the construction trades can also help you decide:

- which remedies are available to you
- when and how to use them, and
- the cost-benefit of using one or more remedies.

A bad lawyer won't do this but will simply want to file litigation immediately in order to generate legal fees.

2. Dealing With Lenders

If you are going after a lender or insurer on the basis of a bonded stop notice, the law governing lien priorities can get very complex. An attorney knowledgeable in mechanics' lien law will be able to sort these questions out and get the best possible recovery for you.

3. Dealing With Sureties

Bonds sometimes play an important role in the mechanics' lien and stop notice areas. If you are in a situation where the party you are suing is covered by a bond, you may be required to proceed against the bonding company rather than against the party directly. Just what you can recover from a surety is a complex area of law not addressed in this book. An attorney who understands this area can be a huge help.

4. Handling Irregularities

Lawsuits are unpredictable. Although we have tried to be thorough in this book regarding the steps you need to take to preserve all your remedies, there is no guarantee that your particular case will be free of twists and turns that we simply couldn't predict. An attorney can deal with these issues as they arise. If you represent yourself, you may find yourself in over your head in a hurry.

5. Dealing With Court Procedures

Last but not least, mechanics' lien and stop notice enforcement lawsuits involve procedures that will take a lot of research on your part to master. Nolo Press publishes several books that can be very helpful in a general sense. (See Section 7, below.) However, Nolo Press has no book that addresses the procedures specific to enforcing a mechanics' lien or stop notice claim. The fact is, the legal system is full of procedural rules. While you may know the merits of your case better than your attorney ever will, if you foul up a procedural aspect of your case you may eliminate your chance of recovery.

Ask the attorney about mediation

Even though you find it necessary to use an attorney, you may nonetheless achieve a better result if you and the other party attend a mediation session. Most construction attorneys are well aware of the benefits of mediation, but if the attorney you contact doesn't bring the subject up, you should.

6. Finding an Attorney

While it may be beneficial for you to use an attorney for all the reasons just mentioned, finding and paying for one can be difficult. Almost all attorneys who conduct this type of litigation charge an hourly fee rather than a contingent fee (a percentage of whatever is collected).

Generally, for an attorney to take a mechanics' lien case on a contingency basis there must either be a decent chance of collecting attorney fees from the defendants or the amount of the claim must be large enough both to pay the attorney and to deliver you a healthy chunk of what you're owed. Fortunately, two of your remedies—the bonded stop notice (Chapter 5) and payment bond (Chapter 7)—provide for attorney fees to the prevailing party if an enforcement lawsuit is necessary. However, getting attorney fees actually awarded by the court and then collecting them from the defendant is not always easy.

Attorneys are plentiful. Try the Yellow Pages, your local bar association's referral panel, a local owner-builder center or referrals from your fellow contractors/materials providers. If you plan to represent yourself but would like to hook up with a lawyer for advice and counsel, read Section O.

7. Alternative Resources

If you are forced to handle your own lawsuit because you can't locate a good construction attorney (or you flat out refuse to deal with lawyers), the following Nolo Press publications will be a big help:

- *Everybody's Guide to Small Claims Court*, by Ralph Warner, will help you handle a breach of contract suit in Small Claims Court.

- *How to Sue for Up to $25,000 and Win*, by Judge Roderic Duncan, will help you bring a breach of contract case. If your mechanics' lien and stop notice claims are less than $25,000, Judge Duncan's book will also help you navigate the court procedures necessary to enforce those claims, but you will probably need some additional help along the way. If your claim is over $25,000, you will need to research the procedures yourself.

- *Represent Yourself in Court,* by Paul Bergman and Sara Berman-Barrett (Nolo Press), will be an indispensable companion to help you through many of the procedures, both in court and out.

Finally, if you are willing to hit the law library, there are several publications designed for attorneys that will take you to the next level of mechanics' lien law. The best of these is *California Mechanics' Lien Law And Construction Industry Practice,* by Matthew and Harry Marsh (Sixth Ed, Parker Publications, 1996).

B. WHAT RELIEF WILL YOU BE SEEKING IN YOUR LAWSUIT?

What relief you will be seeking in your lawsuit depends on what preliminary steps you've taken to preserve your remedies. If you properly served your preliminary notices (Chapter 2), recorded your Claim of Mechanics' Lien (Chapter 3) and served stop notices on the appropriate parties (Chapters 4 and 5), your lawsuit will be seeking the enforcement of all these remedies. You can obtain:

- a money judgment against whoever was subject to your stop notices (Chapters 4 and 5)

- a judgment ordering the property sold to pay off your mechanics' lien (Chapter 3)

- a money judgment for breach of contract against anyone who was contractually bound to pay you, but did not (Chapter 6)

- a money judgment against the issuer of any payment bond (Chapter 7), and

- in some cases, attorney fees and costs.

C. GETTING INTO COURT TO PRESERVE YOUR REMEDIES

As mentioned, getting an attorney to represent you would be wise. However, many of you either will not have an attorney by the time the lawsuit filing deadline rolls around or will have claims that are below most attorneys' radar. Because you can lose the benefit of all the careful preparatory work you've done up to this point (serving the preliminary notice, etc.) if you don't file your lawsuit on time, the purpose of this section is to help you at least get into court before the deadline.

To accomplish this purpose we take you clause by clause through a sample complaint (the first document you file to start a lawsuit) that will at least preserve any mechanics' lien, stop notice and payment bond remedies you may have. We also provide general instructions for how and where to file the complaint. A blank copy of the complaint is included in Appendix B and on the forms disk under the file name COMPLNT.

Unfortunately, the scope of this book does not permit the kind of detailed step-by-step guidance you would probably need to pursue your case through the court process to final judgment. However, the resources mentioned in Section A7, above, may be a big help.

D. WHEN TO FILE THE COMPLAINT

To make sure that all your possible remedies are preserved, you should file your complaint no later than 90 days after the date you recorded your Claim of Mechanics' Lien. If you file on the 91st day, your mechanics' lien remedy will go away. So, if you want to preserve this remedy, make sure you file by the deadline. Our advice: Don't wait until the last day.

If for some reason you didn't record a Claim of Mechanics' Lien, but did serve a stop notice, you should file this complaint no later than 120 days after the project was completed. Again, don't wait until the last day.

If there is a payment bond in the picture and you are not seeking the mechanics' lien or stop notice remedies (perhaps because you didn't comply with the preliminary notice requirement), then you should file the complaint no later than six months after work on the project was completed. If you don't know when work was completed, you should file your lawsuit as soon as possible.

If you are only suing for breach of contract, you must sue within two years of the breach if the contract was oral or implied from the circumstances. You have up to four years to file if the contract was written.

E. CHOOSING THE CORRECT COURT

As part of drafting your complaint, you'll need to know which court to file in. Here are your options.

If you are not suing to enforce your mechanics' lien or stop notice, and your claim is for $5,000 or less (or you are willing to cut back your claim to that amount), you can use the Small Claims Court that has jurisdiction over your contract claim. This will be any of the following places (CCP §395):

- The county where the work of improvement is located.
- If the defendant is a corporation or partnership, the county where the corporation does business.

- If the defendant is an individual or sole proprietor, the county where he or she resides.
- Regardless of what type of entity the defendant is, the county where the contract was entered into (signed).
- If your claim is for more than $5,000, but less than $25,000 (or you are willing to cut your claim back to that amount), you must use the Municipal Court for the judicial district where the property being improved is located.
- If your claim is for more than $25,000, you must use the Superior Court for the district where the property being improved is located.

If the courts have been consolidated, then you will be able to file in the consolidated court (now called the Superior Court) without worrying about the Municipal Court/Superior Court distinction.

Even if your claim is for $5,000 or less, you must still use the Municipal or the consolidated court (Superior Court) to enforce your mechanics' lien and stop notice remedies. Small Claims Courts have no jurisdiction over these enforcement suits.

You can bring all these actions in the same court in the same lawsuit, or you can split them up. For instance, you can file your breach of contract action in Small Claims Court, but bring your mechanics' lien enforcement action in Municipal or consolidated court. However, beware: A loss in your Small Claims action may torpedo your attempt in Municipal or consolidated court to enforce your mechanics' lien, since the court would most likely rule that the small claims loss means that you don't have a valid mechanics' lien claim.

The better practice is to keep all these lawsuits together in one court. For this reason, the complaint described in the next section assumes that you will be choosing one court—Municipal Court, Superior Court or the consolidated court (which will also be called the Superior Court).

F. PREPARING THE COMPLAINT

A properly formatted check-the-boxes, fill-in-the-blanks form complaint is in Appendix B and on the forms disk under the file name COMPLNT. Here are instructions for how to fill it in.

We have created this complaint from scratch. Under the California Rules of Court, this complaint should be sufficient for you to get your case on file. Even if you later have to make changes, the date you get your case on file is what counts for the purpose of preserving your mechanics' lien, stop notice or payment bond remedies. However, don't be surprised if you are later asked or required to file an amended complaint in a format that is more to the court's liking. We only intend this as an emergency complaint for you to file to preserve your remedies.

The complaint is divided into four different claims (called causes of action):

- breach of contract
- enforcement of mechanics' lien
- enforcement of stop notice, and
- recovery under payment bond.

Most of the factual statements made in the complaint will be made at the beginning. Then, for each cause of action one or more of these factual statements will be incorporated by reference. If you are only suing for breach of contract, you will only use one of the causes of action. If you have a breach of contract claim and also wish to enforce a mechanics' lien, you will have two causes of action, and so on.

Caption

The top part of this form is called the caption. Here is how to fill it in:

- Enter your name, address and telephone number in the top left space. Note that the information already in the space shows that you are appearing without an attorney.

- The next blank provides information about the court in which you'll be filing your complaint. After reviewing Section E, above, check the box next to the appropriate court (Superior Court or Municipal Court or consolidated court) and enter the name of the appropriate county. Then enter the address information for that court and the branch name (if it has one). To find out this information, either visit or call the court clerk.

PARTY WITHOUT ATTORNEY (Name and Address): MY TELEPHONE NO:	FOR COURT USE ONLY
_____ **COURT OF CALIFORNIA, COUNTY OF** STREET ADDRESS: MAILING ADDRESS: CITY AND ZIP CODE: BRANCH NAME:	
PETITIONER/PLAINTIFF: RESPONDENT/DEFENDANT:	
	CASE NUMBER:

• Put your name next to the Petitioner/Plaintiff entry. Put the name of the parties you are suing next to the Respondent/Defendant entry. If you don't yet know who you should sue, don't worry. Proceed with the rest of our instructions, paying careful attention to Item 3. You can always come back later and enter the names of these parties.

1. Plaintiffs

_____

Here you enter your name. If you own your business as a sole proprietorship, corporation, limited liability company or partnership, enter the correct business name as a DBA (doing business as), for instance, John Plumber DBA Pipes-R-Us.

2. Plaintiffs' License Qualifications

At all relevant times, Plaintiff was duly licensed by the California State Contractor's Licensing Board under the laws of the State of California as a corporation doing business as such at Hemet, California.

If you are a contractor, subcontractor or licensed professional (architect, engineer, surveyor), here is where you state that you were licensed at the time you made your contribution to the work of improvement.

If you were required to be licensed but weren't, you should speak with an attorney before filing the complaint. In some cases you may still be able to proceed.

3. Defendants

a. ☐ The following persons or entities owe me money under a contract for goods or services more completely described in paragraph 5: _____

_____

In addition, I name DOES 1 through 5 as Defendants whose identities are currently unknown to me. If I later discover their identity, I ask leave to amend this complaint accordingly.

Check the box if you are suing for breach of contract and fill in the names of the person(s) or business(es) who directly hired you to perform labor or services, or who purchased materials from you. Also, you should name the owner if the owner participated in any way in bringing you onto the job. The complaint automatically names five fictitious defendants (called "DOES") just in case you later discover that there are other defendants who you have a breach of contract claim against and want to add them to your suit.

b. ☐ The following persons or entities own, reputedly own or have an ownership interest in the real property described in paragraph 5:

_____

_____

Plaintiff also names Does One through Fifty as Defendants having an interest in the Property. Plaintiff is ignorant of the true names of Defendants Doe One to Doe Fifty, inclusive, and is informed and believes that each of said Defendants claims an interest in the property. Plaintiff therefore asks that when their true names are discovered this complaint may be amended by inserting their true names in lieu of said fictitious names.

Check the box and fill in the names of the people or entities who have an interest in the real estate that was improved by your labor, services, equipment or materials. To find out who has an interest in the property, first call a title insurance company. If you can't get the information that way, you will need to visit the recorder's office for the county where the property is located.

Most often you will be naming the owner or owners of the title to the property and the bank or other lender who is the beneficiary of a deed of trust on the property. You should also name any other lien holders of record, such as taxing agencies, judgment creditors and other mechanics' lien holders. In addition, the complaint automatically names fifty additional fictitious defendants (called Does) who have an interest in the property, just in case you later discover additional owners.

c. ☐ The following persons or entities were served with stop notices under Civil Code §3160:

_____

_____

_____

_____.

Check the box if you are suing to enforce a stop notice and enter the names of the parties who you served with the Stop Payment Notice. Typically, this will be the owner of the property and the lender of the improvement funds.

d. ☐ The following persons or entities, as the Principal and the Surety, are liable to me for the amount of payment bond #_____:

Check the box if you are suing to recover under a payment bond and name the party who purchased the payment bond (typically the general contractor or the owner as principal) and the company that issued the bond as surety. If you need information on whether there is a surety, write and ask the owner and general contractor. If an invitation to bid was used by the owner or general contractor, see whether the invitation required a bond.

4. Agency Relationship

At all times mentioned in this complaint, Defendants other than the owners of the Property described in this complaint were the agents and employees of said owners.

This clause makes the claim that everyone you sue is working at the behest of the owner (that is, the other parties are the owner's agents). If you can prove this, you may be able to make the owner liable for acts of the other defendants, since an agent's acts often are attributed to the "principal" (in this context, the owner).

5. The Property

The property being improved by the work of improvement relevant to this lawsuit (PROPERTY) is located in the City of _____, County of _____, California, and legally described as follows:

_____

_____

_____

_____.

The description of the property will be the same as you entered on your Claim of Mechanics' Lien. (See Chapter 3.)

6. The Contract

On or about _____, Plaintiffs and Defendants entered into an ☐ oral ☐ written agreement in which Plaintiffs agreed to ☐ act as general contractor ☐ furnish labor/services/equipment/materials for a work of improvement on the real property described in paragraph 3 for an agreed contract price of $_____, which Defendants _____ _____ agreed to pay. The whole of the real property and the entire estate of Defendants in the real property are required for the convenient use and occupation of the work of improvement.

Enter here the date you were hired to provide your labor, services or materials, the price agreed to and the names of the defendants who you directly contracted with. Where there are two boxes, check the appropriate box.

7. Plaintiff's Performance of Obligations Under the Contract

Between _____ and _____, at the special instance and request of _____, Plaintiff(s) furnished the following services, labor or materials

_____

_____

_____

☐ Plaintiff(s) has performed all required obligations to be performed under the contract.

☐ Except to the extent prevented and excused by the following actions of Defendant(s), Plaintiff(s) has performed all required obligations to be performed under the contract:

_____

_____

_____

☐ The contribution to the work of improvement described earlier in this paragraph was in addition to that specified in the contract described in paragraph _____ because of the following change orders:

_____

_____

_____

This paragraph identifies:

- who hired you or purchased materials from you,

- what work, services, equipment or materials you contributed to the work of improvement, and

- the degree to which fulfilled your obligations under the contract.

After you enter the appropriate information in the blanks, check the first box if you completed the contract, the second box if the defendant prevented you from completing the contract and the third box if you performed work or supplied materials in addition to those specified in the contract.

If you check the second box, explain what the defendant did to prevent you from completing the contract. If you checked the third box, describe the change order, either referring to a written change order (and attaching a copy to the complaint) or explaining why the change order was not written.

8. Value of Contribution

The Plaintiff's contribution to the work of improvement described in paragraph 7 was furnished at the reasonable and current market rate of $_____, which Defendants agreed ☐ orally ☐ in writing to pay.

This paragraph describes the value of your contribution and states that it was reasonable. Enter the rate you charged for your labor, services, equipment or materials and check the appropriate box (which should match the information you entered in paragraph 6). Note that if the work involved home remodeling or swimming pool work, the contract must be in writing.

9. Breach of Contract: Non-payment

Defendants described in paragraph 3a have breached the contract described in paragraph 6 in that said Defendants have paid Plaintiffs $_____ and no more, and there is due, owing and unpaid since _____, a balance of $_____ plus interest at the legal rate.

Here you enter the details of what you are owed. This may be the total amount listed in your Claim of Mechanics' Lien or stop notice, or it may be less if you have received some payment since you prepared those documents.

10. Attorney Fees

☐ The contract described in paragraph 6 does not provide for the payment of attorney fees.

☐ The contract described in paragraph 6 provides that attorney fees shall be paid in any action brought on the agreement. Plaintiff is entitled to recover reasonable attorney fees incurred in bringing and prosecuting this action, as determined by the court.

If your contract described in paragraph 6 does not address the issue of attorney fees, check the first box. If the contract provides that one or other of the parties (or both parties) is entitled to recover attorney fees in case of a court dispute, check the second box.

☐ 11. First Cause of Action—Breach of Contract

If the above box is checked, as a first cause of action, Plaintiff realleges and incorporates by reference all allegations contained in paragraphs 1 through 10, and further alleges that the Defendants described in paragraph 3a owe Plaintiff the sum of $_____ because of the breach of contract described in paragraph 9.

If you are bringing a breach of contract action against the party who hired you, check the box and fill in the required information. The only reason you wouldn't be bringing a breach of contract action in this lawsuit is 1) that you decided to do it separately in Small Claims Court. (See Section E, above); or 2) your construction contract calls for arbitration and you wish to pursue that remedy for your breach of contract claim.

However, if your contract contains an arbitration clause, you may not be able to take your breach of contract case to court even though you want to. This is because the defendant may ask that the court action be stayed pending arbitration and require you to attend arbitration.

☐ 12. Second Cause of Action— Enforcement of Mechanics' Lien

If the above box is checked, as a second cause of action, Plaintiff realleges and incorporates by reference all allegations contained in paragraphs 1 through 10 and further alleges as follows:

If you are suing to enforce a mechanics' lien, check the box and continue to the next paragraph.

13. Preliminary Notices

On or about _____, Plaintiff(s) served the following Defendant(s) with a preliminary 20-day notice (private works) within the time required by law:

_____

_____

_____.

Copies of the preliminary notices and proofs of service are attached to this complaint as Exhibit _____.

Here you state that you properly served your 20-day preliminary notices. See Chapter 2 for more on this requirement for mechanics' liens. In the blank lines, enter the names of the parties you served. Depending on your role, this will be the owner, the prime (general) contractor and/or the lender. Remember to attach copies of the 20-day notices and the proofs of service you prepared to your complaint. Label them as Exhibits in the order they are mentioned in the complaint (for instance, Exhibit A, Exhibit B and so on).

Note: If you didn't properly serve your preliminary notices, you won't get very far trying to enforce your mechanics' lien or your claim under a stop notice or payment bond. All these remedies require a properly served preliminary notice if a preliminary notice was required in the first place. (See Chapter 2.)

14. Recording of Claim of Mechanics' Lien

☐ **a. Prime Contractor**

Plaintiff recorded a valid Claim of Mechanics' Lien on _____, in the office of the county recorder of _____ County:

☐ after Plaintiff completed ☐ his ☐ her contribution and before the expiration of 90 days after the work of improvement was completed, no notice of completion or cessation having been recorded.

☐ after Plaintiff ceased furnishing ☐ his ☐ her contribution to the work of improvement as alleged above, and before the expiration of 60 days after the notice of completion or cessation was recorded.

☐ **b. Other Lien Claimant**

Plaintiff recorded a valid Claim of Mechanics' Lien on _____, in the office of the country recorder of _____ County:

☐ after Plaintiff completed ☐ his ☐ her contribution and before the expiration of 90 days after the work of improvement was completed, no notice of completion or cessation having been recorded.

☐ after Plaintiff ceased furnishing ☐ his ☐ her contribution to the work of improvement as alleged above and before the expiration of 30 days after the notice of completion or cessation was recorded.

A copy of the recorded Claim of Mechanics' Lien is attached to this complaint as Exhibit_____ and incorporated by reference.

If you are the prime contractor (the general or original contractor who contracted directly with the owner), complete section 14a. If you are anyone other than the general (original) contractor, complete section 14b. In both sections, check the first box if no notice of

completion or cessation was recorded by the owner. Check the second box if either of these documents was recorded. Remember to attach a copy of the recorded Claim of Mechanics' Lien as an exhibit.

15. Costs and Amount Due

At the time Plaintiff recorded the Claim of Mechanics' Lien as described in paragraph 14, the amount shown unpaid on the Claim of Mechanics' Lien was due, owing and unpaid. The cost of verifying and recording the lien claim was $_____, no part of which has been repaid.

This paragraph clarifies the amount that was due you when your Claim of Mechanics' Lien was recorded and describes allowable costs—the fee charged you by the recorder's office for recording your Claim of Mechanics' Lien.

☐ **16. Third Cause of Action—Stop Notice**

If the above box is checked, as a third cause of action, Plaintiff realleges and incorporates by reference all allegations contained in paragraphs 1 through 13 and further alleges as follows:

This clause brings those earlier factual statements into this cause of action and support your claim that you are entitled to a stop notice. If you are suing to enforce a stop notice, check the box to indicate that you are bringing this cause of action.

17. Service of Stop Notice

On or about _____, at which time there remained due, owing and unpaid to Plaintiff $_____ for ☐ his ☐ her contribution furnished to the work of improvement on the Property described in paragraph 5, plaintiff served on the Defendants described in paragraph 3c a stop notice signed and verified by Plaintiff.

☐ The stop notice was accompanied by a bond with good and sufficient sureties conforming to the requirements of Civil Code §3083. Plaintiff expended $_____ as an annual premium on the bond.

A copy of the stop notice and proof of service is attached to this Complaint as Exhibit ___ and is incorporated by reference.

Here you describe the details of the sums subject to the stop notice. If you obtained a bond (which is necessary to bind a lender to the terms of the stop notice), check the box before the second paragraph and fill in the amount of the premium. If you only served a stop notice on the owner, a bond may be desirable but is not necessary. (See Chapter 4.) Be sure to attach a copy of your stop notice and proof of service to your complaint as an exhibit.

18. Funds Due or to Become Due

At the time the stop notice was served, on information and belief, the Defendants described in paragraph 3c had in their possession or in their control funds earmarked to pay construction costs on the work of improvement and therefore due or to become due to the Plaintiff in an amount unknown to Plaintiff but known to Defendants.

This paragraph states that the owner and/or lender did in fact have funds subject to your stop notice.

☐ 19. Fourth Cause of Action—Payment Bond

If the above box is checked, as a fourth cause of action, Plaintiff realleges and incorporates by reference all allegations contained in paragraphs 1 through 13 and further alleges as follows:

Plaintiff is informed and believes and on the basis of such information and belief alleges that the defendants

described in paragraph 3d, as principals and sureties, executed a payment bond in connection with the work of improvement on the Property described in paragraph 5. The bond provides for payment in full of the claims of all claimants and is by its terms made to inure to the benefit of all claimants to give them a right of action to recover on the bond in this action.

This clause alleges the existence of a payment bond and that you are entitled to recover the value of your contribution out of the bond. If there is a payment bond in your case, check the box to indicate that you are bringing this cause of action.

20. Prerequisites to Action on Payment Bond

Plaintiff:

☐ has recorded a Claim of Mechanics' Lien as described in the Second Cause of Action of this Complaint

☐ gave written notice to _____ before expiration of the time for recording a Claim of Mechanics' Lien, a copy of which is attached to this complaint as Exhibit___ and incorporated by reference.

Check the appropriate box. If you check the second box, enter the name of the surety (as it appears in paragraph 3d). Remember to attach the written notice as an exhibit.

WHEREFORE, Plaintiff demands judgment as follows:

☐ For Breach of Contract:

Judgment against the Defendants, and each of them, described in paragraph 3a for $_____ in favor of Plaintiff, together with interest provided by law from _____ until paid, plus costs and ☐ reasonable attorneys fees.

If you have sued for breach of contract, check the first box. In the first blank copy the amount you entered in paragraph 9. In the second blank put the date that you were due payment under your contract. If your contract called for payment of attorney fees to either party, check the second box.

☐ For Foreclosure of Mechanics' Lien

That the sum of $_____, together with interest provided by law until paid and the further sum of $_____ for verifying and recording the Claim of Mechanics' Lien and Plaintiff's costs in bringing this action, be adjudged and decreed to be a lien on the real property described in paragraph 5 of this complaint.

If you have sued to enforce a Claim of Mechanics' Lien, check the first box. In the first blank put the amount you have entered into your Claim of Mechanics' Lien (which you'll be attaching to this complaint). In the second blank enter the amount you entered in Paragraph 15.

That the demands of Plaintiff and all persons having claims of lien, or any interest in the Property described in paragraph 5 of this complaint, be ascertained and adjudged, and that the interests of Defendants described in paragraph 3b and any persons claiming under these Defendants be sold under the decree of this court to satisfy the amount of the liens ascertained and adjudged in favor of Plaintiff.

That, if any deficiency results from the sale of the real property under this court's decree, the Plaintiff have judgment for such deficiency against the Defendants _____.

Here, defendants who actually own the property should be named, not other lienholders.

That the court clerk be directed to docket and enter the personal judgment for breach of contract demanded in this prayer independently of any deficiency judgment

that may be entered after sale of the real property under the court's decree.

☐ For Enforcement of Stop Notice

That Plaintiff's stop notice claim in the amount of $_____, ☐ including the premium on Plaintiff's stop notice bond, together with Plaintiff's costs incurred in bringing this action, be decreed to be an equitable garnishment and lien on the funds that Defendants described in paragraph 3c had in ☐ his ☐ her ☐ its ☐ their possession at the time of service of the stop notice alleged in paragraph 17 of this complaint, and that a trust be imposed on such funds for the benefit of Plaintiff, and that Plaintiff have judgment against Defendant for the amount so adjudged, and if it is determined that Defendants improperly disbursed any part of such funds, and that there now are inadequate funds because of such disbursement to satisfy Plaintiff's claim in full, that Plaintiffs have a personal judgment against Defendants for whatever amount has been improperly disbursed.

If you have sued to enforce a stop notice, check the first box. Then, in the first blank, enter the amount shown on your stop notice (which you will be attaching to this complaint). Check the second box if you served a bond with your stop notice. Check the third, fourth, fifth or sixth box, depending on the nature of the defendant or defendants.

☐ For Recovery Under Payment Bond

Judgment under Payment Bond #_____ against Defendant_____ for $_____ in favor of Plaintiff, together with interest provided by law from _____ until paid, plus costs and ☐ reasonable attorneys fees.

For such other relief as the court considers just and proper.

Dated: _____   Signed: _____

If you have sued for payment under a payment bond, check the box. Then enter the payment bond number in the first blank. Enter the name of the defendant surety in the second blank. Enter the face amount of the bond. In the third blank enter the date you were due payment.

Then date and sign the complaint.

G. PREPARING THE SUMMONS AND CIVIL CASE COVER SHEET

Every complaint must have a Summons and Civil Case Cover Sheet. The Summons is a document that comes from the court (though you have to fill it in for the court) that notifies the defendants that they are being sued and have 30 days to respond in order to contest the case. Tear-out blank copies of the Summons and Cover Sheet are in Appendix B.

Under "Notice to Defendant:" type the names of all of the defendants exactly as you typed them in the form complaint. Under "You Are Being Sued by Plaintiff:" type the names of all of the plaintiffs (in most cases just your name) exactly as you typed them on the complaint.

Below the bold-faced box, insert the name and address of the court. Use the full name and address, including any branch. This should be the same as the address you entered in the caption of your complaint. Under the address, put your name, address and phone number—also, just as you put them in the complaint caption. Leave the "Notice to the Person Served" and all of page two blank.

The Cover Sheet is used by the courts for gathering statistics on the types of cases being filed in California. It will have no bearing on the outcome of your case, but you must prepare and file one in order to get started. You do not serve a copy on the defendant. You don't even need to keep a copy for your records, but do so if you wish.

To fill out the Cover Sheet, enter the same information in the top portion as you entered in the caption of your complaint.

In the box next to the number 1, enter the number 34, and in the blank next to number 34 add "mechanics' lien enforcement."

On line 2, check both monetary and non-monetary.

On line 3, enter the number of causes of action that you are including in your complaint. This will be equal to the number of boxes you checked next to the cause of action titles in paragraphs 11, 12, 16 and 19.

On line 4, check "no."

Sign and date the form and print your name.

H. CHECKLIST

This checklist helps you review your paperwork to make sure you've:

- properly completed the Summons, Cover Sheet and Complaint

- attached all required exhibits to the complaint, and

- made the necessary number of copies.

1. Complaint

☐ Identifies plaintiffs

☐ Identifies defendants

☐ Identifies property owners

☐ Provides legal description of property

☐ Describes contract and contract terms

☐ Describes plaintiff's contribution

☐ Describes value of plaintiff's contribution

☐ Describes amount owed plaintiff under the contract

☐ Describes whether attorney fees owed under the contract

☐ If applicable, describes breach of contract cause of action

☐ If applicable, describes mechanics' lien enforcement cause of action

☐ If applicable, describes stop notice cause of action

☐ If applicable, describes payment bond cause of action

☐ Request applicable relief from the court

☐ Signed and dated

2. Summons

☐ Summons completed

3. Cover Sheet

☐ Cover Sheet completed

4. Exhibits Attached

☐ Preliminary Notices

☐ Proofs of Service of Preliminary Notices

☐ Recorded Claim of Mechanics' Lien (if cause of action for mechanics' lien enforcement)

☐ Stop Notice and Proof of Service (if cause of action for stop notice enforcement)

☐ Notice to Surety (if cause of action for payment bond enforcement)

5. Copies

☐ One copy of the complaint for each person or entity you have named in paragraph 3 of the form complaint

☐ One copy of the complaint for your files

☐ One copy of the Civil Case Cover Sheet

I.   FILING AND SERVING THE COMPLAINT

Now that you've prepared your complaint, identified the exhibits and made the necessary copies, its time to:

- file your complaint, and
- if you plan to proceed on the basis of this complaint, serve copies on the defendants.

If you plan to get help

Earlier we suggested that you use this complaint only for the purpose of preserving your rights, and that you would be well advised to find an attorney to handle your case from this point forward. If you plan to hunt for an attorney, you may want to hold off serving the complaint on the defendants, since the attorney may well want to file an amended complaint.

1. Call the Clerk's Office

Before you physically visit the clerk's office, call and find out the following:

- If the court has any special local rules governing mechanics' lien/stop notice/payment bond enforcement actions. These rules could require that you file additional papers with the Summons and Complaint. Also, the rules might require that you label your exhibits in a certain way.

- The amount of the filing fee. You can pay in cash or by check in many counties, but some courts won't accept checks from self-represented plaintiffs. Be sure to ask. If you can't afford the filing fee, you may qualify for a waiver.

- What hours the office is open to the public. Some clerk's offices close for lunch (usually from noon to 1:00 p.m.), and some others close to the public much earlier than you would expect (for instance, in Lake County the court is only open from 8:30 to 12:30).

2. Filing the Papers

You have at least two and possibly three options for filing your papers:

- file them by mail
- file them by fax (in most but not all courts), or
- file them in person.

Many people prefer to file in person, since they can get some instant feedback about any problems that the clerk spots. However, if time, distance or transportation is an issue, filing by mail or fax are commonly used options. If you want to file in person, read Section 3. If you want to file by mail or fax, read Section 4.

3. Filing the Papers in Person

The first step to filing your papers in person is to find the clerk's office for the court you're filing in. This should be located in the same building as the court. The civil division is the one you want. The other divisions are criminal and, in larger courts, small claims and traffic. These will be combined with the criminal division in small counties. They'll be separate in larger areas.

When you enter the building, look for a directory or information desk. Then locate or ask where the Municipal Court civil division clerk's office is. If you can't find a directory or information desk, look for a court marshal (sheriff) or someone who looks like a lawyer. They'll know where the office is.

With the move to consolidate many functions of Superior and Municipal Courts well under way, you will find that in some courts the Municipal Courts civil filing

window is right next to a similar Superior Court window. In some courts both Municipal and Superior Court filings are accepted at the same window.

When you get to the clerk's office, look for a sign showing where new cases are filed. Be prepared to wait in line awhile.

When it's your turn, walk to the counter and immediately tell the clerk that you are a self-represented plaintiff filing a new action and that you've never done this before. Often the clerk will become quite helpful. This works much better than pretending you are an old experienced litigator who knows the ropes.

Hand the clerk these papers:

- the original complaint you have signed, and one copy if the court requires it
- the Civil Case Cover Sheet, and
- the original Summons you have prepared.

If the clerk rejects your papers

It is unlikely this will happen, but if the clerk rejects your papers be sure you understand exactly what you did wrong. Write down what the clerk tells you and repeat it back. If you have some time to do the repair job before you have to get your complaint on file, don't argue with the clerk. But if you are filing at the last minute, insist that your original complaint and at least one copy be stamped "filed" by the clerk no matter what's wrong. If necessary, speak with the clerk's supervisor. No clerk should be able to deprive you of your right to pursue your mechanics' lien and related remedies simply because you have chosen to represent yourself and have made a technical mistake of some kind in your papers.

If you're not applying for a fee waiver, the clerk will ask you to pay the filing fee. You'll get a receipt, which you should keep.

In the upper right-hand corner of your documents, the clerk will stamp some information on the origin of the Summons and complaint. Included in the information will be a case number. Then the clerk will sign the original Summons and place the official seal of the court in the lower left corner. Ask the clerk if you can use her stamp to fill in the case number on the copies of the complaint you have prepared. If you forget to do this, you can fill in the numbers by hand later.

In many courts, you'll be handed the stamping device and allowed to place the official court stamp on as many copies as you wish. If you'd prefer not to stand at the desk stamping your papers, you can photocopy the forms with the official court stamp on them. A photocopy of a court stamp is as good as the original itself.

The clerk will hand you back the original Summons. You may feel strange walking off with the original, but that's the way it's done. Later, when the defendants have been served, you will file the original with the court.

4. Filing the Papers by Mail

If you do decide to file your complaint by mail, enclose a note asking the clerk to file the original complaint, issue the Summons and file-stamp (put the court's stamp, with the date the papers were filed, on the papers) and return the extra copies to you. The clerk will probably file-stamp only one copy. If that happens, make copies of the file-stamped papers and use those when serving the defendants.

Don't use the mail if your filing deadline looms

It's possible to file your papers by mail. But if time is getting short, don't do it. If there's something wrong with the papers, the clerk will return them to you by mail rather than filing them. If your filing deadline is close, this turnaround time may cause you to miss it.

Be sure to include a check for the filing fee and a large self-addressed, stamped envelope with sufficient postage to mail the forms back to you.

Many courts now accept filing by fax under California Rules of Court §2001 and following. You will have to check with your court.

If the court accepts direct filing by fax and you wish to do so, ask the court for instructions. Applicable filing fees may be paid by noting a Visa or MasterCard number that may be charged. An extra fee of $1 per page is typically added to the standard filing fee.

If your court will not accept direct fax filing, ask whether there is an agency located near the courthouse where documents may be faxed. For a fee, the agency will copy your fax onto plain paper and personally deliver it to the clerk's office for filing. They pay the filing fee and charge you.

5. Deciding Whether to Serve the Complaint

Once you file your papers with the court, your next task is to serve the defendants. Earlier we noted that you might wish to forego this next step if you only filed the complaint to preserve your rights and plan to retain the services of a lawyer. The reason for not serving the defendants is that the lawyer you do retain probably will want to file an amended complaint that is more in tune with how that lawyer practices. This is more efficient and avoids the possibility of confusion if the only complaint served on the defendants is the one that will carry the case to its conclusion—the one that your lawyer prepares.

If you plan to represent yourself, however, you will want to have the defendants served with the Summons and complaint as soon as possible. The reason for the rush is that many courts have local rules that require prompt service.

Each defendant must be served with two documents:

- a copy of the Summons (be sure to keep the original), and
- a copy of the complaint.

6. Preparing the Summons Copies for Service

Your first step is to make as many copies of the Summons as there are defendants, plus one copy for your records.

Your next step is to fill in the bottom portion of the Summons copy for each defendant:

Check Box 1 if you are suing the defendant in his own name, such as William Lambroso.

Check Box 2 if the defendant does business under a fictitious business name (and fill in the fictitious business name).

Check Box 3 if the defendant is a corporation, defunct corporation, unincorporated association, partnership, minor or person subject to a conservatorship. Specify the name of the defendant and check and the applicable sub-box. Don't check item 4 (since service has not yet been effected).

If you are suing a particular defendant in more than one capacity—such as an individual who does business under a fictitious name, or an officer of a corporation who is being sued as an individual and as the corporation's representative—check all boxes that apply.

7. Prepare Sets of Papers to Serve

Next, prepare one set of papers for each defendant by attaching the copy of the Summons prepared for each defendant to a copy of the complaint.

8. Serving the Papers

Once you've prepared the papers to be served on the defendants, you need to select someone to do the actual serving. The basic rule is: Anyone *but you* who is over 18 years of age and not a party in the case can deliver the papers to the defendants. You can use a friend or other non-professional process server, but you shouldn't use an employee or other person under your direction and control. Nor should you use your spouse. Other relatives are okay.

Even though it will cost you more, we strongly recommend that you pay a sheriff (some sheriff's offices provide this service, others don't) or professional process server to do the job. First of all, they know how to do it. Second, if later there is a dispute over whether a particular party was served, the word of the sheriff or professional service in this matter will go much further than will that of your friend or relative.

If you do use a friend, relative or other non-professional process server, you will need to tell them how to accomplish the service. The papers must be personally served on the defendants in this way:

- If the defendant is an individual, the papers must be physically delivered to him or her. This means either handing the papers to the individual or, if the individual refuses to accept them, placing the papers in front of the defendant on a counter or desk.

- If the defendant is a corporation, service may be made on the corporation's general manager, any officer or the agent designated by the corporation for this purpose (in papers on file with the California Secretary of State).

- If the defendant is a partnership, service may be made on any partner.

9. Completing the Proof of Service

Once your process server serves a defendant, she must fill out a form called a "Proof of Service," which describes how and when service was accomplished. A professional process server, sheriff or marshal will complete the form and give it to you.

If you use a friend or other non-professional, your server will have to complete a Proof of Service as well. If there is only one defendant, the back of the original Summons (which you still have at this point) can be used. But if there is more than one defendant (which is common in mechanics' lien cases), you can use separate copies of the back of the Summons for each defendant served. Here is how to complete the Proof of Service:

1a. Check the boxes for Summons and complaint

1b. Fill in the name of the defendant, using the name exactly as it appears in the complaint. Remember to use a separate form for each defendant served.

1c. If your friend served the defendant, check the first box. Otherwise, check the second box and fill in the name of the person who served the defendant.

1d. Indicate where and when service occurred.

1e. Skip this. It's for the more complicated methods of service.

2. Check box 2a. The others are normally used by professional process servers for the more complicated methods of service.

3. Check the same boxes that are checked on the front of the Summons for that defendant.

4. Nothing needs be done here.

5. Skip this; your friend can't recover a fee.

6. Your friend (or other non-professional process server) should check box d and fill in her name and address at f.

Date and Signature: Make sure she dates and signs the form in the date and signature slots on the left.

Once you have the completed Proof of Service—from the sheriff, marshal, professional process server or your friend—make two copies of it. If there's more than one (more than one defendant was served), make two copies of each. Send the originals and one copy of each Proof of Service to the court clerk. Ask the clerk to file the original Proof(s) of Service, stamp the copies and return them to you. Don't forget to enclose a self-addressed, stamped envelope.

When all the named defendants have been served and you have completed Proofs of Service for each, file the original Summons with the Court Clerk.

J.   IF YOUR CONSTRUCTION CONTRACT CALLS FOR ARBITRATION

Many written construction contracts require the parties to submit their disputes to arbitration rather than take them to court. Yet the California statutes governing mechanics' liens, stop notices and payment bonds require you to file enforcement actions in court.

The way out of this apparent contradiction is pretty simple: If you want your underlying breach of contract suit to be decided by arbitration rather than in court, at the same time you file your court action (to satisfy the statutes) you can also file a motion asking the court to stay the court action and compel arbitration. If the court grants your request, you can then submit your basic payment dispute to the arbitrator and then, assuming you win, restart your enforcement lawsuit (which will now go a lot faster because the basic issue of whether you are owed money will be settled).

This book does not tell you how to prepare, file and argue the Motion to Stay Proceedings and Compel Arbitration. For that you will need to visit the law library or call the Construction Law Help Line at 831-476-8784 for assistance.

You are now on your own

We have cautioned you throughout this chapter that handling your own court case can be difficult and that you should try to find an attorney to represent you or at least provide some coaching. The purpose of this chapter is to help you get into court. However, helping you to stay there is beyond the scope of this book. If you do intend on handling your own case, you will most definitely need to become familiar with the law library. To help you find your way around, we recommend *Legal Research: How to Find and Understand the Law*, by Elias and Levinkind (Nolo Press).

Suppose that you don't want arbitration. If you file your enforcement lawsuit and don't ask the court to stay the action, your right to arbitrate under the contract will be deemed waived by you. If the other party to the contract (one of the defendants in your enforcement lawsuit) wants to submit the payment dispute to arbitration, it will be up to that party to seek a stay of the court proceedings pending arbitration. If no such stay is sought by the other party, than that party too will be deemed to have waived its arbitration right.

(See Chapter 12, Section G, for more on arbitration and available resources.)

K. PROCEEDING TO JUDGMENT

As we have emphasized, once you are in court, you will either need to find an attorney or do some additional research. Assuming that the case isn't settled and you are ultimately successful in your lawsuit, your ultimate recovery will not exceed the value of your contract, and usually not be more than the value of the goods or services you contributed to the work of improvement. Even though you may be suing under four distinct remedies—mechanics' lien, stop notice, payment bond and breach of contract—your ultimate recovery is restricted to what you are owed, plus certain additional costs described in Chapters 3 through 7.

L. NOTICE OF LIS PENDENS

Once you've filed your lawsuit, you are entitled to record what's known as a Lis Pendens or, in English, a Notice of Pending Action. This notice will alert any potential buyers of the owner's property that you have sued to enforce your mechanics' lien and that the mechanics' lien of record is still valid. A blank copy of a Notice of Pending Action is in Appendix B and on the forms disk under the file name LISPEND. As with other documents, it will cost between $10 and $20 to record this document, depending on the county.

NOTICE OF PENDING ACTION, CCP §409

NOTICE IS HEREBY GIVEN that the above-entitled action concerning and affecting real property as described below was commenced on _(date complaint filed)_, in the above-named court by Plaintiff___(your name)___, against the Defendants ___(all defendants named in complaint]___ , and Does 1 through 5 inclusive. The action is now pending in the (name of court and county), State of California.

The action affects title to real property situated in ___(name of county)___ , State of California, and is legally described as follows:___(describe property as it is described in the complaint)___

_____

_____.

The object of Plaintiff's action is to enforce Plaintiff's Claim of Mechanics' Lien against the property described above.

Dated: _____

M. ENFORCEMENT OF MONEY JUDGMENT

Let's say that the result of all your hard work is a court judgment against one or several parties for money damages. Unfortunately, money judgments can be difficult to enforce. However, you may be in luck: If your judgment is against anyone who is required to be licensed by the California State Contractor's Licensing Board, you can enforce the judgment by sending it to the Board. If the judgment, plus costs and interest, is not paid within 90 days, the Board will suspend the person's license (or refuse to renew it if it is coming up for renewal) until you are paid. (California Business and Professions Code §7191.)

If your judgment is against someone who is not required to be licensed, you will have the same rights as other holders of civil money judgments. These include:

- recording a judgment lien against the debtor's real estate and foreclosing on it if necessary

- garnishing wages

- attaching bank accounts

- seizing luxury personal property items

- seizing accounts receivable

- seizing receipts as they are collected by a business, and

- recording a lien against business assets.

For more information on how to collect a money judgment in California, see *Collect Your Court Judgment*, by Scott, Elias and Goldoftas (Nolo Press).

N. IF A DEFENDANT FILES FOR BANKRUPTCY

In the construction world as in the larger world, people and businesses file for bankruptcy for a variety of reasons. *Collect Your Court Judgment*, by Scott, Elias and Goldoftas (Nolo Press), has a chapter telling you how to deal with it from a creditor's perspective. Here we only need cover several brief points peculiar to mechanics' lien law:

1. Filing a Mechanics' Lien or Stop Notice Enforcement Action

When a person files for bankruptcy, the law automatically provides what's called an Order of Relief. The Order of Relief is an automatic stay that preserves the bankruptcy filer's economic status quo while the case is before the bankruptcy court. Part of preserving this status quo is a bar on all attempts to collect on a debt. As a general matter, filing a lawsuit is considered such an attempt. Under ordinary circumstances, you can get cited for contempt of court by the bankruptcy judge if you file a lawsuit against a defendant who has already filed for bankruptcy.

The problem, of course, is that California law requires you to file your enforcement lawsuit within 90 days of recording your Claim of Mechanics' Lien. It is possible to file a motion in bankruptcy court asking the court's permission to file your lawsuit. However, this may not be possible, either because you aren't able to handle the bankruptcy procedures or because you don't have enough time.

Fortunately, the bankruptcy law contains provisions (11 USC §546(b), §362(b)(3)) that appear to allow actions necessary to preserve an interest in real estate. Although there is no legal decision that says so, you are probably safe if you file your enforcement lawsuit and then take no further action on the lawsuit pending the outcome of the bankruptcy.

If you've already filed the lawsuit when the person files for bankruptcy, all further proceedings in the lawsuit are stayed while the bankruptcy is active. If you are representing yourself and you are faced with a time limit of some type, simply file a motion requesting a continuance pending resolution of the bankruptcy case. Information about filing motions can be found in two Nolo Press books: *How to Sue for Up to $25,000 and Win*, by Roderic Duncan, and *Represent Yourself in Court*, by Bergman and Berman-Barrett. (See Section A, above.)

2. What Happens to Your Lien in a Bankruptcy Case?

If the owner files for bankruptcy, you may be told that your lien has probably gone down the drain. This is not necessarily true. The extent to which you will be able to still collect will depend on how much equity there is in the real estate after certain deductions are made. But at the very least, your claim will be afforded a higher priority than that given to most other creditors who don't have liens.

O. FINDING AND USING A LAW COACH

Much of the information in this section comes from *Represent Yourself in Court*, by Paul Bergman and Sara Berman-Barrett (Nolo Press). If you are representing yourself in a breach of contract action or an action to enforce a mechanics' lien, stop notice or payment bond, you should make *Represent Yourself in Court* your constant companion.

In addition to *Represent Yourself in Court*, you will want to have a consultation with Gary Ransone of the Construction Law Help Line. As we pointed out earlier in this chapter, Attorney Ransone specializes in construction law and can provide wise and experienced counsel regarding your lawsuit. Call 831-476-8784 for more information about the services that the Construction Law Help Line provides and what these services cost.

1. What Is a Law Coach and How Can a Law Coach Help You?

When a lawyer advises you on how to conduct your own case but does not actually represent you, the lawyer is serving as what we call a "law coach." Instead of turning your case over to the lawyer, you pay—by the hour, usually—for limited help and advice. This arrangement can be an affordable way to get the help you need.

Your law coach may be able to help you make sure any legal document you prepare is correct, logical and persuasive. A law coach can help you draft or respond to the initial pleadings (the complaint or answer) or proofread pleadings you have prepared.

A lawyer acting as your law coach, not your attorney, will not sign your legal documents but simply help you prepare them. You will sign all papers you file with the court in your own name. The caption (heading) on your legal documents will state your name, address and phone number, and that you are representing yourself.

You may also wish to ask your coach to go over any pre-trial motions or discovery documents, such as interrogatories (written questions), which you want to send to your adversary. Or you may want assistance responding to your adversary's motion for summary judgment.

Your coach may also be a big help if the judge asks you to write some legal document—for example, if she asks you to "brief" a question (write a persuasive argument about a legal issue) or draft a court order or factual or legal findings.

If you have to prepare a pleading or other legal document, ask your coach to see a sample of a pleading she filed in a similar case so that you can see what it's supposed to look like. Once a document has been filed in court, it is almost always public record and therefore no longer confidential. Reviewing a sample before preparing your own draft will give you a good place to start, and your coach can edit what you did instead of starting from scratch.

In addition to helping you draft documents, your coach, or assistants in her office, such as paralegals or legal secretaries, may be able to help you put those documents together in the correct format. Legal documents often have to be written up in certain ways—sometimes even on a specific kind of paper—and filed and served according to detailed rules. Your law coach may be able to assist you a great deal by typing court documents into final form and filing and serving them on your opponent for you.

Ultimately, what to say and do at trial will be your judgment call. But preparing and trying a case necessarily involves maneuvering within a complex and impersonal system. You not only need to understand legal rules, but also to plug them into a winning strategy—a strategy you'll typically have to fine-tune as your adversary reacts to your actions. It can help you a lot to run your general plans by an experienced lawyer. You may also come to particular points of confusion where some expert legal advice can save you much time and frustration. For example, you may want assistance planning a deposition, subpoenaing documents or deciding whether to accept a settlement proposal from your opponent.

It may be especially helpful to have your coach review your outlines of what you expect to testify to and what you plan to ask witnesses on direct and cross-examination. Your coach may spot areas where you reveal information you are better off keeping to yourself or questions that are likely to get you into trouble. For example, your proposed questions might give a hostile witness too much of a chance to expand upon testimony that might damage your case. And asking your adversary's expert witness certain questions would allow the expert to repeat harmful information.

You may know right now that there is no way you can afford to hire a lawyer and that you will try your whole case from start to finish no matter what. But, although you want to save as much as possible on legal fees by handling the case yourself, don't rule out hiring a lawyer to take over if you really need help and can afford it. If you have consulted a law coach from time to time in preparing for trial, that lawyer may be in a good position to step in for you if you feel you are unable to continue representing yourself.

2. Finding a Law Coach

Increasingly, lawyers understand that the legal system has become overly costly and complicated, and they are opening up to new approaches. They also understand and are sympathetic to the fact that the average person can no longer afford to pay for full service representation.

Many lawyers also need work. Some may view law coaching as a good way to develop future business. By providing helpful consultations in one case, the lawyer may generate repeat business and word-of-mouth referrals for full-service representation on bigger, more complex matters. Some lawyers may even view helping pro pers as combining the concept of pro bono work (free services provided for the public good or public assistance) with earning a modest fee.

But many lawyers won't go for the law coach arrangement. Some simply don't want to get involved in what they see as the messy world of self-representation. Others will claim that their malpractice insurance won't allow them to or that they don't want to risk being legally liable if you make a mistake.

The bottom line, however, is that lawyers can and do sell advice by the hour without being responsible for every use to which their counsel is put. This is especially true of business lawyers, and most construction lawyers (being business lawyers) are already used to working with clients on an advice-only basis.

Finding a good law coach isn't impossible, but it is likely to require some searching. You want a lawyer who is familiar with construction law and mechanics' lien/ stop notice enforcement actions. You also want someone you are comfortable with—someone who understands, respects and agrees to perform the role of law coach.

Probably the best approach is to ask other contractors or materials providers whether they have had to use a lawyer, and if so, who they might recommend. After you have several names, start calling. Explain that you want to file a lawsuit to enforce a mechanics' lien and ask whether the lawyer will be willing to advise you as you go along. If the lawyer insists on an all or nothing approach ("Sorry, I don't consult on ongoing litigation."), you can either politely disengage from the conversation or inquire further about services the lawyer might provide you.

BAR ASSOCIATION REFERRAL SERVICES

Many local bar associations have lawyer referral services. For a few dollars, or sometimes without charge, you will be referred to a lawyer who will give you an initial consultation for a reduced fee or free of charge. Unfortunately, bar associations usually provide minimal screening for lawyers they list. In many areas, any local lawyer who has joined the association (paid the required dues) will be listed. Despite the obvious weakness of an uncritical referral system, it can be a starting point.

Offering piecemeal (sometimes called "unbundled") legal services as a self-help law coach is a fairly new approach for lawyers. It may not be clear from the first consultation how much you can do on your own and how much help you will need as your case proceeds. You and the lawyer you choose may have to decide together what the fairest approach is for you to pay for the lawyer's services. For this reason and many of the others stated above, be sure to choose a lawyer whom you feel comfortable enough with to frankly discuss fee arrangements and other thorny issues.

The lawyer may reasonably request that you sign an agreement that makes it clear that the lawyer is merely advising you, and that you are making your own decisions and are responsible for the results in the case. It may also be to your benefit to have an agreement so that the terms don't change in the middle of the relationship. California requires a written agreement whenever a lawyer and client expect legal fees to exceed $1,000, or if the client agrees to a contingency fee. ■

Mechanics' Liens:
An Owner's Perspective

I f you are the owner of real estate that is undergoing improvement work of some type, including home improvement projects, you should make sure that all people who contribute to the project get paid what's coming to them. This includes the prime (general) contractor if there is one, and all subcontractors, laborers, architects, materials providers, equipment lessors and anyone else who contributes time, labor or services to the project.

Why should you care whether these people get paid? Because any of them can record a Claim of Mechanics' Lien against your property, which ultimately can lead to the property being sold at auction. In addition, anyone other than the general contractor can serve a notice on you (called a stop notice) ordering you to withhold payment from the general contractor until you have settled up with the person serving the notice. If you don't withhold the money, you can be personally sued for that amount. Finally, if you were involved in lining up any of the labor or materials contributors, you can be sued for breach of contract.

This chapter provides an overview of mechanics' liens and how you might deal with them. In Chapter 10 we tell you how to decide whether the mechanics' lien and/or stop notice remedies being used against you are valid. In Chapter 11 we tell you how to have a mechanics' lien removed from your property record. In Chapter 12 we provide some heartfelt advice on how to negotiate a solution and get some help from a mediator if you need it.

A. HOW AND WHY MECHANICS' LIENS ARISE

There are several basic reasons why you may get hit with one or more mechanics' lien claims:

- there is a dispute between you and the general contractor involving payment
- you paid the general contractor what you were supposed to, but another person down the line—a laborer, materials provider or subcontractor—wasn't paid for some reason, or

- you acted as your own general contractor and for some reason didn't pay the subcontractors and materials providers who contributed to the project.

If you refused to pay a general contractor because of a dispute over the pace, quality or completeness of the work, chances are high that the contractor passed the problem down the line to any subcontractors or materials providers who contributed to the improvement. By not paying the general contractor, you have greatly increased the odds that both the contractor and the other people involved in the project will all record mechanics' liens.

There is no limit to the number of mechanics' liens that can be recorded against your property. They all have equal priority—they are treated as coming into existence at the time the work of improvement started. This means that the mechanics' liens claimants will have first claim on any equity in the property after the liens held by the original and construction lenders are subtracted.

Even if you did pay the general contractor in full, the general contractor may have decided not to pay certain subcontractors or materials providers. If these unpaid contributors record mechanics' liens, you are left with the possibility of having to pay the unpaid contributors out of your own pocket to get the liens removed from your property. You must then go after the contractor for reimbursement for this double payment.

Can this really happen to you? The answer is, "yes, quite easily." The reason is that the law is more concerned about those who provide labor, services or materials to a work of improvement getting paid than it is about the possibility of owners having to pay double. In essence, the law says, any contributor to a work of improvement is entitled to hold the improved property hostage for payment.

As mentioned, anyone who contributes labor, services, equipment or materials to the improvement of your real estate potentially can record a mechanics' lien against your property as a means of securing payment. This is so no matter how small the contribution and no matter how slight the improvement. The lien is good for 90 days after it is recorded. Its life may be extended by the filing of a lawsuit to enforce it, which may ultimately mean the lien claimant can have the property sold at auction if you lose the enforcement action in court and can't reach settlement with the claimant.

Example of Worst Case Scenario: You hire Home Additions 2000 to add a separate-entrance apartment to your home. Home Additions 2000 acts as a general contractor and hires various subcontractors and laborers to work on the project. To fund this project, you obtain a home improvement loan from your mortgage lender. After the project is well underway, and after you have paid out $100,000 to Home Additions 2000, you find out that Home Additions 2000 has not been paying the subcontractors and that the subcontractors have therefore not been paying their materials providers. All of the people who have not been paid record mechanics' lien claims against your property.

Home Additions walks off the job and goes out of business. Shortly after work stops, you are informed that if you don't satisfy the mechanics' liens, the mechanics' lien claimants will sue you in court to have your property sold. You are in a bind, because you have no more equity to fund another loan to pay off the unpaid subcontractors and materials providers. You can sue Home Additions 2000, get a judgment and then have Home Addition's owner's contractor's license suspended, but this will take too long. In fact, you are in jeopardy of losing your property through no fault of your own.

Fortunately, worst case scenarios are just that—things seldom happen that way. There are steps that an owner can take going into a work of improvement to protect against this type of horror show, and other steps that can be taken during construction to avoid the mechanics' lien minefield. In Section B, below, we explain a few of these procedures. For more information

on how to protect yourself as the owner of a home improvement project, see *How to Hire a Home Improvement Contractor Without Getting Chiseled,* by Tom Philbin (St. Martin's Press), or *Renovating with a Contractor,* by Brenner and Kelly (Taylor Publishing Co.).

B. How to Avoid Mechanics' Liens

In this section we explain:

- when and how you can obtain mechanics' lien waivers from potential and actual mechanics' lien claimants (statutory conditional and unconditional waiver forms)

- how to pay your prime (general) contractor to minimize your exposure to mechanics' lien liability (joint signature requirement)

- how to shorten the period in which potential mechanics' lien claimants have to record their Claims of Mechanics' Lien and serve their stop notices (the notice of completion or cessation)

- when you can keep your interest in real estate from being affected by mechanics' liens, and how to do it (the Notice of Non-Responsibility), and

- how to limit your property's liability for mechanics' lien claims (recording the construction contract and payment bond).

1. Obtain Waivers Before Making Progress Payments

Wouldn't it be nice for a real estate owner if he or she could require all people contributing to the work of improvement to give up (waive) their mechanics' lien rights in advance? One simple way to accomplish this would be to require all such contributors to sign a binding legal document giving up their right to use the mechanics' lien remedy. Such a document is called a "waiver and release" because the person signing it is waiving (giving up) his or her lien rights and releasing the owner from liability for nonpayment.

Unfortunately for owners, the California mechanics' lien law has long recognized that the mechanics' lien remedy wouldn't be worth much if owners could require a potential lien claimant to surrender his or her mechanics' lien rights as a condition of coming to work on the project. To make sure that owners don't find a way around this rule, the law requires that all owners use one of four statutory waiver and release forms that have been written by the Legislature. These are:

- Conditional Waiver and Release Upon Progress Payment

- Unconditional Waiver and Release Upon Progress Payment

- Conditional Waiver and Release Upon Final Payment, and

- Unconditional Waiver and Release Upon Final Payment.

The "conditional" forms are used when the potential lien claimant is asked to sign a waiver and release prior to actually having the payment in hand. Even if the potential claimant has received or endorsed a check, the waiver and release will not take effect until the bank actually pays the check. When the release does take effect, it will apply to all potential mechanics' lien claims that existed prior to the signing date.

The unconditional forms are used when the potential lien claimant has been paid. Once these forms are signed, the potential mechanics' lien claimant surrenders any mechanics' lien claims that exist prior to the date of the signing. In other words, the unconditional forms operate as a type of receipt and settlement of all existing mechanics' lien claims.

Note that none of these waivers take effect unless the potential mechanics' lien claimant has been paid (although the unconditional waiver takes effect when a check is delivered, even though the check later bounces). These restrictions on the effectiveness of waivers protect contributors to works of improvement, but make them far from foolproof for owners. If, for example, a subcontractor who has signed a conditional waiver is not paid by the prime contractor, the waiver will be worthless and the subcontractor can pursue his or her mechanics' lien remedy against the owner.

Retentions, extras and breach of contract claims

The waiver and release forms only apply to potential mechanics' lien claims (as well as stop notice and payment bond claims that we discuss in Chapters 4, 5 and 7). It is quite possible for you to obtain a waiver and release from a subcontractor but still be sued by the subcontractor for breach of contract or other monetary obligations arising out of the work of improvement that aren't subject to a mechanics' lien claim.

HOME IMPROVEMENT CONTRACTS

Civil Code Section 7159 sets out mandatory provisions for the written contract that home improvement contractors must offer homeowners. One of these provisions (Section f) requires the contractor to furnish the owner with an unconditional waiver of the mechanics' lien remedy for all work done for which the contractor has been paid before accepting any further payment for additional work. For example, if the owner pays the contractor $25,000 upon completion of phase one of a new addition, the contractor cannot collect any additional money from the contractor until the contractor signs an unconditional waiver of his mechanics' lien rights for the previous work. However, this requirement does not apply if the contractor obtains a performance or payment bond. (See Chapter 7 for a discussion of bonds.)

A common strategy for owners is to require their prime (general) contractor to obtain waivers from all contributors to the construction phase before making a progress payment to the general contractor. However, since few general contractors can afford to pay their subcontractors and the materials providers before receiving the progress payment, the waivers that they obtain under this approach are of the conditional variety. This, of course, means that the waivers won't be any good unless and until there is proof of payment (an endorsed check paid by the bank or a written acknowledgment of payment). However, if the contractor does pay as indicated on the waivers, the owner will already have the waivers in hand and won't have to worry about mechanics' liens.

For examples of the four waiver forms, and instructions for filling them in, see Chapter 12, Section I.

2. Make Out Checks to Joint Payees

Instead of writing one check to the prime (general) contractor for a particular phase, some owners write several checks. Each check is jointly made out to the general contractor and to a particular subcontractor or to a subcontractor and a materials provider the prime contractor has used. The idea here is that the check may only be cashed if the ultimate beneficiary (subcontractor or materials provider) endorses it. This helps assure payment and eliminate the risk of mechanics' liens. This is a common procedure, especially near or at the end of a project.

3. Record a Notice of Completion or a Notice of Cessation

Under the mechanics' lien and stop notice statutes, the mechanics' lien claimant has a limited period of time in which to record a Claim of Mechanics' Lien or serve a stop notice. (See Chapter 10, Section A3.) This time period starts to run from the date the project is deemed completed. If the deadline is blown, so is the Claim of Mechanics' Lien and stop notice. By recording a document that, depending on the facts, is known alternatively as a Notice of Completion or a Notice of Cessation, you can shorten the deadline, thereby increasing the chances that mechanics' lien and stop notice claimants will miss the deadline.

Note that there are other reasons for filing a notice of cessation or completion that are not related to mechanics' liens, such as closing out the construction loan and selling the property (especially if that was the plan all along).

DATES OF COMPLETION

It is important to find out when your project will be deemed completed. There are five possible dates of completion (CC §3086):

- The date the work of improvement is actually completed.

Example: Jonas hires Franco Construction Co. to add a bathroom to his house. After Franco is finished, no further work is done on the bathroom. The bathroom will be deemed completed.

- The date you accept the work of improvement.

Example: Jonas hires Franco Construction Co. to add a bathroom to his house. Payments are to be made in three phases: a down payment, a progress payment and a final payment. When Franco is done, Jonas tenders the final payment. The bathroom will be deemed completed.

- The date you occupy the work of improvement.

Example: Jonas hires Franco Construction Co. to add a bathroom to his house. When Franco is done, Jonas is pleased with the result and starts using the bathroom. The bathroom will be deemed completed.

- The date upon which there has been no labor on the project for 60 continuous days and you haven't recorded a notice of completion or cessation.

Example: Jonas hires Franco Construction Co. to add a bathroom to his house. Payments are to be made in three phases: a down payment, a progress payment and a final payment. Although Franco thinks he's done with the project, Jonas doesn't agree, but doesn't file a notice of completion or cessation. 60 continuous days pass without any labor being done on the project. The bathroom will be deemed completed.

- The date upon which here has been no labor on the project for 30 continuous days and you record a notice of completion or cessation.

Example: Jonas hires Franco Construction Co. to add a bathroom to his house. Payments are to be made in three phases: a down payment, a progress payment and a final payment. Although Franco thinks he's done with the project, Jonas doesn't agree. 30 continuous days pass without any labor being done on the project, and Jonas records a Notice of Cessation. Franco records a Claim of Mechanics' Lien. The project will be deemed completed on the thirtieth day.

Clearly, your first task is to know when your particular work of improvement was completed (see sidebar, above). Unfortunately, there is no general rule. Each completion date depends on your individual circumstances. However, your next step is very definite. At the earliest possible moment after your project is deemed completed, you should visit the recorder's office for your county and record the proper notice.

If your project really is completed, this notice will be called a Notice of Completion. If your project isn't completed but no work has occurred on it for at least 30

continuous days, then the notice will be called a Notice of Cessation. Once you record the document, the deadline for recording a Claim of Mechanics' Lien and serving a stop notice starts to run.

Example: Jonas hires Franco Construction Co. to add a bathroom to his house. Payments are to be made in three phases: a down payment, a progress payment and a final payment. Although Franco thinks he's done with the project, Jonas doesn't agree. Jonas refuses to tender the final payment and does not use the bathroom. Thirty continuous days pass without any labor being done on the bathroom. Jonas records a Notice of Cessation. Franco doesn't understand the ins and outs of mechanics' lien law and fails to record his mechanics' lien on time. He is disqualified from using the mechanics' lien remedy.

Here are the deadlines that apply to anyone seeking to record a Claim of Mechanics' Lien on your property or serve a stop notice on you:

- If the mechanics' lien claimant is a general (prime) contractor and you have not recorded a notice of completion or cessation, the claimant has 90 days to record the Claim of Mechanics' Lien and serve a stop notice from the date work on the project actually ceased.

- If the mechanics' lien claimant is a general (prime) contractor and you have recorded a Notice of Completion or a Notice of Cessation, the claimant has 60 days from the date you recorded your notice to record the Claim of Mechanics' Lien and serve a stop notice.

- If the mechanics' lien claimant is anyone other than the prime (general) contractor and you have not recorded a completion or cessation notice, the claimant has 90 days from the date work on the project actually ceased to record the Claim of Mechanics' Lien and serve a stop notice.

- If the mechanics' lien claimant is anyone other than the general (prime) contractor and you have recorded a Notice of Completion or a Notice of Cessation, the claimant has 30 days from the date you recorded your notice to record the Claim of Mechanics' Lien and serve a stop notice.

By recording the proper completion document, you can shorten the period that the mechanics' lien claimant has to record the Claim of Mechanics' Lien and serve the stop notice by between 30 and 60 days.

Example: Jonas hires Franco Construction Co. to add a bathroom to his house, to be paid for in three installments. Franco uses a plumbing subcontractor to install the plumbing and an electrical subcontractor to install the wiring. The project is finished and Jonas makes the final payment to Franco. Franco, however, doesn't pay the plumbing or electrical subcontractors. Because Jonas has accepted the work, the project is completed. Jonas immediately records a Notice of Completion. The subcontractors have 30 days to record their Claims of Mechanics' Lien. If Jonas had not recorded a Notice of Completion, the subcontractors would have 90 days to record their mechanics' lien.

Time limits for recording notices

The Notice of Completion must be recorded within 10 days after the date of completion. The Notice of Cessation may not be recorded until 30 days have passed since labor on the project stopped.

To properly prepare and record a Notice of Cessation or Notice of Completion, take these steps:

a. Step One: Complete the Form

Complete your Notice of Completion or Notice of Cessation form. The Notice of Completion is in Appendix B and on the forms disk under the file name NOTCMPLT. Fill in the form following the filled-in sample and instructions that follow:

Notice of Completion

State of California

County of _____Santa Barbara_____

NOTICE IS HEREBY GIVEN THAT:

1. I am ☒ the owner of a fee simple interest ☐ the purchaser under contract ☐ the lessee of real property (Property) described in Paragraph 5.

2. The full names and addresses of the owner or co-owners of Property are:

a. _____Horace Harvey, 26 Mill Lane Road, Carpenteria, CA_____

b. _____

c. _____

3. On the day of ___2/24/99___ a work of improvement on Property was completed as follows: ___The new room added to the house was finished except for punch list work, and we moved furniture into the room.___

4. The name of the original (prime, general) contractor for the work of improvement as a whole was: ___Arthur Stephenson___.

5. The Property is situated in the City of __Santa Barbara__, County of __Santa Barbara__, State of California and described as follows: ___A single family residence and adjoining property___

6. The street address of Property is: ___4444 Mission Place, Santa Barbara___

_____Horace Harvey_____

Signature

VERIFICATION [CCP § 446]
I declare under penalty of perjury under the laws of the State of California that the foregoing is true and correct, this ___25th___ day of ___February___ at ___Santa Barbara___, California.

_____Horace Harvey_____

Signature

Notice of Cessation

State of California

County of _____ Santa Barbara _____

NOTICE IS HEREBY GIVEN THAT:

1. I am ☒ the owner of a fee simple interest ☐ the purchaser under contract ☐ the lessee of real property (Property) described in Paragraph 5.

2. The full names and addresses of the owner or co-owners of Property are:

a. _____ Joan Eiger _____

_____

b. _____

_____

c. _____

_____

3. A cessation from labor on a work of improvement on Property commenced on or about the _____ 5th _____ day of _____ March _____, and the cessation from labor has continued for a period of more than 30 days and until the date of this notice.

4. The name of the original (prime, general) contractor for the work of improvement as a whole was: _____ Arthur Stephenson _____.

5. The Property is situated in the City of _____ Santa Barbara _____, County of _____ Santa Barbara _____, State of California and described as follows: A single family residence and adjuoining property _____

_____

_____.

6. The street address of Property is: _____ 4218 Draft Way Terrace, Santa Barbara, CA _____

_____.

_____ *Joan Eiger* _____
Signature

VERIFICATION [CCP § 446]

I declare under penalty of perjury under the laws of the State of California that the foregoing is true and correct, this _____ day of _____ at _____, California.

_____ *Joan Eiger* _____
Signature

Instructions for Notice of Completion

Enter the county where the property is located in the top blank.

1. Check the appropriate box. This will be the first box if you are an actual owner.

2. Enter the names and addresses of all owners of the property.

3. Enter the date the project was completed, and briefly describe the project. See the sidebar above for what constitutes completion.

4. Enter the name of the general contractor, if any. If there was no general contractor (for instance, you did your own contracting as an owner), put N/A.

5. Enter the city and county where the property is located, and describe the property in sufficient detail to uniquely identify it.

6. Enter the street address of the property.

7. Sign the Notice of Completion and the verification statement.

The Notice of Cessation is in Appendix B and on the forms disk under the file name NOTCESS. Follow the filled-in sample and instructions below.

Instructions for Notice of Cessation

Enter the county where the property is located in the top blank.

1. Check the appropriate box. This will be the first box if you are an actual owner.

2. Enter the names and addresses of all owners of the property.

3. Enter the date work on the project ceased, and briefly describe the project.

4. Enter the name of the general contractor, if any. If there was no general contractor (for instance, you did your own contracting as an owner), put N/A.

5. Enter the city and county where the property is located, and describe the property in sufficient detail to uniquely identify it.

6. Enter the street address of the property.

7. Sign the Notice of Completion and the verification statement.

b. Step Two: Record the Notice of Completion or Cessation

Mail or take the notice of completion or cessation to the recorder's office for the county where the property is located. There will be a recording fee of between $10 and $20. Call the recorder's office for further details.

4. Notice of Non-Responsibility

Most often, the owner of the real estate being improved is also the party who has arranged for the improvements to take place. But occasionally the owner is not involved. Instead, a person or business holding a long-term lease on the property will voluntarily set about to improve the property without going through the owner. Under many commercial leases, such improvements are permitted, either as part of the lease or on condition that the owner approves them.

> **Example:** Sharktalk Press, a self-help law book publisher, has a ten-year lease on a commercial building owned by Tom Gunn. The lease permits Sharktalk to carry out improvements that Gunn approves in advance. Sharktalk decides to create a storefront outlet on its own initiative.

If you are the owner of property being leased or purchased by someone who wants to improve it, you should make very sure that the activities of the lessor don't result in mechanics' liens. The best way to do this is to prepare a Notice of Non-Responsibility, post the notice on a prominent place at the site of the improvement and record the notice with the county recorder. This posting and recording must be done within ten days of the date you discover that the work of improvement has begun.

The Notice of Non-Responsibility is very simple. All it requires is:

- a description of the site of the work of improvement, sufficient for identification

- the name and nature of the title or interest of the person giving the notice

- the name of the party who is causing the improvements to be made (usually the lessee, or a purchaser under contract who is buying the property but who doesn't yet own it)

- a statement that the person giving the notice will not be responsible for any claims arising from it

- the owner's signature, and

- a place for the owner to *verify* that he or she posted the notice in a prominent place at the work of improvement.

A blank Notice of Non-Responsibility is included in Appendix B and on the forms disk under the file name NOTNORES.

Here is a sample notice:

Notice of Non-Responsibility

TO WHOM IT MAY CONCERN:
NOTICE IS HEREBY GIVEN that _____Thomas Hashimoto_____ is the owner ☒ in fee simple ☐ _____ (other type of ownership) of real property (Property) situated in __Weaverville__ , __Trinity__ County, described as follows: _____
_____The house and adjoining property located at 5647 Miner's Lane, Weaverville, CA_____
_____
_____.

The name of the ☐ contract purchaser ☒ lessee of Property is __Norcal Graphics__
_____.

Within the previous 10 days I obtained knowledge that a work of improvement best described as _____Addition of a workshop_____ has been commenced (is being made) upon Property.

The Provider of Notice will not be responsible for this work of improvement, nor for the payment of any labor, services or materials used or to be used in connection with this work of improvement.

Thomas Hashimoto
Signature of Owner or Other Provider of Notice

VERIFICATION
I, _____Thomas Hashimoto_____ , say that this notice is a true copy of a notice posted at __5647 Miner's Lane on the front door__ in the City of __Weaverville__ , County of __Trinity__ , State of California, on the day of __April 9, 1999__ , by __me__ and that the facts stated in this notice are true of my own knowledge.

I declare under penalty of perjury that the foregoing is true and correct and that this document was executed at _____Weaverville_____ , California, on __April 10, 1999__ .

Thomas Hashimoto
Signature

Note that you shouldn't complete the verification until the notice has first been posted on the property. Once the posting is done, the next step is to sign the verification and record the notice with the recorder for the county where the property is located. As mentioned, this recording must also be done within 10 days of discovering that the work of improvement has commenced.

If the lease requires the improvements

Some leases require that certain improvements be made, often in exchange for a reduction in rent. Improvements required by a lease are deemed to be made at the property owner's behest, and the owner cannot avoid mechanics' liens on his interest by posting and recording the Notice of Non-Responsibility.

5. Recording the Construction Contract and Payment Bond

Often, an owner will enter into a master contract with a prime (general) contractor under which the contractor agrees to carry out a specific work of improvement to its completion for a set amount of money. Depending on the size of the project, various subcontractors and/or materials providers will make at least some contribution that might give rise to a mechanics' lien claim somewhere down the road. In these situations, the owner's overall mechanics' lien risk, coupled with payments actually made to the prime (general) contractor, may far exceed the contract price for the project.

Example: Jose Esparza contracts with Jonas and Gomez Construction, Inc., a general contractor firm, to build a new house on the outskirts of El Centro, California, for a total contract price of $200,000. For a variety of reasons, the project is plagued with cost overruns. After a fitful year of on-again, off-again progress, the house is finished. Jose has paid Jonas and Gomez $150,000 and still owes them $50,000 under the

contract. Jonas and Gomez record a mechanics' lien for the $50,000, and additional mechanics' lien claims are recorded by subcontractors and materials providers for an aggregate sum of $100,000. If all mechanics' liens are paid, Jose Esparza will end up paying $300,000 instead of $200,000 for his house.

To prevent this from happening, a California law (CC §3235) permits the owner of a work of improvement that is described in a master (general) contract to limit his or her mechanics' lien liability. To accomplish this, before the work of improvement begins the owner must:

- record the general contract (including any plans and specifications referred to by the contract) with the county recorder, and
- record a payment bond in the name of the general contract that is worth at least 50% of the general contract price.

If these two recordings are made, and mechanics' liens are later recorded against the property, the aggregate recovery against the owner under all the mechanics' liens will be limited to what the owner owes the general contractor. Any additional amount will be assessed against the general contractor and the payment bond.

Example: As in the previous example, Jose Esparza owes the general contractor $50,000 and also is at risk for $100,000 worth of mechanics' lien claims. However, assume that before work on the house began, Jose required Jonas and Gomez to take out a $100,000 bond which Jose recorded along with the general contract. Jose's total mechanics' lien liability is limited to $50,000, the amount he owes the general contractor. The other mechanics' lien claimants can collect against the $100,000 payment bond.

Although this approach to reducing mechanics' lien risk may seem like a good idea, most general contractors will not qualify for a payment bond equal to 50% of the overall project cost. In our example, not only would

Jonas and Gomez have to have enough credit or collateral to qualify for a $100,000 bond, but the cost of the bond would be somewhere in the neighborhood of $10,000, which would be economically unfeasible as well. As a general rule, this owner protection is seldom used except on extremely large projects involving highly bondable general contractors and price tags that allow the cost of the bond to be absorbed in the larger project.

C. WHAT TO DO IF YOU'RE HIT WITH A MECHANICS' LIEN

The fact that the law provides considerable bargaining leverage to people who furnish labor services or materials to a work of improvement doesn't mean that you have no recourse.

Here, in order of their simplicity, are your possible remedies if your property has been hit with a Claim of Mechanics' Lien:

- Negotiate a settlement with the mechanics' lien claimant. In exchange for your payment, the claimant signs a mechanics' lien waiver and release that will result in removal of the lien from your title. (See Section E and Chapter 12 for more on negotiating the release of a mechanics' lien.)

- If the amount of the dispute is enough to justify it, pay a mediator to help you and the mechanics' lien claimant negotiate a settlement that leads to a release of the lien. (See Section E and Chapter 12 for more on mediation.)

- Purchase a bond that covers the amount of the mechanics' lien; however, this is not a viable option for most small property owners and not covered further in this book.

- If more than 90 days has passed since the Claim of Mechanics' Lien was recorded, no en-

forcement lawsuit has been filed and you didn't grant the mechanics' lien claimant an extension of time in which to file the lawsuit, demand that the mechanics' lien claimant execute a release of claim. This release will completely free your property's title from the mechanics' lien.

- If the mechanics' lien claimant refuses to cooperate, file a court action to remove the lien. Although the lien is by law void and of no legal effect if no enforcement lawsuit is filed within the 90-day period (CC §3144), you may need the court order removing the lien if you ever want to sell or finance your property and establish good credit. We tell you in Chapter 11 how to get this done. This is a surprisingly simple and straightforward procedure that also permits recovery of up to $1,000 in attorney fees.

- If the mechanics' lien claimant filed a mechanics' lien enforcement action and also recorded a Notice of Lis Pendens (see Chapter 8, Section L, for more on what this document means), you can request a hearing on whether there is any basis for the enforcement action. If the mechanics' lien claimant is unable to prove to the court that a basis exists for the enforcement lawsuit, the court will order the Lis Pendens removed from the recorder's office. This will also have the effect of defeating the underlying enforcement action. We do not cover this procedure in this book; to defend the enforcement action you'll need an attorney.

- If the mechanics' lien claimant files a mechanics' lien enforcement action, and you are unable to dispose of the lawsuit by attacking the Lis Pendens (one isn't recorded or you lose your motion to have the Lis Pendens expunged), determine whether you have grounds to successfully defend the action on its merits. We tell you how to make this assessment in Chapter 10. If you do have grounds to defend, find an attorney to represent you, assuming the amount in dispute is enough to pay the attorney's legal fees.

LIEN WAIVERS MAY PROVE HELPFUL

As a condition of payment to the general contractor, you may have required the general contractor to obtain mechanics' lien waivers from the subcontractors and materials providers who contributed to the work of improvement during the phase for which the payment is being made. There are two basic types of waivers: unconditional and conditional. (See Section B1.)

If the waiver is labeled "Unconditional," you should have a good defense in a mechanics' lien enforcement action. And if no action has been filed, the waiver will be helpful in your petition to have the court order the lien removed from the record.

If the waiver is labeled as "Conditional," however, it may not be worth much. That's because the waiver only goes into effect when payment has actually been made, and if the person who signed the waiver is also alleging that he or she wasn't paid, a conditional waiver won't help you.

The law is very specific about which waivers you can use. For more on what these waivers look like and mean, and which ones will do the best job of protecting you, see Chapter 12, Section I.

MORE ABOUT MECHANICS' LIENS

If you want to understand more about what mechanics' liens are and what someone has to do to record one against your property, read Chapters 1 and 3 of this book. While those chapters have been written for potential mechanics' lien claimants rather than for owners, you will learn all you want, and probably more.

D. IF YOU GET HIT WITH A STOP NOTICE

The mechanics' lien remedy ultimately depends upon the ability of the property being improved to produce enough money to pay off the lien claimant. However, many construction projects are abandoned well short of completion. In this event, the property itself possibly would produce less than is owed on it if it were sold at auction—which means there would be nothing left to pay off the mechanics' lien.

With this in mind, with one exception, the law authorizes anyone who is qualified to pursue the mechanics' lien remedy to also go after any funds that have been loaned for the purpose of paying for the construction. They do this by serving what's called a "stop notice" on the holder of the funds. For larger projects, this will usually be a construction loan bank, which typically disburses the loan funds in phases. For smaller projects—especially home improvement projects—this typically will be the owner, who has deposited the loan proceeds in a bank account. Despite the availability of the stop notice remedy in home improvement situations, it tends to be used only for larger construction projects.

The stop notice requires the holder of the funds to continue holding onto the amount claimed in the notice. For example, if you are a homeowner building a deck and one of the laborers serves a stop notice on you telling you to withhold funds the laborer is allegedly owed by the deck contractor, you could not legally disburse those funds to the contractor. Instead, you would have to hold on to them pending further developments.

As with a mechanics' lien, the stop notice is only good for a certain period of time unless an enforcement action is filed. And as with mechanics' liens, a lot more stop notices are served than enforcement actions filed. This is because serving a stop notice doesn't require an attorney, while the filing an enforcement action in court generally does. The court action may be filed ten days after the stop notice was served, but must be filed no later than 90 days after the mechanics' lien period expires (120-180 days after work on the project stops).

1. Stop Notices Can't Be Used by Prime Contractors

Earlier we mentioned that there was exception. A general contractor can't file a stop notice against the property owner. For instance, if you have hired a general contractor to build an addition to your home and a payment dispute arises between you and the general contractor, the general contractor can't serve a stop notice on you.

2. Bonded and Non-Bonded Stop Notices

There are two types of stop notices: bonded and unbonded. To force a lender to withhold construction funds, the stop notice must be covered by a bond that is worth 125% of the amount claimed in the stop notice. This bond requirement is not required when the stop notice is directed against the owner as holder of the construction funds.

3. What to Do If You're Served With a Stop Notice

Here are your potential remedies if you are served with a stop notice:

- Attempt to negotiate or mediate a settlement. (See Section E.) If you are unable to settle, you should place the amount of the claim in a separate account and wait to see whether the stop notice claimant files an enforcement action on time. If not, you are free to use the money.

- Alternatively, you can purchase a bond in an amount that covers the stop notice claim. This approach is not recommended for home repair or small construction projects because of the hassle and expense.

- Finally, you can determine whether the person who served the stop notice followed all required procedures. If not, and you can prove it, you should feel free to ignore the stop notice. We tell you in Chapter 10 how to check whether all requirements have been met.

- If an enforcement action is filed, you can defend it (you'll probably need an attorney).

> **MORE ABOUT STOP NOTICES**
>
> If you want to understand more about what stop notices are and what a person has to do to have them properly served and enforced, you should read Chapters 4 and 5 of this book. By pretending that you are the stop notice claimant instead of the owner of the property, you will learn all you want, and probably more.

E. NEGOTIATION AND MEDIATION

In almost every case, you will be better off negotiating a resolution of your dispute, either on your own or with the help of a third-party neutral facilitator—a mediator. Although the law may seem clear enough when you contemplate filing or fighting a lawsuit, the ultimate outcome is usually unpredictable. It is much better to retain control of the decision-making process and work towards a settlement that both sides can live with.

In Chapter 12, Section E, we suggest some resources that may help you improve your negotiation skills and some tips that should make it much more likely that your negotiations will be successful. In Chapter 12, Section F, we explain how mediation might work for you and suggest some resources in case you are interested in using that technique. It will be to your benefit to review that material before assuming that you will have to become involved in court. Even if you have already been sued, it is never too late to negotiate or mediate. ■

Do You Have a Defense?

In Chapter 9 we described two important remedies enjoyed by people who are not paid for their contributions to works of improvement—the mechanics' lien and the stop notice. Whether or not you are at fault for the nonpayment, the buck will usually stop with you—the owner of the real estate being improved. This chapter is intended to help you assess whether the person invoking these remedies has done the job right. If not, you can use this fact when negotiating a settlement. And, if negotiations fail and you end up in court, you'll know that your position is a strong one.

Although this chapter outlines the possible defenses available to you regarding the mechanics' lien and stop notice remedies, you can also get a good idea of whether the claimant did everything right by studying Chapters 2 through 5. Since those chapters are addressed to potential lien and stop notice claimants to help them get it right, you can turn the information around for the purpose of deciding whether they did it wrong.

You may have additional rights

As the owner, you may have defenses against a mechanics' lien or stop notice claimant in addition to those discussed here. For instance, you may have recorded a Notice of Non-Responsibility (CC §3094) or a payment bond that should have precluded the mechanics' lien foreclosure suit. Or, you may have recorded the original construction contract and a payment bond that together limited your liability to the total amount of the contract. (CC §§3235, 3236). These preventative measures are discussed in Chapter 9, Section B.

You also may have some claims of your own, such as an action against the lien claimant for breach of contract or for intentional misuse of the mechanics' lien process. As suggested in Chapter 9, if you want to be up to speed regarding all possible rights and remedies in your situation, see a lawyer.

A. DEFENSES TO A CLAIM OF MECHANICS' LIEN

The basic premise of the mechanics' lien remedy is that your improved property should serve as the ultimate security for anyone who contributed work or materials to help create the improvement. However, to successfully use this remedy, a mechanics' lien claimant must comply with complex procedural requirements. If you can find one or more instances where the mechanics' lien claimant didn't follow the prescribed procedures, you can win in court if the claimant files a mechanics' lien enforcement lawsuit.

1. Does the Person Qualify as a Mechanics' Lien Claimant?

To qualify as a mechanics' lien claimant, a person's labor, services, equipment or materials must be:

- contributed to the improvement of a real estate site, or

- contributed to an actual work of improvement.

a. Site Improvement

A "site improvement" includes the following types of work on any lot or tract of land:

- demolishing or removing improvements, trees or other vegetation

- drilling test holes

- grading, filling or otherwise improving any lot or tract of land on the street, highway or sidewalk in front of or adjoining any lot or tract of land

- constructing or installing sewers or other public utilities, or

- constructing any areas, vaults, cellars or rooms under sidewalks or making any improvements thereon.

b.   Work of Improvement

A "work of improvement" includes, but is not limited to:

- the construction, alteration, addition to or repair—in whole or in part—of any building, wharf, bridge, ditch, flume, aqueduct, well, tunnel, fence, machinery, railroad or road
- the seeding, sodding or planting of any lot or tract of land for landscaping purposes
- the filling, leveling or grading of any lot or tract of land, and
- the demolition and removal of buildings.

The "work of improvement" is the entire structure or scheme of improvement as a whole.

c.   Work on Project Must Have Begun

If the mechanics' lien claimant did work preparatory to either a site improvement of work of improvement—for example, evaluating a site for drainage or stress tolerance, or evaluating the structural integrity of a home for the purpose of adding a second story—such work will not support a mechanics' lien unless the project for which the work was done is actually undertaken (but not necessarily finished).

Example: Sam owns a large house in Santa Monica that was slightly damaged in a recent earthquake. He hires Lee, a structural engineer, to performs a study on how to make the house as earthquake proof as possible. Lee completes the study. Sam ultimately decides not to do the work Lee recommends because it will cost too much. Sam fails to pay Lee for the study. Lee's work was preparatory to a contemplated "work of improvement"—earthquake proofing qualifies as such. However, Lee cannot use the mechanics' lien remedy against Sam because the earthquake proofing work was never begun.

Design professionals' lien

A design professional (architect, engineer, surveyor) has a separate lien remedy for work that is undertaken on a work of improvement that never happens. For more on this remedy, see Chapter 3, Section H.

d.   Claimant's Contribution Must Be Direct

To support a mechanics' lien claim, a person's contribution must be direct. For example, a wholesale materials provider will not qualify for a mechanics' lien simply because the wholesaler sold materials to a retailer who actually provided the materials used in the project. Similarly, mechanics who service equipment at the site of an equipment lessor don't qualify for a mechanics' lien, since their contribution is indirect at best. However, if the mechanic is called to the work site to repair the equipment, then he or she would qualify.

e.   Materials Must Be Actually Used

For a materials provider to qualify for mechanics' lien, the materials have to actually be used or consumed in the work of improvement. Even if the materials were delivered to the site or picked up by the contractor who ordered them, the materials provider must still be able to prove that they were actually used on the specific work of improvement, rather than, for example, being diverted to another project or sold off to another builder.

f.   Two-Part Test for Lien Validity

If this is all getting a bit murky, here is a basic two-part test:

- Was work done on your real estate with the intent that the real estate be improved in some way, no matter how small?
- Is it fair to say that the mechanics' lien claimant directly contributed to the work intended to

improve the property, no matter how slight the contribution?

If you can answer "no" to either question, then you have a good argument that the mechanics' lien is not valid.

Example: You live in a rural area and get your water from a well via a water pump and pressure holding tank. Because your pump frequently freezes during the winter, you hire a water consultant to suggest some alternatives that would eliminate the freezing problem. The consultant spends two hours walking your property, measuring grades and testing the soil. He then suggests that you dig a new well and use gravity rather than an electric pump. He bills you $500 for this "advice." Since you feel that $500 is far too much money, you refuse to pay him. He records a mechanics' lien against your property. In the meantime, you bring in another expert who suggests a new type of pump insulation that will work except in the most extreme of situations. You hire the second expert, who installs the new insulation for a combined total of $700, $200 for the installation and $500 for the insulation material.

Because the first expert's services did not contribute to the improvement of your real estate, the mechanics' lien is invalid. However, if you also decided not to pay the second expert who contributed services directed towards an improvement, the second expert could record a valid mechanics' lien against the property (as could the supplier of the insulation if he or she also wasn't paid).

2. Was the Preliminary Notice Served on All Necessary Parties?

With certain exceptions, anyone who wants to use the mechanics' lien remedy is required to serve what's called a "preliminary notice" on the owner, lender and, if the claimant is a subcontractor or materials provider, the prime (general) contractor. The function of the prelimi-

nary notice is to provide notice that the work is being done or materials contributed and that failure to pay for the work or materials may result in a mechanics' lien being recorded against the property.

If the preliminary notice was not served within 20 days after the work or materials were first provided, the mechanics' lien will not cover the work or materials from the very beginning. It will only apply to work or materials contributed during a 20-day period prior to when the preliminary notice was finally served, as well as to all work and materials provided after that date.

Example: Tony Tamorello, a landscape architect, contracts with Davila Developer (the owner) to landscape a 37-unit planned development. He starts his activity on August 10, 1998 and works steadily until October 10. At no time does he serve a preliminary notice. On October 11th he submits an invoice to Davila for $50,000, including labor and materials. Davila refuses to pay him because the plants all died in an unexpected freeze on October 12th. Because Tony didn't serve a preliminary notice on Davila, he can't use the mechanics' lien remedy to get paid.

However, if Tony immediately realized his mistake and served Davila a preliminary notice on October 12, Tony could record a Claim of Mechanics' Lien for the work done during the 20 day period prior to October 12.

People who fall into the following categories *do not* have to serve a preliminary notice on the owner in order to use the mechanics' lien remedy:

- the prime (general) contractor
- wage laborers who work at the work site
- anyone else who contracts directly with the owner, such as an architect or a landscape designer.

However, if there is a lender in the picture, anyone other than the prime (general) contractor and on-site wage laborers does have to at least serve the lender. If they didn't, this too can be used to defeat the mechanics' lien.

3. Were the Preliminary Notices Timely Served?

If a person is required to serve a preliminary notice as a condition of using the mechanics' lien remedy, there are three rules for when it must be served:

- To make sure the mechanics' lien remedy covers all contributions to the work of improvement, the preliminary notice must be served on all necessary parties within 20 days of when the potential mechanics' lien claimant first started work or delivered materials or equipment.

Example: Peter Carpenter begins framing a new house on September 20, 1998. Peter can serve his preliminary notices as soon as he gets the job, but must serve them no later than October 10, 1998.

- If the preliminary notice is not served within 20 days of when the work first began, it can still be served. However, the mechanics' lien remedy will only apply to contributions made during the 20-day period prior to mailing the notice and during future periods.

Example: Peri Plumber is hired to provide all the plumbing on a new home. Peri has been working for 30 days before she learns that she should have served her preliminary notices. Peri serves the notices and continues working for 10 more days. Peri's mechanics' lien remedy applies to all Peri's work except that done during the first 10 days.

- If the contribution is made before the work of improvement begins (for instance, blueprints, surveys, soil tests), the preliminary notices must be served not later than 20 days after the actual work of improvement begins.

Example: Artie Architect prepares blueprints for an A-frame mountain cabin in the fall. Due to an early winter, actual construction on the cabin doesn't start until April 10th the following spring. Artie has until April 30th to serve his preliminary notices.

If the preliminary notices in your situation violated any of these rules, then the mechanics' lien is invalid and you should be able to prevail in court (if it becomes necessary).

4. Was the Preliminary Notice Properly Served on You?

Not only must the preliminary notices be served on the correct people within the correct time limits, they must also be served in the correct manner. The options for correctly serving a preliminary notice on the owner are as follows:

- It can be served by handing it to you.
- It can be served by leaving it at your home or place of business with someone in charge.
- It can be served by mailing it to your residence or place of business *by registered mail or certified mail,* return receipt requested.

If the preliminary notice was not served in one of these ways, it may be considered invalid, in which case the mechanics' lien remedy can't be used. Sending the preliminary notice by regular first class mail is not sufficient, nor is handing it to a friend or employee to deliver to you (unless the friend or employee is at and in charge of your business or residence).

5. Was the Claim of Mechanics' Lien Timely Recorded?

Preliminary notices generally are served long before a payment problem surfaces. If and when payment becomes an issue, the person who served the preliminary notices must take the next step in a timely manner—which is to record a Claim of Mechanics' Lien with the recorder for the county where the work of improvement is located. If the Claim of Mechanics' Lien was not recorded within the applicable time limit, the claim is invalid and can be defeated in court.

There are three rules governing when the Claim of Mechanics' Lien must be recorded:

- If you, as owner of the work of improvement, didn't record a document declaring the project completed (a Notice of Completion) or work on the project finished (a Notice of Cessation), the Claim of Mechanics' Lien may be recorded anytime prior to 90 days after work on the project actually ceased. (See Chapter 9, Section B3, for more on when work on a project is considered to have ceased.)

Example: Lucern Sheet Metal Inc. is hired to install the sheet metal for the roof and heating ducts for three new residences which are part of a single development. Lucern promptly serves the necessary preliminary notices and finishes its share of the work within 20 days. The work on the project drags on for another six months after Lucern has completed its job. When the job is finished, the owner does not record a Notice of Completion or a Notice of Cessation. Lucern has an additional 90 days after the date the entire project was completed to record its Claim of Mechanics' Lien.

- If you did record a Notice of Completion or a Notice of Cessation, everyone except the prime (general) contractor has 30 days after that recording date to record their Claim of Mechanics' Lien. (See Chapter 9, Section B3, for more on what these notices are and how to use them.) The prime (general) contractor has 60 days after the Notice of Completion or Notice of Cessation recording date.

Example: Assume the same facts as the previous example, except that the owner recorded a Notice of Completion on April 1. Because Lucern is a subcontractor, it has 30 days after April 1 to record its Claim of Mechanics' Lien.

6. Was the Claim of Mechanics' Lien Recorded in the Proper County?

The Claim of Mechanics' Lien must be recorded in the county where the work of improvement occurred. If it is recorded in a different county, then it is no good. For example, if the property where the work of improvement occurs is in Los Angeles County, then the Claim of Mechanics' Lien must be recorded in Los Angeles County and not in a neighboring county.

7. Does the Claim of Mechanics' Lien Have All Necessary Information?

The law requires that the Claim of Mechanics' Lien include all of the following information:

- A statement of the demand after deducting all just credits and offsets.
- The name of the owner or reputed owner, if known.
- A general statement of the kind of labor, services, equipment or materials furnished by the claimant.
- The name of the person by whom the claimant was employed or to whom the claimant furnished the labor, services, equipment or materials.
- A description of the site sufficient for identification.

If any of these are missing, you have a good argument that the mechanics' lien claim is invalid. If some of the information is inaccurate, however, the Claim of Mechanics' lien will probably not be invalid unless the court finds that the inaccuracy was deliberate or could have been avoided with reasonable care. Even then, the Claim of Mechanics' Lien will probably be considered valid unless you have been harmed in some way by the inaccuracy.

8. Have 90 Days Elapsed Since Claim of Mechanics' Lien Recorded?

A Claim of Mechanics' Lien expires 90 days after it is recorded unless a lawsuit to enforce the lien is filed in the appropriate court. This 90-day period can be extended with your permission in writing (called a Notice of Credit), but if you don't agree to extend it, and the 90-day period passes, the mechanics' lien is by law considered to be void and of no effect. Nonetheless, it will be to your interest to obtain a court order to that effect. (See Chapter 11.)

9. Was Lien Enforcement Lawsuit Properly and Timely Filed?

The mechanics' lien enforcement lawsuit must be filed in the county where the property containing the work of improvement is located, and in the court with the right jurisdictional limits. If the Claim of Mechanics' Lien is for less than $25,000, then the enforcement lawsuit must be filed in Municipal Court. If the Claim of Mechanics' Lien is for $25,000 or more, the enforcement lawsuit must be filed in Superior Court. If the courts have been consolidated in the county where the lien was recorded, then it makes no difference which court is used.

If the filing is done in the wrong court and the 90-day period expires before it is refiled in the proper court, the mechanics' lien expires. You will know what court the enforcement lawsuit was filed in because this information will be on the summons and complaint that are served on you by the party bringing the enforcement action.

B. Defenses to Stop Notices

Another remedy available to unpaid contributors to a work of improvement is called a "stop notice." This is designed to force you (or a lender) to withhold loan funds in your possession earmarked to pay the prime (general) contractor for the work of improvement until the unpaid contributor's claim is resolved and he or she signs a release of stop notice.

As with the mechanics' lien discussed in Section A, the stop notice expires after a certain time period unless the stop notice claimant files an enforcement lawsuit. If the lawsuit is timely filed, and you did not withhold the funds as required, you become personally liable for the funds.

Anyone who is entitled to use the mechanics' lien remedy may also use the stop notice remedy against you as the owner of the work of improvement. But there is one big exception: The prime (general) contractor may not use this remedy.

There are two types of stop notices: bonded stop notices and unbonded stop notices. As the name implies, a bonded stop notice is a demand that you withhold funds that is accompanied by a bond that will pay you up to 125% of the stop notice demand if it turns out that you weren't legally required to withhold the funds in the first place. An unbonded stop notice is a stop notice that isn't accompanied by a bond.

Both types of stop notices are directed at funds that have been earmarked for the work of improvement. However, a bonded stop notice typically is directed to a construction lender that still has funds loaned for the purpose of completing the work of improvement (See Chapter 5). The unbonded stop notice is directed to the owner of the work of improvement—that is, to you. (See Chapter 4.) Here we only cover the unbonded stop notice, since this chapter is addressed to you as the owner.

As with the mechanics' lien remedy, a stop notice claimant must meet complex procedural requirements to successfully use the stop notice remedy. If you can find one or more instances where the stop notice claimant didn't follow the prescribed procedures, you can win in the event the matter ends up in court in a stop notice enforcement lawsuit.

Following are the procedural questions you should ask whenever you are served with a stop notice.

1. Does the Claimant Qualify to Use the Stop Notice Remedy?

Everyone who qualifies to use the mechanics' lien remedy can also use the stop notice remedy against you—except for the prime (general) contractor, who is prohibited from serving you with a stop notice. For more information on who qualifies for a mechanics' lien, see Section A1, above. Also review Chapter 1, Section C.

2. Were Preliminary Notices Properly Served?

The same preliminary notice requirements apply to stop notices as to mechanics' liens. For more details on the preliminary notice requirements, review Sections A2, A3 and A4, above.

3. Was the Stop Notice Timely Served on You?

For a stop notice to be valid, it must be served on you no later than the time for recording a mechanics' lien. This is either 30 days from the date a Notice of Completion or a Notice of Cessation is recorded by you, or 90 days from the time the work of improvement is completed if no Notice of Completion or Notice of Cessation was recorded. (See Section A5, above, for more on this time period.)

4. Does the Stop Notice Have All Necessary Information?

The law requires that the stop notice include all of the following information:

- the stop notice claimant's name and address
- the kind of labor, services, equipment or materials the claimant contributed to the work of improvement

- the name of the person the claimant contracted with to provide the labor, services, equipment or materials
- the value of the labor, services, equipment or materials the claimant actually contributed, and
- the total value of the labor, services, equipment or materials the claimant agreed to contribute.

The stop notice also must be dated, signed and verified (signed under penalty of perjury).

If the information required for the stop notice is provided but is inaccurate, the stop notice will most likely be considered valid unless you can show that the inaccuracy was deliberate or could have been avoided with reasonable care. Even then, unless you have been harmed in some way by the inaccuracy, it probably won't affect the validity of the stop notice.

5. Has a Stop Notice Enforcement Lawsuit Been Timely Filed?

A stop notice only lasts for 90 days past the deadline for recording a Claim of Mechanics' Lien. If you, as the owner, didn't record a Notice of Completion or a Notice of Cessation (see Chapter 9, Section B3), this deadline was 90 days after work on the project stopped. This means the stop notice enforcement lawsuit must be filed by the claimant within 180 days after the work stopped. If you did record a Notice of Completion or a Notice of Cessation, then the deadline was 30 days from the recording date. This means the stop notice enforcement suit must be filed within 120 days after the recording date. (See Chapter 9, Section B3, for more on when a project is considered to be completed.)

Example: Toastie Furnace Co. is hired by the prime (general) contractor to install a furnace in a newly constructed home. The funds for the new home were borrowed by Larry Lewis from a bank, with the land as collateral. Some of these funds remain in Larry Lewis's bank account. Larry pays the general contractor the funds due Toastie, but the general contractor doesn't like the work Toastie did and withholds the funds.

Toastie serves a stop notice on Larry. The house is completed on October 31, 1999. Larry records a Notice of Completion on November 5, 1999. Toastie has 120 days from November 5, 1999 to file their stop notice enforcement lawsuit, which is March 4, 2000.

For most owners, the project will be completed when final payment is made or when they occupy the improvement. Otherwise, the date when the project is completed can be a little fuzzy. For instance, if all the work called for in the prime contract has been done, the project may be considered completed even though some warranty or "punchlist" work remains to be done (this is referred to as "substantial completion"). ■

CHAPTER 11

Removing a Mechanics' Lien From Your Property Record

Once a mechanics' lien has been recorded against your property, you may not be able to sell it without first getting the lien removed from your property record. The easiest way to get the lien removed is to have the lien claimant to sign a Release of Lien. (See Section B, below.) Unfortunately this seldom works. This chapter focuses on the easiest and cheapest way to get the lien removed in the absence of the lien claimant's cooperation: filing in court a document called a Petition to Release Property From Mechanics' Lien. This procedure can be used whenever the lien claimant fails to timely file a mechanics' lien enforcement action with the court.

A. WHY YOU NEED TO FILE A PETITION TO RELEASE LIEN

It's very common for claimants who record mechanics' liens to fail to file a court action to enforce the lien within the legal time limit—90 days from the date the mechanics' lien was recorded. This may be because they don't understand the deadline, don't know how to file such an action and/or can't find or afford an attorney to file the action. Whatever the reason, you're in luck: If the lien claimant doesn't file within 90 days of recording the mechanics' lien (and you haven't signed an agreement extending this deadline), the lien is no longer valid. However, title companies often don't recognize the fact that by law a mechanics' lien automatically becomes invalid when the lien claimant fails to timely file suit. This means that you may not be able to pass clear title to a buyer.

For this reason, it is necessary to take further steps to have the lien permanently removed. You can do this by filing in court a document called a Petition to Release Property From Mechanics' Lien. (CC §3154) If you are successful, the court will issue a Decree Releasing Lien which, when recorded, will satisfy the title company.

This is a simple procedure that you can handle yourself. It involves obtaining a certified copy of the Claim of Mechanics' Lien from the recorder's office, preparing three documents, filing the documents, mailing the documents to the lien claimant, showing up in court for a brief hearing, obtaining the decree and recording the decree with the county recorder's office. The remainder of this chapter shows you how to handle each step in the process.

If you think doing this yourself is too much trouble, you can hire an attorney to do the work for you. The court can award you up to $1,000 in attorney fees if you decide to use an attorney. This should be enough to pay the attorney fees involved. Indeed, this might be one time when you should hire an attorney, since you probably won't have to pay for it out of your own pocket.

Possible effects on credit

Unfortunately, even if the lien is removed, your credit report may show that the lien used to be there, a fact that may adversely affect your credit. An explanation may clear the matter up. But if you run into computer credit scoring, you may be out of luck even though you never did anything wrong. The fact is, the mechanics' lien remedy was created long before the modern credit reporting system, and as with many other areas of life, the law has not caught up with modern developments.

THE RELEASE BOND OPTION

You can always get a mechanics' lien removed by purchasing and recording a "release bond" in the amount of 150% of the lien claim (CC §3194). However, this remedy is problematic. The release bond can be expensive, and you may have trouble obtaining a bond (depending on your creditworthiness). If you later lose on the underlying lien claim, you would have been better off settling for the amount of the lien, since by paying for the bond you would have thrown good money after bad.

Obtaining a waiver and release from the lien claimant requires settlement, and for a number of reasons you may not be able or willing to settle.

B. REQUEST THAT THE LIEN CLAIMANT SIGN A RELEASE OF LIEN

To obtain an order from the court releasing the lien, you have to allege that the lien claimant refused to voluntarily sign a Release of Lien. The only way you'll be able to allege this is to request a Release of Lien from the lien claimant. To do this you'll want to send a request letter and a completed Release of Lien for the lien claimant to sign. This should be sent certified mail, return receipt requested.

Below we provide samples of the request letter and Release of Lien. Copies of both are in Appendix B and on the forms disk under the file names LNRELREQ and RELIEN, respectively.

John Contractor
1111 Fourth St.
Carlsbad, CA 90000
February 20, 2000

Re: Mechanics' lien on my property

Dear Mr. Contractor:

On November 15, 1999 you recorded a Claim of Mechanics' Lien against my property at the San Diego County Recorder's Office. It is now February 20, 2000, more than 90 days since that recording date. Because you have not filed an action to enforce the mechanics' lien within the 90-day period set by law (Civil Code §3144), your lien is null and void. I would now like to have the lien removed from my property record.

The easiest way for this to happen is for you to sign the enclosed Release of Lien in front of a notary public and return it to me. I'll then record the Release and the lien will be removed from my record.

If you are unwilling to sign the enclosed Release of Lien in front of a notary and return it to me, I'll be forced to petition the court to order the lien released. Please be aware that the law allows me to collect attorney fees up to $1,000 from you if I am successful in that action.

I hope we can resolve this without involving the court. Please let me know your intentions no later than 10 days from the date of this letter.

Sincerely,

Owen Owner

Owen Owner

Release of Lien

That certain Claim of Mechanics' Lien recorded _____May 15, 1999_____, in

Book __187__ of Official Records, page ___29___, records of _____Lake_____

County, California, against _____Allen Fourhi_____ is hereby

fully satisfied, released and discharged.

The property affected by this release is described as follows: *(Same description that is on the recorded Claim of Mechanics' Lien)*

Two residential buildings and adjoining property located at _____

4344 Lakeshore Dr., Lakeport, CA _____

_____

_____.

Date:_____   Signature: _____

VERIFICATION [CCP § 446]

I declare under penalty of perjury under the laws of the State of California that the

foregoing is true and correct, this ____16th____day of _____June_____ at

_____Lakeport_____, California.

_____

Signature

C. PREPARING THE PETITION FOR RELEASE OF LIEN

Assuming that you do not receive a positive response from the lien claimant, you will need to go to court. A blank Petition for Release of Lien is in Appendix B and on the forms disk under the file name PETITION. You may have to conform some of its language to your own situation. For now, tear or print out a copy of the petition and follow these step-by-step instructions.

Instruction for one lien only

The instructions for preparing the petition and accompanying documents assume you are only interested in removing one mechanics' lien from your record. However, it is possible that there are several mechanics' liens on record that you can remove by using this method. If you want to go after more than one mechanics' lien, you will need to modify these documents accordingly. To avoid confusion, we don't provide instructions for how to do that, since the great majority of cases involve only one mechanics' lien. If you can't get help from an attorney, you can always file a separate petition for each lien. This will be more costly because of the extra filing fees, but will get the job done.

1. Caption

Caption

The top part of this form is called the caption. Here is how to fill it in:

- Enter your name, address and telephone number in the top left space. Note that the information already in the space shows that you are appearing without an attorney.

- The next blank provides information about the court you'll be filing your petition in. The proper court will depend on the amount of the lien claim. If it is over $25,000 you must file in the Superior Court for the county where your property is located. If it is for less than $25,000, you must file in the Municipal Court for the judicial district where your property is located. If you are in a consolidated county, you will file in the Superior Court. Enter the address information for the appropriate court and the branch name (if it has one).

Merger of municipal and superior courts

As this book goes to print, a recently passed ballot initiative requires that the municipal and superior courts be merged. Except in Los Angeles and a few other counties, there is now only one court—the Superior Court.

- Put your name next to the Petitioner/Plaintiff entry. Put the name of the parties you are suing next to the Respondent/Defendant entry. If you don't yet know who you should sue, don't worry. Proceed with the rest of our instructions, paying careful attention to Item 3. You can always come back later and enter the names of these parties.

2. Title of Document

Petition to Release Property From Mechanics' Lien [CC §3154]

This tells the court what kind of relief you are seeking. You need add no information here.

3. Petitioner and Respondent

I.   Petitioner and Respondent

Petitioner _____ is the

☐ owner ☐ owner of an interest in the property described in paragraph II. Respondent (Lien Claimant) is, and at all times herein mentioned was, a:

    ☐ corporation organized and existing under the laws of _____

    ☐ limited liability company organized and existing under the laws of

    _____

    ☐ partnership existing under the laws of

    _____

    ☐ sole proprietor or individual residing in the county of _____

These provisions tell the court who is bringing the case—you—and which person or entity is on the other side of the case (the lien claimant). You are entitled to bring this petition if you either own the property outright, or you own an interest in it. For instance, you would own an interest in the property if you held a deed of trust in the property as security for a loan. The best way to tell whether you own an interest is whether you would be financially harmed if the property were sold to pay the mechanics' lien.

You must check one of the boxes to describe the lien claimant. You can tell whether the lien claimant is a corporation, partnership, partnership or sole proprietor from the Claim of Mechanics' Lien that was recorded against your property.

4. Property

II.   The Property

The property that is the subject of this petition is described as follows:

Here is where you enter the legal description of your property. This entry can be taken directly from the mechanics' lien claim that was recorded against your property (assuming it's correct). Otherwise, describe your property in enough detail for it to be identified in the recorder's office. It is a good idea to double-check your property description against that contained in your deed.

5. The Claim of Mechanics' Lien

III. The Claim of Mechanics' Lien

On or about _____, 19_____, Lien Claimant caused to be recorded in the Official Records of the County of _____, Book____, page_____, a duly verified Claim of Mechanics' Lien against the Property. A copy of the Claim of Mechanics' Lien is attached hereto as Exhibit A and made a part hereof.

Here you enter the date the claim of lien was recorded and exactly where in the records it is recorded. This date sets the time limit for filing a mechanics' lien enforcement action. This date is important because you can't legally file your Petition until 90 days have passed. You'll need to visit the recorder's office to get a certified copy of the Claim of Mechanics' Lien to attach to the petition as Exhibit A. This certified copy will provide the information you need to complete this part of the Petition.

WHEN CLAIM OF MECHANICS' LIEN MUST BE RECORDED

The mechanics' lien law requires a Claim of Mechanics' Lien to be recorded no later than 90 days after work on the project ceased, and sooner if you recorded a Notice of Completion or a Notice of Cessation. See Chapter 9, Section B3, for more on these notices. Assuming you didn't record a Notice of Completion or Notice of Cessation, you will be able to tell whether a mechanics' lien has been recorded by visiting the recorder's office 90 or more days after work on the project has stopped. You can usually get this information from the customer service division of any title insurance company. Or, you can ask the recorder's office staff for instructions.

6. No Enforcement Action or Extension

IV. No Foreclosure Action Filed nor Extension of Credit Granted

No action has been filed to foreclose the lien, no extension of credit has been recorded and the time period during which suit can be brought to foreclose the lien has expired.

Here you state that to your knowledge the lien claimant has not filed a mechanics' lien enforcement action and that you have not agreed to an extension of the deadline (called a Notice of Credit). If you have signed a Notice of Credit, you won't be able to file your Petition until the period of time for the extension (typically 90 days) has passed.

7. Lien Claimant's Non-Cooperation

V. Lien Claimant's Non-Cooperation

Lien Claimant _____

is ☐ unable ☐ unwilling to execute a release of

the lien in that _____

_____.

or ☐ Lien Claimant cannot with reasonable diligence

be found in that _____

_____.

Here you state that the lien claimant was unable or unwilling to prepare and record a Release of Mechanics' Lien Claim removing the mechanics' lien from your property record. You must provide what details you can describing why the claimant refused or was unable to do so. For instance, if the claimant failed to respond to your request letter (Section B, above), state that you unsuccessfully requested a Release of Lien from the claimant and attach the request letter and Release of Lien form to the petition as exhibits.

If you were unable to locate the mechanics' lien claimant after diligent attempts to do so, leave the first part of this clause blank and check the box stating that you couldn't locate the claimant. You must then provide details of your "diligent attempts" to locate the claimant. As a general rule, "diligent attempts" means you have made at least three attempts to find the claimant by visiting the claimant's last known address. In this event you would state, for example: "I was unable to locate claimant despite three visits to his last known address at 100 Main St., Marred Vista, CA on January 3, 5 and 8, 1999."

8. No Bankruptcy or Restraint

VI. No Bankruptcy or Restraint

Petitioner has not filed for relief under any law governing bankrupts, and Petitioner knows of no other restraint that exists to prevent the lien claimant from filing to foreclose his or her lien.

Here you state that the lien claimant has not been restrained from filing an enforcement action because of any bankruptcy petition filed by you, or for any other reason known to you.

9. Attorney Fees

VII. Attorney Fees

Petitioner ☐ has not ☐ has incurred attorney's fees in bringing and prosecuting this petition.

The law permits you to recover up to $1,000 in attorney fees. If you are filing the Petition yourself, you can't recover attorney fees for your own time, even though you technically are acting as your own attorney. However, if you spend money consulting with an attorney regarding this remedy, you are entitled to recover that money.

10. Prayer

WHEREFORE, Petitioner prays:

1. That the Property be released from the lien claimant's claim of lien;

2. For attorney fees in the amount of $_____

3. For costs of suit herein incurred; and

4. For such other and further relief as the court deems proper.

Dated: _____

_____
Signature (or attorney's signature)

Here is where you ask the court to grant you the relief you are seeking in the Petition. As you can see, the only thing you need to do is include an amount for attorney fees (if you incurred any).

11. Verification

Verification [CCP §§446, 2015.5]

I, _____, am the petitioner in this proceeding. I have read the foregoing petition and know the contents thereof. The same is true of my own knowledge, except as to those matters which are therein alleged on information and belief, and, as to those matters, I believe it to be true.

I declare under penalty of perjury under the laws of the State of California that the foregoing is true and correct, this ____ day of _____ of 19____.

Signature _____

Here you date and sign the Petition under penalty of perjury.

12. Copies

Remember to attach a copy of the Claim of Mechanics' Lien certified by the county recorder.

Prepare at least two copies of your Petition, one for your records and one to serve on the claimant.

D. PREPARING NOTICE OF HEARING

When you file the Petition, you will receive a date on which a hearing on your Petition will be held by the court. In addition to a copy of your Petition, you will need to serve a Notice of Hearing on the lien claimant. (See Section F for how to serve these documents.) A blank copy of the Notice of Hearing is in Appendix B and on the forms disk under the file name HEARNOT.

Tear or print out a copy of the petition and then follow along.

- Enter the same information in the Caption and Court sections as you did on your Petition.
- Enter the place, date and time set for the hearing on your Petition.
- Enter the information requested in the notice—that is, your name and a description of the property (this should be the same as in your Petition).
- Date and sign the notice.

Leave the Proof of Service blank for now.

Make at least two copies: one for your records and one to send to the lien claimant. You will later file the original Notice of Hearing in court.

E. PREPARING THE DECREE FOR RELEASE OF LIEN

Although you have not yet gone to court, you will want to prepare the order the judge will sign if you are successful. A blank Decree for Release of Lien is in the forms appendix and on the forms disk under the file name DECREE. You may have to conform some of its language to your own situation. For now, tear or print out a copy of the petition. You only need to fill out the following portions of the form:

1. Caption

This should be the same as on the petition you prepared in Section C1, above.

2. Case History

This proceeding came on for hearing before the court on _____, the Honorable

_____ presiding.

Petitioner appeared ☐ in pro persona ☐ by counsel

_____, and

Respondent appeared ☐ in pro persona ☐ by

Counsel _____.

Since you probably are preparing this decree before the hearing, you may not know what to put in these blanks (for example, the name of the judge hearing the case). If so, leave them blank. After the judge rules, you can complete them then, or perhaps the judge or clerk will complete them.

3. Paragraph 2

2. On _____, a claim of

lien was recorded in the office of the Recorder of

_____County, California, in

Book _____ of Official Records, against the following

described property: _____

_____

_____;

The information for this paragraph should be the same as that contained in paragraphs II and III of your Petition. (See Sections C4-5.)

Make two copies of the Decree Releasing Lien.

F. FILING THE PETITION IN COURT

Your next step is to file your Petition to Release Lien in the appropriate court. As mentioned, this will be either the Municipal or Superior Court for the county in which the property in question is located. If the amount of the Claim of Mechanics' Lien is more than $25,000, you will file your Petition in Superior Court. If the amount of the claim is less than $25,000, you will file in Municipal Court. If there are two or more courts in the county where you live, you will usually want to file in the nearest court. But to be on the safe side, call the court clerk to find out for sure.

Although it is possible to accomplish the actual filing by mail, we recommend that you visit the court. Even though the court clerks will not give you legal advice, you can often learn a lot just through the casual conversation you will have when filing the papers.

IF YOU FILE BY MAIL

If you decide to file your documents by mail, you should include in your mailing:

- the originals and two copies of each document

- a self-addressed, stamped envelope (SASE)

- the necessary filing fee, and

- a brief cover letter telling the clerk what you have enclosed in your mailing and what you want the clerk to do (file the original, conform the copies and mail the copies back to you in the enclosed SASE).

You should take the original and two copies of your Petition to the court. The court will accept the original for filing and file stamp your copies. One of these copies will be for your own use and one will be sent to the lien claimant.

There will be a fee for filing the petition, often about $150-$200. Call the court in advance to find out the correct amount.

Upon filing of the petition, the clerk (or judge if there is no clerk) is supposed to set a date for the hearing not more that 30 days following the filing of the petition. The court may continue the hearing beyond the 30-day period, but good cause must be shown for any continuance. There is no definition of what "good cause" means, and ultimately it is up to whoever is seeking the continuance to convince the judge why it is required. Illness and legitimate conflicting business or personal obligations usually are considered to be good cause.

When you get the hearing place, date and time, enter that information in the Notice of Hearing you already prepared. If you have already made copies, enter the information in the copies as well as the original. If you haven't yet made copies, enter the information on the original and then make the copies.

G. SERVING THE PETITION AND NOTICE OF HEARING ON THE LIEN CLAIMANT

Your next step is to have the lien claimant officially served with a copy of your Petition and Notice of Hearing. This service must be accomplished by someone *other than you* who is a resident of California and over age 18. The service must be made at least *10 days prior to the date set for hearing.* There are several basic ways to accomplish this service:

- have the lien claimant personally served by handing him or her the papers

- have the lien claimant personally served by having the papers delivered to the lien claimant's home or business and handing them to a responsible person, or

- use first class registered or certified mail to send the papers to the lien claimant.

If registered or certified mail is used, the date the mail is deposited with the post office must be at least *15 days before the date set for hearing.* The mail must be addressed to the lien claimant at his or her address as shown on any of the following documents:

- the preliminary 20-day notice served by the claimant pursuant to Section 3097 (see Chapter 10, Section A, for more on the preliminary notice)

- the Contractor State Licensing Board records

- the contract on which the lien is based, or

- the Claim of Mechanics' Lien itself.

Have someone else do the serving

Remember that for the service to be valid it must be accomplished by someone else. While this can be a friend or relative—anyone other than you or your spouse or employee—by far the best option is to use a professional process server (use the Yellow Pages) or the sheriff if the local sheriff's office provides this service. While this will cost you more than would a friend or relative, you will be in much better shape if the lien claimant doesn't show up in court and then later argues that he or she never got the papers.

H.　PROOF OF SERVICE

As soon as the lien claimant has been served with the Petition and Notice of Hearing, a Proof of Service must be prepared and filed. If you follow our advice and use a professional process server or the sheriff, that person will prepare the Proof of Service for you. If, however, you use a friend or relative, you should complete the document called Proof of Service and have your server sign it. This will establish that the service of the documents was correctly carried out as required by law. The Proof of Service is contained on the Notice of Hearing. If the service was accomplished by mail, remember to attach the registration or certification receipt to the Proof of Service document.

After completing the Proof of Service and having your server sign it, you have two options: file the proof of service with the court or take it with you to court when you appear for the hearing. The better practice is to file the Proof of Service with the court. While this can be done by mail, the better practice is to personally accomplish the filing so that if there is some problem, the clerk will tell you in time for you to correct it before the hearing.

I.　PROVING YOUR CASE IN COURT

You must show up at the court hearing at the appointed time to convince the judge that the lien should be released. Under the law, you will be required to establish that you properly served all the required documents on the lien claimant. (CC §3154(d).) The way this will normally be accomplished is for the judge

to swear you in and ask you whether the information in your proof of service is correct.

Whether or not the lien claimant shows up, your main evidence to justify the Decree Releasing Lien will be the certified copy of the recorded Claim of Mechanics' Lien attached to your Petition. That document will show the date the Claim was recorded in the County Recorder's Office. The only other facts that the judge will need to rule in your favor were alleged in your Petition:

- that as far as you know, the lien claimant has not filed a lawsuit to enforce the lien
- that you have not granted the lien claimant an extension of time in which to file the lawsuit, and
- that you haven't filed for bankruptcy or taken any other steps to prevent the lien claimant from filing the enforcement petition.

In court, the judge may want you to testify to these three facts; or, the judge may simply accept them as true based on your Petition (which you filed under oath). No fancy or legalistic language is necessary. Just be prepared to explain what is in your papers or answer the judge's questions.

Assuming that the lien claimant doesn't show up, or shows up and is unable to disprove your testimony or statements in your Petition, the court should rule in your favor.

J.　GETTING THE JUDGE TO SIGN THE DECREE

Sometimes the judge will rule right in the courtroom. Other times the judge will take the matter under advisement. If the judge rules in your favor on the spot, you can present your prepared Decree Releasing Lien for the judge's signature. If the judge takes the case under submission, the courtroom clerk may be willing to accept your prepared Decree, or you may have to place it with the court clerk (in the main clerk's office) for further action by the judge (called lodging the

Decree). Make sure you find out from the court clerk what you should do with your prepared Decree. It is even possible that the court will issue its own Decree, although this would be an exception to how most courts operate.

K. OBTAINING A CERTIFIED COPY OF THE DECREE

Once the judge signs the Decree and places it in the court file, you should ask the court clerk to issue you a certified copy of the Decree. It is this certified copy that you will use to record the Decree with the county recorder's office, which in turn will remove the lien from your property.

L. RECORDING THE DECREE RELEASING LIEN

Record your certified copy of the Decree with the county recorder. Once the Decree is recorded, your property record will be clear of the mechanics' lien. The staff in the recorder's office will provide you any necessary help. ■

Negotiating a Settlement

This chapter explains by far the most common way that mechanics' lien disputes are resolved: by voluntary agreement. It provides some pointers for negotiating a solution and getting outside help if you are having trouble reaching a settlement. Since arbitration is commonly called for in construction contracts, this chapter also provides an overview of arbitration: what it is, how it works and when it might be a good remedy for you.

Unlike the other chapters of this book, this one is written for both mechanics' lien claimants and for property owners. In many ways, you are both in the same boat. You both have a common interest in avoiding the expense of going to court and the risk of losing. The potentially sizable costs of lawyers and expert witnesses won't flow into either of your pockets, even if you're the one who wins.

You also both have a common interest in knowing what the very best voluntary resolution might be if only you could agree to it. Then you can make an informed choice about whether you would rather take your chances in court or arbitration. Remember that virtually everyone who comes into court or arbitration sees things only from their own perspective and so believes they're going to win. They often tell their attorneys only their own side of the story, and so hear honestly from counsel that they appear to have a strong case. At least half of these folks end up pretty mad—when they finally lose.

A. WHY NEGOTIATE?

The specter of a court action provides a powerful motivation for settlement. No one ever wants to go to court, and with good reason. Courts can get expensive and, like Murphy's law, everything that can go wrong, will. As long as you're still negotiating, you still control the outcome. If the very best potential settlement you can construct isn't good enough, you still keep all your rights to go to court or arbitration (assuming it's provided for in the contract).

It's almost always wise to make serious efforts to settle things early on, before everyone has sunk a lot of time and money into preparing for battle. Those resources are usually better spent on getting the problems solved. The time period after a contributor to a work of improvement records a Claim of Mechanics' Lien and/or serves a stop notice on the owner, and before the claimant goes to court, is typically the time you are most likely to negotiate a settlement.

B. WHO SHOULD BE IN ON THE NEGOTIATIONS?

Theoretically, everyone who may be asked to pay money or believes they are due money should be in on the negotiations.

If you are a contributor to a work of improvement, you should always try to include the owner in your negotiations. You are most likely to be paid because the owner wants you paid, which means either that the owner will pay you or will arrange for the prime (general) contractor to do so.

If you're the owner, you may firmly believe you should not have to pay the contributor to your work of improvement. Perhaps you already paid the general contractor for this work, or the work or materials were not satisfactory. You will probably want to talk with the subcontractor or materials supplier and the general contractor.

Unfortunately, it is often next to impossible to get all these people in a room at the same time. If you become frustrated in your attempt to call an all-inclusive meeting, consider meeting with the individual who has the most to gain in settling the dispute, and then contact the other people with a proposal as needed.

C. INITIATING NEGOTIATIONS

It's relatively easy to negotiate with people at the beginning of a project, when everyone is looking to make the deal work. But it's a real challenge to negotiate with people who are angry and feel they've been cheated. Most people on all sides of construction disputes feel this way. Often they believe someone is withholding their money when they have worked hard to earn it, or believe they haven't received the quality work they're entitled to. If you're heading into a lawsuit, sitting down and talking cooperatively with the other side is probably the last thing you or they feel like doing.

The first, and often the hardest, step is to get everyone to sit down with the honest intention of seeing what things look like from the other side and what's the best potential agreement you can work out. Many of us are afraid that any hint of willingness to talk settlement will be considered a sign of weakness. Most of us are caught up in building our own case to ourselves and to our friends about why we are right, what awful folks they are on the other side and how we have no choice but to fight it out.

As soon as possible after the mechanics' lien is recorded, consider writing a letter suggesting settlement negotiations. Send copies to all persons whose participation might help you settle the dispute. The purpose of the letter is to set a tone which encourages everyone to meet for serious settlement efforts. Here are some samples that vary slightly depending on who is writing and receiving them. The text of these letters is included on the forms disk under the file name SETLTRS.

LETTER FROM GENERAL CONTRACTOR TO OWNER

Mike Toyama
Toyama Contracting Co.
9922 Bay Blvd.
San Diego, CA 90001

April 29, 1999

RE: Settlement of payment dispute

Dear Owner:

When it recently became clear that our bill was not getting paid we felt it prudent to record a mechanics' lien against your property. To keep the mechanics' lien alive we will have to file an enforcement action in court no later than May 15, 1999, unless of course, we are able to settle this matter among ourselves.

Certainly there have been some serious misunderstandings along the way. To get negotiations started, we would like to briefly describe how we understood our agreements when we first decided to work together on this project, and how things changed as we got into the job. Then we would like to know how you see the situation. Would you be willing to review the following and make notes on where you think we are not seeing things clearly? It's important to us to understand your perspective on this.

 [Insert brief, strictly factual chronology of key events as accurately as you can reconstruct them from receipts, contracts, canceled checks, job logs and your memory.]

We want to work something out that feels fair to you. At this stage we still control the outcome of this ourselves and have a common interest in avoiding a legal fight with an unknown ending handed down by a court (or arbitrator). I'm convinced that we can work out something we can all live with. We look forward to hearing from you in the next week.

Sincerely,

Mike Toyama

Mike Toyama

LETTER FROM SUBCONTRACTOR OR MATERIALS SUPPLIER TO OWNER

Jeff Bluestone
Bluestone Suppliers
1720 Virginia St.
Berkeley, CA 94704

October 15, 1999
RE: Settlement of unpaid balance

Dear Owner:

When it recently became clear that our bill was not getting paid we felt it prudent to record a mechanics' lien against your property. To keep the mechanics' lien alive we will have to file an enforcement action in court no later than [insert last day to file], unless of course, we are able to settle this matter among ourselves.

Towards that end, we would like to briefly describe our view of the situation.

 [Insert brief, strictly factual chronology of key events as accurately as you can reconstruct them from receipts, contracts, canceled checks, job logs, and your memory.]

At this stage we still control the outcome of this dispute ourselves and have a common interest in avoiding a legal fight with an unknown ending handed down by a court (or arbitrator). I'm convinced that we can work out something we can both live with. We look forward to hearing from you in the next week.

Sincerely,

Jeff Bluestone

Jeff Bluestone

LETTER FROM OWNER TO GENERAL CONTRACTOR

Betty Hudson
2020 Cadberry Lane
Kensington, CA 94709

May 30, 1999
RE: Settlement negotiations

Dear General Contractor:

We recently learned that you have recorded a mechanics' lien against our property. In the hope that we can settle this matter without further legal proceedings, we would welcome an opportunity to meet with you.

To get negotiations started, we would like to briefly describe how we understood our agreements when we first decided to work together on this project, and how things changed as we got into the job. Then we would like to know how you see the situation. Would you be willing to review the following and make notes on where you think we are not seeing things clearly? It's important to us to understand your perspective on this.

 [Insert brief, strictly factual chronology of key events as accurately as you can reconstruct them from receipts, contracts, canceled checks, job logs and your memory.]

We want to work something out that feels fair to you. At this stage we still control the outcome of this ourselves and have a common interest in avoiding a legal fight with an unknown ending handed down by a court (or arbitrator). I'm convinced that we can work out something we can all live with. We look forward to hearing from you in the next week.

Sincerely,

Betty Hudson

Betty Hudson

LETTER FROM SUBCONTRACTOR OR MATERIALS SUPPLIER TO GENERAL CONTRACTOR OR SUBCONTRACTOR

Jeff Bluestone Suppliers
1720 Virginia St.
Berkeley, CA 94704

October 15, 1999
RE: Payment of balance due

Dear Mr. Toyama,

As you know, I have not been paid for my roofing supplies contributed to the work of improvement on the property located at 4732 5th St., Yreka, on June 20, 1999.

Unless we can settle this matter I will be forced to file a lawsuit in the near future to enforce my remedies, which would include a breach of contract claim against you.

As a first step to settlement, I would like to briefly describe how I interpret our contract and how things changed as we got into the job. Then I would like to know how you see the situation. Would you be willing to review the following and make notes on where you think I am not seeing things clearly? It's important to me to understand your perspective on this.

    [Insert brief, strictly factual chronology of key events as accurately as you can reconstruct them from receipts, contracts, canceled checks, job logs and your memory.]

I want to work something out that feels fair to you. Because I would also be proceeding against the owner's property in any lawsuit that I file, I think the best approach would be for you, the owner and me to sit down and reach a solution that is satisfactory to all of us.

At this stage we still control the outcome of this dispute ourselves and have a common interest in avoiding a legal fight with an unknown ending handed down by a court (or arbitrator). I'm convinced that we can work out something we can all live with. I look forward to hearing from you in the next week.

Sincerely,

Jeff Bluestone

Jeff Bluestone

cc Betty Hudson, Owner

D. EXPLORING POSSIBLE SETTLEMENT TERMS

If the reason payment isn't being made is purely economic—that is, it has nothing to do with job performance, delay or the quality of the materials—the negotiations should be pretty straightforward. The trick here is to be flexible about what you are willing to accept. Starting with the full amount of what is allegedly owed, you may be able to work out payments over time. Or you may be able to work out an agreement combining partial payment with future work on another project.

Although it may not seem desirable, offering a discount in exchange for payment of a flat amount (perhaps 80-90% of the full amount due) may be a better choice for all parties than going to court. The more flexible you are, the better your chance of settlement.

If the quality of the work or materials is also in dispute, you have a different set of issues to deal with. The owner or general contractor may not want to pay for work or materials they feel didn't measure up to industry standards. The person providing the work or materials, on the other hand, may feel they were perfectly adequate and that the quality issue is being raised in bad faith. Especially if there have been previous conversations about this issue, you may think that there's not much point talking about it again. This point of view is understandable, but wrong. The fact that you are about to embark on litigation will likely provide an impetus for satisfactory negotiations that may not have been there before.

What do you have to negotiate about? If you believe that there is no basis for the other side's claims, then you at least might consider getting part of the money or work you feel you are owed—and getting on with the rest of your life—in exchange for giving up your full claim.

Many construction payment disputes snowball into multiple complex claims involving alleged delays, unpaid extras, cost overruns, quality of work or materials, deviation from plans and specs and unforeseen conditions. When owners find a mechanics' lien has been filed against them, they often run to an attorney. The attorney, in turn, may then begin preparing to file counterclaims against the contractor for construction defects and delay damages. Everyone then gets into a costly legal battle.

Is there some basis to expect these kinds of claims and counterclaims in your case? If so, you and everyone else involved may be much better off figuring out together what it takes to get the problems solved and get people paid before you put all your time, energy and money into a legal battle. For contractors and suppliers, you may be able to advance the interests of your business by admitting the problem and finding a way to satisfy both your sense of what's fair and what the other party is willing to accept.

Resolving disputes this way is much more likely to produce future business relationships than pushing for every cent. For owners, this is often a much better path to getting your property in usable shape sooner, and assuring that the contractor will come back to fix it if something else starts leaking next winter.

E. SPECIALIZED NEGOTIATION TECHNIQUES

Many of us are pretty good negotiators in our normal lives. When we are caught up in feelings of anger and mistrust, however, we're often pretty lousy at negotiating with other people who are feeling the same way about us—even our own loved ones. This situation requires some specialized approaches to negotiation. If there is any significant amount of money and emotion involved, you will want to invest time in planning and preparing yourself to make these negotiations successful. Here are several good resources to help you gain the insights and approaches needed for this kind of negotiating:

*   *Field Guide to Negotiation,* by Gavin Kennedy (Harvard Business School Press)

*   *Getting to Yes: Negotiating Agreement Without Giving In,* by Roger Fisher and William Ury (Penguin Books)

*   *Negotiating Rationally,* by Max H. Bazeman and Margaret A. Neale (Free Press), and

*   *Win-Win Negotiating,* by Fred E. Jandt (John Wiley & Sons).

In addition, taking the time to write out the answers to the following questions will help you prepare for your upcoming negotiation. After the questions, we provide some phrases that can help this tricky kind of negotiation go better. Both the questions and the phrases come, with permission, from a World Wide Web site operated by Ron Kelly, a well-known construction arbitrator and mediator, at http://www.ronkelly.com.

1. Key Questions Before You Meet

If you are headed into negotiations, you'll be making the very best use of your time by working through these questions and issues before you meet. Even better, do your best to see that all sides to the negotiation receive these questions beforehand.

- List your basic interests, and then number their order of importance to you. (For instance: time, money, security, get even, get on with life, minimize risk, fairness, future plans, maintain a working relationship, etc.). To help identify your real interest in each area, ask yourself— "Suppose they agree to what I want—exactly what will that do for me?"

- How do you think they see their interests? List and rank them.

- In what areas could you cooperate to see that both of your interests are met—assuming you want to?

- What significant things do you think you already agree about?

- Where do you think you disagree most strongly?

- In the areas of your disagreement, what objective criteria could you use together to develop fair and constructive voluntary resolutions?

- How will you know when a potential agreement is a better choice than fighting it out? What criteria will you use to measure how well it satisfies the interests you've identified?

- From your perspective, what important understandings did you think you had when you originally got involved together? (Time, money, working conditions, rights and duties, decision-making, who was responsible for what, who was on the hook for the unforeseen risks, methods for resolving differences, etc.)

- What important shifts in these understandings happened as the situation developed, and where do you think their perspective differs from yours?

- What feelings of trust and goodwill supported your original agreements?

- Exactly when and over what did you first have any feelings of betrayal, bad faith or loss of confidence? How strong are these feelings still? Do you feel like they might owe you something to specifically make up for this?

- In areas where you have sharply different perspectives, what useful evidence can you bring in that will be credible to them, to help them see your view? (For example: receipts, photographs, witnesses, notes, written industry standards, copies of laws or rules, expert reports, etc.)

- What could they say or do in your meeting that would really push your buttons all over again? How will you keep things on track if this happens?

- In resolving this dispute, how will you balance your shorter-term emotional interests with your longer-term financial interests? (For instance: Are you willing to risk your future financial interests to avoid uncomfortable discussions now? Will you accept a satisfactory offer even if you're very resentful about how you've been treated?)

- If you're unable to agree on a voluntary settlement, what do you currently believe is your next best alternative in the real world? You can make an informed choice between the best voluntary agreement available and your next best alternative only if you have a clear picture of each one. List as much as you can about potential risks and benefits of your next best alternative.

- What are their next best alternatives?

- List every issue which might reasonably be disputed if this is argued before a court, arbitrator, boss, etc. (For example: verbal representations, unforeseen problems, mistakes, different versions of facts, breaches of agreements, contract language, delay, scope and quality of work, interpretations of law, methods of calculating direct and consequential damages, coverage issues, etc.)

• List the possible consequences of not reaching agreement. Suppose you're unable to settle the dispute between yourselves and you end up in litigation and the judge, jury, board or arbitrator eventually agrees completely with the other side's arguments. What's the maximum amount of your financial risk for: 1) the difference between your likely claims; 2) everyone's attorney fees, expert witness fees and procedural costs; 3) the value of your time lost from work and family? If you don't know, get the most accurate information you can.

• What are two different potential settlements that 1) you believe will satisfy their main interests as you understand them; 2) you can live with; and 3) will address all your key issues? (Important note: You can kill the best possible resolution by suggesting it too soon. It's often seen as a threatening demand instead of a possible solution to a joint problem. Almost any solution will feel better to the other side if you both develop it together.)

• How could a neutral third party help you develop your best voluntary settlement? Defuse emotions, and take some of the heat? Be a confidential sounding board to help you evaluate your options and approaches? Provide for safe and productive direct negotiations? Help you to break logjams and generate creative options? Help you develop specific written language to ensure a lasting resolution?

2. Key Phrases for Problem Solving

Negotiations often flow more smoothly when certain phrases that indicate an attitude of openness, receptivity and flexibility are used. We list some of these below. You would be wise to practice them before you meet or write.

"Right now we (you) can still decide this ourselves. We have a common interest in avoiding a long fight with an unknown ending handed down by some court (arbitrator, board, boss) a year from now."

"Can we agree that what we want to do here is work together, develop the best voluntary agreement possible, then let everyone look at it and see if it's good enough?"

"Can we figure out together what it takes to fix this problem? Then maybe we can talk about who might take responsibility for doing what, if we can work out a voluntary agreement."

"I'll bet we (you) can each make a pretty good case for why it's not our (your) fault. I don't think it's going to help us much to be arguing about whose fault this is."

"I'm convinced we can work out something we can both live with."

"It's important to me to understand how you see this."

"Let me see if I understand you right. Are you saying...?"

"I'm not saying I'm right. May I just explain how I honestly understood our original agreement?"

"Let's suppose for a minute that your attorney (friend, mother) is absolutely right. Does that mean...?"

"I can really understand how you'd feel that way. I had no business saying that (doing that), and I'm sorry. Is there something you'd like to see in our agreement to address how you feel?"

"Leaving all the feelings aside for a moment, what do you think two prudent business people would do if they were in our current situation?"

"Whose responsibility do you think this should be? What objective standards led you to that view?"

"One fair solution might be....Can you think of others?"

"What would that do for you? What other ways are there of accomplishing that?"

"Is this helping (working)? Are we still going the right direction with this?"

"We can deal with that issue next if you like. Right now we're talking about...."

"Is our agreement not to interrupt each other (badmouth each other to John) still in effect?"

"If we don't resolve this between ourselves, I wonder where it will be settled?"

"I'm feeling pretty stirred up right now. I've just got to step outside for some fresh air, and I'll meet you back here in five minutes."

"Are you saying you believe it's in your best interest to gamble on the outcome that the jury (judge, arbitrator, board, boss) will impose on us (you), instead of...? Suppose the jury...?"

"When you explain our proposed agreement to your strongest critic, what's she/he going to tell you is wrong with it? How will you explain why you want to agree to it?"

"What would it take to get you back into trying to work this out ourselves? If you could have this turn out any way you wanted, how would that be?"

F. MEDIATION

Even if the dispute has become so heated that negotiations seem impossible, consider paying a third-party mediator to help you reach agreement. Although much has been written about mediation in recent years, it is really a very old concept—as old as the concept of village elders. The basic idea of mediation is that a skilled neutral third party can bring parties to agreement in situations where the parties couldn't reach agreement by themselves. No coercion or threats are involved. The mediator is not in a position to make a decision or ruling, the way an arbitrator does.

The role of the mediator is to provide the framework and tools that disputing parties often need to voluntarily resolve their differences. Amazingly, most owners and contractors who enter into voluntary mediation successfully negotiate their own settlements, on terms everyone can live with. Once they've come to agreement, people actually send the checks and perform the work they agree on. Of course, if you don't resolve everything in mediation, you still keep all your rights to go on to court.

If you want to know more about mediation in general, get a copy of *Mediate Your Dispute,* by Peter Lovenheim (Nolo Press). If you want to consult with a mediator and arbitrator who for many years has specialized in owner-contractor disputes, we recommend Ron Kelly at 510-843-6074 (or visit his Website at http://www.ronkelly.com). There's no charge for information about his services.

G. WHAT ABOUT ARBITRATION?

Arbitration is a very different process than mediation. In many ways arbitration is like court. Arbitration involves a hearing in which the parties introduce evidence, question witnesses and produce written and oral arguments. Sometimes there is one arbitrator to preside over the proceeding, while other times there are three arbitrators. This will depend on what the parties agree to or what the construction contract provides. Like a judge, the arbitrator makes a decision. Whether this decision ends up being 100% supportive of one side's position or awards the winner less than they feel they deserved, at least half the people involved often leave dissatisfied.

JUDICIAL ARBITRATION

Don't confuse the final and binding form of arbitration discussed here with a different and non-binding form which many courts order as a preliminary step before trial. This second kind of arbitration is called "judicial arbitration." If either side doesn't like the outcome of this non-binding kind, they can simply say they are going on to trial.

Unlike a judge's decision, the arbitrator's decision almost always is non-appealable—that is, you can't ask another court or arbitrator to review the decision. The finality of the arbitration process is one of its major benefits. Also, unlike a judge, the arbitrator isn't bound by legal rules of evidence in the hearing or by legal principles when making his or her decision. This means that the outcome may be even more unpredictable than if you went to court. On the other hand, arbitration procedures generally are simpler than court procedures, and it is therefore common for parties to represent themselves in arbitration proceedings without an attorney.

You are most likely to encounter arbitration if the construction contract you signed calls for it in case of a dispute. Check your contract carefully to see if it requires you to arbitrate. If this is your situation, then either you or the other party can invoke the arbitration process as provided in the contract. Often this is done by calling the American Arbitration Association and asking them to start an arbitration proceeding. The American Arbitration Association is a non-profit organization which provides neutral administration of most construction arbitrations. Here are the phone numbers of their three California offices:

- San Francisco: 415-981-3901

- Los Angeles: 213-383-6516

- San Diego: 619-239-3051

The American Arbitration Association has recently adopted special fast-track procedures for construction cases under $50,000, which includes a fairly low flat rate total charge for the arbitration.

1. Structuring Your Arbitration

Unlike court, the parties have the option to structure their arbitration process almost any way they can all agree on. For example, you can legally choose anyone you trust to be your arbitrator. However, it's a good idea to choose someone with experience in construction arbitration.

Suppose much of your dispute involves questions of why something is leaking and what it really costs to fix it, rather than strictly legal issues. You can choose a construction professional experienced in this area as your arbitrator rather than a lawyer.

You can also customize your procedures by agreeing to hold the hearings by phone, or limit your risk by limiting the arbitrator's authority to a certain dollar range. But before you do this, it would be best to attempt a negotiated settlement, and try mediation if unassisted negotiations fail. You are much more likely to be satisfied with a settlement that you reach voluntarily, with or without the help of a mediator, than you will be with a settlement that is imposed on you by an arbitrator.

2. Preserving Your Legal Remedies

In Chapter 8 we point out that the existence of an arbitration clause in your contract doesn't relieve claimants of the need to file a mechanics' lien, stop notice and payment bond enforcement action in court if they want to preserve these remedies. If you are unable to settle and would rather handle the matter in court, you can go ahead and do so even if the contract requires arbitration. If neither you nor the other party to the litigation raises the issue of arbitration when filing the complaint or the answer, the arbitration clause will be deemed waived. (Code of Civil Procedure §1281.5.) On the other hand, if you do want to arbitrate the dispute but don't want to give up your other remedies, you can ask the court where the lawsuit is filed to stay the proceedings pending the outcome of the arbitration.

H. GETTING SOME BREATHING ROOM FOR NEGOTIATIONS

Throughout this book we've emphasized that if the mechanics' lien enforcement action is not filed within 90 days of the date the Claim of Mechanics' Lien was recorded, the mechanics' lien becomes void. However, it is possible to extend the 90-day period by any additional period up to one year if the claimant and the owner agree. For example, if you enter negotiations, but you don't think you can wrap matters up before the 90-day deadline, you can extend the period for the addi-

tional time you think you'll need. You do this by recording a Notice of Credit, a document that must be signed by both of you and notarized. (CC §3144.) A blank Notice of Credit is set out below. A blank form is in Appendix B and on the forms disk under the file name CREDIT.

Mechanics' lien claimants should be cautious

We recommend that you act cautiously here. The longer the extension of the deadline to file your enforcement suit, the longer the period that will pass before you can enforce your mechanics' lien remedy. Also, the pressure that the mechanics' lien enforcement action puts on negotiations may be a motivating factor for all parties to deal seriously with the problems. Eliminating the pressure may eliminate the need for settlement.

On the other hand, if you have let things get down to the wire without talking seriously about settlement and you are all heading for a costly court battle over money, quality of work and other complex issues, agreeing to a short time extension may be a solid first step towards working out a potential voluntary agreement together.

EXTENSION OF TIME TO ENFORCE LIEN AND NOTICE OF CREDIT

_____(Claimant)_____ and _____(Owner)_____ agree as follows:

1. On _____, Claimant recorded a Claim of Mechanics' Lien for $_____ in Book _____, Page _____ of Official Records in the Office of the County Recorder of _____ County, State of California against the following property:

_____

_____

_____.

2. To preserve his/her Claim of Mechanics' Lien, Claimant must file a lawsuit to enforce Claimant's Claim of Mechanics' Lien in the near future unless Owner is willing to extend the time for filing such lawsuit by agreeing to a credit in the manner permitted in Section 3144 of the California Civil Code.

3. Owner and Claimant agree that a credit of _____ days from and after the date this agreement is signed shall be given, and Claimant's Claim of Mechanics' Lien shall be extended for a period of 90 days after the credit period expires.

4. Owner waives any and all right to object to a lawsuit brought by Claimant to foreclose on Claimant's Claim of Mechanics' Lien if the lawsuit is filed within the period of time permitted by this Notice of Credit.

5. Owner waives the right to raise any statute of limitations defense against an action brought by Claimant to foreclose Claimant's Claim of Mechanics' Lien.

Dated: _____   Signed: _____

I. WAIVERS AND RELEASES

If you do reach agreement, the owner will want the lien claimant to sign a form giving up his or her mechanics' lien rights and releasing the recorded Claim of Mechanics' Lien. For projects that are completed (we assume that is your situation) there are two statutory forms, one of which must be used—the conditional waiver and release or the unconditional waiver and release. The claimant should use the first one if whatever payment is negotiated has not yet shown up in his or her bank account. The second one should be used if the check has cleared. Copies of the forms are in Appendix B and on the forms disk under the file names CONWVR and UNCONWVR, respectively.

Conditional Waiver and Release
Upon Final Payment

Upon receipt by the undersigned of a check from _____ Joe Owner _____ in the sum of

$ __2,572__ payable to ___ Sammy Subcontractor ___, and when the check has

been properly endorsed and has been paid by the bank upon which it is drawn, this document

shall become effective to release any mechanics' lien, stop notice or bond right the undersigned

has on the job of _____ Construction _____ located at

_____ 4745 Tree Lane, Ukiah, CA _____.

This release covers the final payment to the undersigned for all labor, services, equipment or

material furnished on the job, except for disputed claims for additional work in the amount of

$_____. Before any recipient of this document relies on it, the party should verify

evidence of payment to the undersigned.

Dated: _____ 7/23/99 _____

North Coast Carpentry
_____

[Company Name]

By: _____ *Sammy Subcontractor* _____

[Title]   President

Unconditional Waiver and Release
Upon Final Payment

The undersigned has been paid in full for all labor, services, equipment or material furnished

to ___Bob Contractor_____ on the job of _____Kitchen remodel_____

_____ located at _____92 Main St., King City, CA_____

_____ and does hereby waive and

release any right to a mechanic's lien, stop notice or any right against a labor and material

bond on the job, except for disputed claims for extra work in the amount of

$_____.

Dated: _____

_____

[Company Name]

By: _____

[Title]

NOTICE: THIS DOCUMENT WAIVES RIGHTS UNCONDITIONALLY AND STATES THAT
YOU HAVE BEEN PAID FOR GIVING UP THOSE RIGHTS. THIS DOCUMENT IS
ENFORCEABLE AGAINST YOU IF YOU SIGN IT, EVEN IF YOU HAVE NOT BEEN PAID.
IF YOU HAVE NOT BEEN PAID, USE A CONDITIONAL RELEASE FORM. ■

Appendices

Relevant Statutes

CIVIL CODE SECTIONS 3081.1-3081.10

3081.1. For purposes of this chapter, "design professional" means any certificated architect, registered professional engineer, or licensed land surveyor who furnishes services pursuant to a written contract with a landowner for the design, engineering, or planning of a work of improvement.

Except as otherwise expressly provided, the definition in this section does not apply to, or limit or expand the meaning of, provisions of law other than this chapter.

3081.2. A design professional shall, from the date of recordation pursuant to Section 3081.3, have a lien upon the real property for which the work of improvement is planned to be constructed, notwithstanding the absence of commencement of actual construction of the planned work of improvement, if the landowner contracted for the design professional's services and is also the owner of the real property at the time of recordation of the lien. The lien of the design professional shall be for the amount of the design professional's fee for any services rendered prior to commencement of the work of improvement or the reasonable value of those services, whichever is less. The amount of the lien shall be reduced by the amount of any deposit or prior payments, as specified by a written contract entered into by the design professional and by the landowner or his or her agent. However, no lien shall arise pursuant to this chapter, and a design professional may not record a notice of lien pursuant to subdivision (c) of Section 3081.3, unless a building permit or other governmental approval in furtherance of the work of improvement has been obtained in connection with or utilizing the services rendered by the design professional.

3081.3. In order for the design professional to be entitled to a lien pursuant to Section 3081.2, all of the following shall occur:

(a) The landowner defaults in any payment required pursuant to the terms of the written contract or refuses to pay upon the demand of the design professional made in accordance with the written contract.

(b) Not less than 10 days prior to recordation pursuant to subdivision (c), the design professional mails by first-class registered or certified mail, postage prepaid, addressed to the landowner, a written demand for payment specifying that a default has occurred pursuant to the contract or agreement and the amount of the default.

(c) The design professional records, in the office of the county recorder in the county in which the real property or some portion thereof is located, a notice of lien which specifies that a lien is created in favor of the named design professional, specifies the amount thereof, identifies the current owner of record of the real property, provides a legal description of the real property to be improved, and specifies the building permit or other governmental approval for the work of improvement required as a condition of recording the notice of lien by Section 3081.2.

3081.4. (a) Upon recordation of the notice of lien pursuant to subdivision (c) of Section 3081.3, a lien is created in favor of the named design professional.

(b) The lien created pursuant to subdivision (a) shall automatically expire and be null and void and of no further force or effect on the occurrence of either of the following:

(1) The commencement of the work of improvement for which the design professional furnished services at the request of the landowner.

(2) The expiration of 90 days after recording the notice of lien, unless the design professional files suit to enforce the lien within 90 days of recordation.

(c) In the event the landowner partially or fully satisfies the lien of the design professional, the design professional shall execute and record a document which evidences a partial or full satisfaction and release of the lien, as the case may be.

3081.5. Any design professionals' lien perfected pursuant to this chapter shall be enforced pursuant to the provisions contained in Article 7 (commencing with Section 3143) of Chapter 2 of Title 15.

3081.6. This chapter does not affect the ability of a design professional to obtain a mechanic's lien pursuant to Title 15 (commencing with Section 3082) of this part.

3081.7. A design professional shall record a notice of lien pursuant to subdivision (c) of Section 3081.3 no later than 90 days after the design professional knows or has reason to know that the landowner is not commencing the work of improvement.

3081.8. The lien of a design professional perfected pursuant to this chapter shall not affect the ability of the design professional to pursue other remedies.

3081.9. (a) No lien created by this chapter shall affect or take priority over the interest of record of a purchaser, lessee, or encumbrancer, if the interest of the purchaser, lessee, or encumbrancer in the real property was duly recorded before recordation of the design professionals' lien.

(b) No lien created by this chapter shall affect or take priority over an encumbrance of a construction lender which funds the loan to commence the work of improvement for which the design professional furnished services at the request of the landowner.

3081.10. The design professionals' lien provided in this chapter shall not apply to a work of improvement relating to a single-family owner occupied residence where the construction costs are less than one hundred thousand dollars ($100,000) in value.

3082. Unless the context otherwise requires, the provisions in this chapter govern the construction of this title.

3083. "Bonded stop notice" means a stop notice, given to any construction lender, accompanied by a bond with good and sufficient sureties in a penal sum equal to 11/4 times the amount of such claim conditioned that if the defendant recovers judgment in an action brought on such verified claim or on the lien filed by the claimant, the claimant will pay all costs that may be awarded against the owner, original contractor, construction lender, or any of them, and all damages that such owner, original contractor, or construction lender may sustain by reason of the equitable garnishment effected by the claim or by reason of the lien, not exceeding the sum specified in the bond. To be effective such bonded stop notice shall be delivered to the manager or other responsible officer or person at the office of the construction lender or must be sent to such office by registered or certified mail. If such notice is delivered or sent to any institution or organization maintaining branch offices, it shall not be effective unless delivered or sent to the office or branch administering or holding such construction funds.

3084. (a) "Claim of lien" means a written statement, signed and verified by the claimant or by the claimant's agent, containing all of the following:

(1) A statement of the claimant's demand after deducting all just credits and offsets.

(2) The name of the owner or reputed owner, if known.

(3) A general statement of the kind of labor, services, equipment, or materials furnished by the claimant.

(4) The name of the person by whom the claimant was employed or to whom the claimant furnished the labor, services, equipment, or materials.

(5) A description of the site sufficient for identification.

(b) A claim of lien in otherwise proper form, verified and containing the information required by this section shall be accepted by the recorder for recording and shall be deemed duly recorded without acknowledgment.

3085. "Claimant" means any person entitled under this title to record a claim of lien, to give a stop notice in connection with any work of improvement, or to recover on any payment bond, or any combination of the foregoing.

3086. "Completion" means, in the case of any work of improvement other than a public work, actual completion of the work of improvement. Any of the following shall be deemed equivalent to a completion:

(a) The occupation or use of a work of improvement by the owner, or his agent, accompanied by cessation of labor thereon.

(b) The acceptance by the owner, or his agent, of the work of improvement.

(c) After the commencement of a work of improvement, a cessation of labor thereon for a continuous period of 60 days, or a cessation of labor thereon for a continuous period of 30 days or more if the owner files for record a notice of cessation.

If the work of improvement is subject to acceptance by any public entity, the completion of such work of improvement shall be deemed to be the date of such acceptance; provided, however, that, except as to contracts awarded under the State Contract Act, Chapter 3 (commencing with Section 14250), Part 5, Division 3, Title 2 of the Government Code, a cessation of labor on any public work for a continuous period of 30 days shall be a completion thereof.

3087. "Construction lender" means any mortgagee or beneficiary under a deed of trust lending funds with which the cost of the work of improvement is, wholly or in part, to be defrayed, or any assignee or successor in interest of either, or any escrow holder or other party holding any funds furnished or to be furnished by the owner or lender or any other person as a fund from which to pay construction costs.

3088. "Contract" means an agreement between an owner and any original contractor providing for the work of improvement or any part thereof.

3089. "Laborer" means any person who, acting as an employee, performs labor upon or bestows skill or other necessary services on any work of improvement.

3090. "Materialman" means any person who furnishes materials or supplies to be used or consumed in any work of improvement.

3092. "Notice of cessation" means a written notice, signed and verified by the owner or his agent, containing all of the following:

(a) The date on or about when the cessation of labor commenced.

(b) A statement that such cessation has continued until the recording of the notice of cessation.

(c) The name and address of the owner.

(d) The nature of the interest or estate of the owner.

(e) A description of the site sufficient for identification, containing the street address of the site, if any. If a sufficient legal description of the site is given, the validity of the notice shall not, however, be affected by the fact that the street address is erroneous or is omitted.

(f) The name of the original contractor, if any, for the work of improvement as a whole.

(g) For the purpose of this section, "owner" means the owner who causes a building, improvement, or structure, to be constructed, altered, or repaired (or his successor in interest at the date of a notice of cessation from labor is filed for record) whether the interest or estate of such owner be in fee, as vendee under a contract of purchase, as lessee, or other interest or estate less than the fee. Where such interest or estate is held by two or more persons as joint tenants or tenants in common, any one or more of the cotenants may be deemed to be the "owner" within the meaning of this section. Any notice of cessation signed by less than all of such cotenants shall recite the names and addresses of all such cotenants.

The notice of cessation shall be recorded in the office of the county recorder of the county in which the site is located and shall be effective only if there has been a continuous cessation of labor for at least 30 days prior to such recording.

3093. "Notice of completion" means a written notice, signed and verified by the owner or his agent, containing all of the following:

(a) The date of completion (other than a cessation of labor). The recital of an erroneous date of completion shall not, however, affect the validity of the notice if the true date of completion is within 10 days preceding the date of recording of such notice.

(b) The name and address of the owner.

(c) The nature of the interest or estate of the owner.

(d) A description of the site sufficient for identification, containing the street address of the site, if any. If a sufficient legal description of the site is given, the validity of the notice shall not, however, be affected by the fact that the street address recited is erroneous or that such street address is omitted.

(e) The name of the original contractor, if any, or if the notice is given only of completion of a contract for a particular portion of such work of improvement, as provided in Section 3117, then the name of the original contractor under such contract, and a general statement of the kind of work done or materials furnished pursuant to such contract.

The notice of completion shall be recorded in the office of the county recorder of the county in which the site is located, within 10 days after such completion. A notice of completion in otherwise proper form, verified and containing the information required by this section shall be accepted by the recorder for recording and shall be deemed duly recorded without acknowledgment.

If there is more than one owner, any notice of completion signed by less than all of such co-owners shall recite the names and addresses of all of such co-owners; and provided further, that any notice of completion signed by a successor in interest shall recite the names and addresses of his transferor or transferrors.

For the purpose of this section, owner is defined as set forth in subdivision (g) of Section 3092.

3094. "Notice of nonresponsibility" means a written notice, signed and verified by a person owning or claiming an interest in the site who has not caused the work of improvement to be performed, or his agent, containing all of the following:

(a) A description of the site sufficient for identification.

(b) The name and nature of the title or interest of the person giving the notice.

(c) The name of the purchaser under contract, if any, or lessee, if known.

(d) A statement that the person giving the notice will not be responsible for any claims arising from the work of improvement.

Within 10 days after the person claiming the benefits of nonresponsibility has obtained knowledge of the work of improvement, the notice provided for in this section shall be posted in some conspicuous place on the site. Within the same 10-day period provided for the posting of the notice, the notice shall be recorded in the office of the county recorder of the county in which the site or some part thereof is located.

3095. "Original contractor" means any contractor who has a direct contractual relationship with the owner.

3096. "Payment bond" means a bond with good and sufficient sureties that is conditioned for the payment in full of the claims of all claimants and that also by its terms is made to inure to the benefit of all claimants so as to give these persons a right of action to recover upon this bond in any suit brought to foreclose the liens provided for in this title or in a separate suit brought on the bond. An owner, original contractor, or a subcontractor may be the principal upon any payment bond.

3097. "Preliminary 20-day notice (private work)" means a written notice from a claimant that is given prior to the recording of a mechanic's lien, prior to the filing of a stop notice, and prior to asserting a claim against a payment bond, and is required to be given under the following circumstances:

(a) Except one under direct contract with the owner or one performing actual labor for wages, or an express trust fund described in Section 3111, every person who furnishes labor, service, equipment, or material for which a lien or payment bond otherwise can be claimed under this title, or for which a notice to withhold can otherwise be given under this title, shall, as a necessary prerequisite to the validity of any claim of lien, payment bond, and of a notice to withhold, cause to be given to the owner or reputed owner, to the original contractor, or reputed contractor, and to the construction lender, if any, or to the reputed construction lender, if any, a written preliminary notice as prescribed by this section.

(b) Except the contractor, or one performing actual labor for wages, or an express trust fund described in Section 3111, all persons who have a direct contract with the owner and who furnish labor, service, equipment, or material for which a lien or payment bond otherwise can be claimed under this title, or for which a notice to withhold can otherwise be given under this title, shall, as a necessary prerequisite to the validity of any claim of lien, claim on a payment bond, and of a notice to withhold, cause to be given to the construction lender, if any, or to the reputed construction lender, if any, a written preliminary notice as prescribed by this section.

(c) The preliminary notice referred to in subdivisions (a) and (b) shall contain the following information:

(1) A general description of the labor, service, equipment, or materials furnished, or to be furnished, and an estimate of the total price thereof.

(2) The name and address of the person furnishing that labor, service, equipment, or materials.

(3) The name of the person who contracted for purchase of that labor, service, equipment, or materials.

(4) A description of the jobsite sufficient for identification.

(5) The following statement in boldface type:
NOTICE TO PROPERTY OWNER If bills are not paid in full for the labor, services, equipment, or materials furnished or to be furnished, a mechanic's lien leading to the loss, through court foreclosure proceedings, of all or part of your property being so improved may be placed against the property even though you have paid your contractor in full. You

may wish to protect yourself against this consequence by (1) requiring your contractor to furnish a signed release by the person or firm giving you this notice before making payment to your contractor or (2) any other method or device that is appropriate under the circumstances.

(6) If the notice is given by a subcontractor who is required pursuant to a collective bargaining agreement to pay supplemental fringe benefits into an express trust fund described in Section 3111, the notice shall also contain the identity and address of the trust fund or funds.

If an invoice for materials contains the information required by this section, a copy of the invoice, transmitted in the manner prescribed by this section shall be sufficient notice.

A certificated architect, registered engineer, or licensed land surveyor who has furnished services for the design of the work of improvement and who gives a preliminary notice as provided in this section not later than 20 days after the work of improvement has commenced shall be deemed to have complied with subdivisions (a) and (b) with respect to architectural, engineering, or surveying services furnished, or to be furnished.

(d) The preliminary notice referred to in subdivisions (a) and (b) shall be given not later than 20 days after the claimant has first furnished labor, service, equipment, or materials to the jobsite. If labor, service, equipment, or materials have been furnished to a jobsite by a claimant who did not give a preliminary notice, that claimant shall not be precluded from giving a preliminary notice at any time thereafter. The claimant shall, however, be entitled to record a lien, file a stop notice, and assert a claim against a payment bond only for labor, service, equipment, or material furnished within 20 days prior to the service of the preliminary notice, and at any time thereafter.

(e) Any agreement made or entered into by an owner, whereby the owner agrees to waive the rights or privileges conferred upon the owner by this section shall be void and of no effect.

(f) The notice required under this section may be served as follows:

(1) If the person to be notified resides in this state, by delivering the notice personally, or by leaving it at his or her address of residence or place of business with some person in charge, or by first-class registered or certified mail, postage prepaid, addressed to the person to whom notice is to be given at his or her residence or place of business address or at the address shown by the building permit on file with the authority issuing a building permit for the work, or at an address recorded pursuant to subdivision (j).

(2) If the person to be notified does not reside in this state, by any method enumerated in paragraph (1) of this subdivision. If the person cannot be served by any of these methods, then notice may be given by first-class certified or registered mail, addressed to the construction lender or to the original contractor.

(3) When service is made by first-class certified or registered mail, service is complete at the time of the deposit of that registered or certified mail.

(g) A person required by this section to give notice to the owner, to an original contractor, and to a person to whom a notice to withhold may be given, need give only one notice to the owner, to the original contractor, and to the person to whom a notice to withhold may be given with respect to all materials, service, labor, or equipment he or she furnishes for a work of improvement, that means the entire structure or scheme of improvements as a whole, unless the same is furnished under contracts with more than one subcontractor, in which event, the notice requirements shall be met with respect to materials, services, labor, or equipment furnished to each contractor.

If a notice contains a general description required by subdivision (a) or (b) of the materials, services, labor, or equipment furnished to the date of notice, it is not defective because, after that date, the person giving notice furnishes materials, services, labor, or equipment not within the scope of this general description.

(h) Where the contract price to be paid to any subcontractor on a particular work of improvement exceeds four hundred dollars ($400), the failure of that contractor, licensed under Chapter 9 (commencing with Section 7000) of Division 3 of the Business and Professions Code, to give the notice provided for in this section, constitutes grounds for disciplinary action by the Registrar of Contractors.

Where the notice is required to contain the information set forth in paragraph (6) of subdivision (c), a failure to give the notice, including that information, that results in the filing of a lien, claim on a payment bond, or the delivery of a stop notice by the express trust fund to which the obligation is owing constitutes grounds for disciplinary action by the Registrar of Contractors against the subcontractor if the amount due the trust fund is not paid.

(i) Every city, county, city and county, or other governmental authority issuing building permits shall, in its application form for a building permit, provide space and a designation for the applicant to enter the name, branch, designation, if any, and address of the construction lender and shall keep the information on file open for public inspection during the regular business hours of the authority.

If there is no known construction lender, that fact shall be noted in the designated space. Any failure to indicate the name and address of the construction lender on the application, however, shall not relieve any person from the obligation to give to the construction lender the notice required by this section.

(j) A mortgage, deed of trust, or other instrument securing a loan, any of the proceeds of which may be used for the purpose of constructing improvements on real property, shall bear the designation "Construction Trust Deed" prominently on its face and shall state all of the following: (1) the name and address of the lender, and the name and address of the owner of the real property described in the instrument, and (2) a legal description of the real property which secures the loan and, if known, the street address of the property. The failure to be so designated or to state any of the information required by this subdivision shall not affect the validity of the mortgage, deed of trust, or other instrument.

Failure to provide this information on this instrument when recorded shall not relieve persons required to give preliminary notice under this section from that duty.

The county recorder of the county in which the instrument is recorded shall indicate in the general index of the official records of the county that the instrument secures a construction loan.

(k) Every contractor and subcontractor who is required pursuant to a collective bargaining agreement to pay supplementary fringe benefits into an express trust fund described in Section 3111, and who has failed to do so shall cause to be given to the trust fund and to the construction lender, if any, or to the reputed construction lender, if any, not later than the date the payment due to the trust fund became delinquent, a written notice containing all of the following:

(1) The name of the owner and the contractor.

(2) A description of the jobsite sufficient for identification.

(3) The identity and address of the express trust fund.

(4) The total number of straight time and overtime hours on each job, payment for which the contractor or subcontractor is delinquent to the express trust.

(5) The amount then past due and owing.

Failure to give this notice shall constitute grounds for disciplinary action by the Registrar of Contractors.

(l) Every written contract entered into between a property owner and an original contractor shall provide space for the owner to enter his or her name and address of residence; and place of business if any. The original contractor shall make available the name and address of residence of the owner to any person seeking to serve the notice specified in subdivision (c).

(m) Every written contract entered into between a property owner and an original contractor, except home improvement contracts and swimming pool contracts subject to Article 10 (commencing with Section 7150) of Chapter 9 of Division 3 of the Business and Professions Code, shall provide space for the owner to enter the name and address of the construction lender or lenders. The original contractor shall make available the name and address of the construction lender or lenders to any person seeking to serve the notice specified in subdivision (c). Every contract entered into between an original contractor and subcontractor, and between subcontractors, shall provide a space for the name and address of the owner, original contractor, and any construction lender.

(n) Where one or more construction loans are obtained after commencement of construction, the property owner shall provide the name and address of the construction lender or lenders to each person who has given the property owner the notice specified in subdivision (c).

(o) (1) Each person who has served a preliminary 20-day notice pursuant to subdivision (f) may file the preliminary 20-day notice with the county recorder in the county in which any portion of the property is located. A preliminary 20-day notice filed pursuant to this section shall contain all of the following:

(A) The name and address of the person furnishing the labor, service, equipment, or materials.

(B) The name of the person who contracted for purchase of the labor, service, equipment, or materials.

(C) The common street address of the jobsite.

(2) Upon the acceptance for recording of a notice of completion or notice of cessation the county recorder shall mail to those persons who have filed a preliminary 20-day notice, notification that a notice of completion or notice of cessation has been recorded on the property, and shall affix the date that the notice of completion or notice of cessation was recorded with the county recorder.

(3) The failure of the county recorder to mail the notification to the person who filed a preliminary 20-day notice, or the failure of those persons to receive the notification or to receive complete notification, shall not affect the period within which a claim of lien is required to be recorded. However, the county recorder shall make a good faith effort to mail notification to those persons who have filed the

preliminary 20-day notice under this section and to do so within five days after the recording of a notice of completion or notice of cessation.

(4) This new function of the county recorder shall not become operative until July 1, 1988. The county recorder may cause to be destroyed all documents filed pursuant to this section, two years after the date of filing.

(5) The preliminary 20-day notice which a person may file pursuant to this subdivision is for the limited purpose of facilitating the mailing of notice by the county recorder of recorded notices of completion and notices of cessation. The notice which is filed is not a recordable document and shall not be entered into those official records of the county which by law impart constructive notice. Notwithstanding any other provision of law, the index maintained by the recorder of filed preliminary 20-day notices shall be separate and distinct from those indexes maintained by the county recorder of those official records of the county which by law impart constructive notice. The filing of a preliminary 20-day notice with the county recorder does not give rise to any actual or constructive notice with respect to any party of the existence or contents of a filed preliminary 20-day notice nor to any duty of inquiry on the part of any party as to the existence or contents of that notice.

(p) The change made to the statement described in subdivision (c) by Chapter 974 of the Statutes of 1994 shall have no effect upon the validity of any notice that otherwise meets the requirements of this section. The failure to provide, pursuant to Chapter 974 of the Statutes of 1994, a written preliminary notice to a subcontractor with whom the claimant has contracted shall not affect the validity of any preliminary notice provided pursuant to this section.

3097.1. Proof that the preliminary 20-day notice required by Section 3097 was served in accordance with subdivision (f) of Section 3097 shall be made as follows:

(a) If served by mail, by the proof of service affidavit described in subdivision (c) of this section accompanied either by the return receipt of certified or registered mail, or by a photocopy of the record of delivery and receipt maintained by the post office, showing the date of delivery and to whom delivered, or, in the event of nondelivery, by the returned envelope itself.

(b) If served by personally delivering the notice to the person to be notified, or by leaving it at his address or place of business with some person in charge, by the proof of service affidavit described in subdivision (c).

(c) A "proof of service affidavit" is an affidavit of the person making the service, showing the time, place and manner of service and facts showing that such service was made in accordance with Section 3097. Such affidavit shall show the name and address of the person upon whom a copy of the preliminary 20-day notice was served, and, if appropriate, the title or capacity in which he was served.

3098. "Preliminary 20-day notice (public work)" means a written notice from a claimant that was given prior to the assertion of a claim against a payment bond, or the filing of a stop notice on public work, and is required to be given under the following circumstances:

(a) In any case in which the law of this state affords a right to a person furnishing labor or materials for a public work who has not been paid therefor to assert a claim against a payment bond, or to file a stop notice with the public agency concerned, and thereby cause the withholding of payment from the contractor for the public work, any such person having no direct contractual relationship with the contractor, other than a person who performed actual labor for wages or an express trust fund described in Section 3111, may file the preliminary notice, but no payment shall be withheld from the contractor pursuant to that notice unless the person has caused written notice to be given to the contractor, and the public agency concerned, not later than 20 days after the claimant has first furnished labor, services, equipment, or materials to the jobsite, stating with substantial accuracy a general description of labor, service, equipment, or materials furnished or to be furnished, and the name of the party to whom the same was furnished. This notice shall be served by mailing the same by first-class mail, registered mail, or certified mail, postage prepaid, in an envelope addressed to the contractor at any place the contractor maintains an office or conducts business, or his or her residence, or by personal service. In case of any public works constructed by the Department of Public Works or the Department of General Services of the state, such notice shall be served by mailing in the same manner as above, addressed to the office of the disbursing officer of the department constructing the work, or by personal service upon the officer. When service is by registered or certified mail, service is complete at the time of the deposit of the registered or certified mail.

(b) Where the contract price to be paid to any subcontractor on a particular work of improvement exceeds four hundred dollars ($400), the failure of that contractor, licensed under Chapter 9, (commencing with Section 7000) of Division 3 of the Business and Professions Code, to give the notice provided for in this section, constitutes grounds for disciplinary action by the Registrar of Contractors.

(c) The notice requirements of this section shall not apply to an express trust fund described in Section 3111.

(d) If labor, service, equipment, or materials have been furnished to a jobsite by a claimant who did not give a preliminary notice pursuant to subdivision (a), that claimant shall not be precluded from giving a preliminary notice at any time thereafter. The claimant shall, however, be entitled to assert a claim against a payment bond and file a stop notice only for labor, service, equipment, or material furnished within 20 days prior to the service of the preliminary notice, and at any time thereafter.

(e) The failure to provide, pursuant to Chapter 974 of the Statutes of 1994, a written preliminary notice to a subcontractor with whom the claimant has contracted shall not affect the validity of any preliminary notice provided pursuant to this section.

3099. "Public entity" means the state, Regents of the University of California, a county, city, district, public authority, public agency, and any other political subdivision or public corporation in the state.

3100. "Public work" means any work of improvement contracted for by a public entity.

3101. "Site" means the real property upon which the work of improvement is being constructed or performed.

3102. "Site improvement" means the demolishing or removing of improvements, trees, or other vegetation located thereon, or drilling test holes or the grading, filling, or otherwise improving of any lot or tract of land or the street, highway, or sidewalk in front of or adjoining any lot or tract of land, or constructing or installing sewers or other public utilities therein, or constructing any areas, vaults, cellars, or rooms under said sidewalks or making any improvements thereon.

3103. "Stop notice" means a written notice, signed and verified by the claimant or his or her agent, stating in general terms all of the following:

(a) The kind of labor, services, equipment, or materials furnished or agreed to be furnished by such claimant.

(b) The name of the person to or for whom the same was done or furnished.

(c) The amount in value, as near as may be, of that already done or furnished and of the whole agreed to be done or furnished.

(d) The name and address of the claimant.

The notice, in the case of any work of improvement other than a public work, shall be delivered to the owner personally or left at his or her residence or place of business with some person in charge, or delivered to his or her architect, if any, if the notice is served upon a construction lender, holding construction funds and maintaining branch offices, it shall not be effective as against the construction lender unless given to or served upon the manager or other responsible officer or person at the office or branch thereof administering or holding the construction funds. The notice, in the case of any public work for the state, shall be filed with the director of the department which let the contract and, in the case of any other public work, shall be filed in the office of the controller, auditor, or other public disbursing officer whose duty it is to make payments under the provisions of the contract, or with the commissioners, managers, trustees, officers, board of supervisors, board of trustees, common council, or other body by whom the contract was awarded. No stop notice shall be invalid by reason of any defect in form if it is sufficient to substantially inform the owner of the information required.

Any stop notice may be served by registered or certified mail with the same effect as by personal service.

3104. "Subcontractor" means any contractor who has no direct contractual relationship with the owner.

3105. "Subdivision" means a work of improvement consisting of two or more separate residential units or two or more buildings, mining claims, or other improvements owned or reputed to be owned by the same person or on which the claimant has been employed by the same person. A separate residential unit means one residential structure, together with any garage or other improvements appurtenant thereto.

3106. "Work of improvement" includes but is not restricted to the construction, alteration, addition to, or repair, in whole or in part, of any building, wharf, bridge, ditch, flume, aqueduct, well, tunnel, fence, machinery, railroad, or road, the seeding, sodding, or planting of any lot or tract of land for landscaping purposes, the filling, leveling, or grading of any lot or tract of land, the demolition of buildings, and the removal of buildings. Except as otherwise provided in this title, "work of improvement" means the entire structure or scheme of improvement as a whole.

CIVIL CODE SECTION 3109

3109. This chapter does not apply to any public work.

CIVIL CODE SECTIONS 3110-3112

3110. Mechanics, materialmen, contractors, subcontractors, lessors of equipment, artisans, architects, registered engineers, licensed land surveyors, machinists, builders, teamsters, and draymen, and all persons and laborers of every class performing labor upon or bestowing skill or other necessary services on, or furnishing materials or leasing equipment to be used or consumed in or furnishing appliances, teams, or power contributing to a work of improvement shall have a lien upon the property upon which they have bestowed labor or furnished materials or appliances or leased equipment for the value of such labor done or materials furnished and for the value of the use of such appliances, equipment, teams, or power whether done or furnished at the instance of the owner or of any person acting by his authority or under him as contractor or otherwise. For the purposes of this chapter, every contractor, subcontractor, sub-subcontractor, architect, builder, or other person having charge of a work of improvement or portion thereof shall be held to be the agent of the owner.

3111. For the purposes of this chapter, an express trust fund established pursuant to a collective bargaining agreement to which payments are required to be made on account of fringe benefits supplemental to a wage agreement for the benefit of a claimant on particular real property shall have a lien on such property in the amount of the supplemental fringe benefit payments owing to it pursuant to the collective bargaining agreement.

3111.5. (a) Every trust fund as described in Section 3111 shall, upon written demand by a subcontractor, give to the subcontractor in person, or by first-class mail, addressed to the address of the subcontractor as stated on the demand, within five working days of the receipt of the demand, a written statement which shall contain the following information:

(1) The name and address of the subcontractor.

(2) A list of those months in the 12 months preceding the demand, commencing with the last

month of record in possession of the trust fund, for which the subcontractor has paid supplemental fringe benefit payments.

(3) The facts, if such be the case, that the trust fund has no information or belief that the subcontractor is further indebted to the trust fund for those months.

(b) The statement of the trust fund provided for in subdivision (a) above shall be, without prejudice to the trust fund, sufficient to satisfy any creditors of the subcontractor to whom it is given that the subcontractor is not indebted to the trust fund for the months so stated, without further release from the trust fund.

3112. Any claimant who, at the instance or request of the owner (or any other person acting by his authority or under him, as contractor or otherwise) of any lot or tract of land, has made any site improvement has a lien upon such lot or tract of land for work done or materials furnished.

CIVIL CODE SECTIONS 3114-3118

3114. A claimant shall be entitled to enforce a lien only if he has given the preliminary 20-day notice (private work) in accordance with the provisions of Section 3097, if required by that section, and has made proof of service in accordance with the provisions of Section 3097.1.

3115. Each original contractor, in order to enforce a lien, must record his claim of lien after he completes his contract and before the expiration of (a) 90 days after the completion of the work of improvement as defined in Section 3106 if no notice of completion or notice of cessation has been recorded, or (b) 60 days after recordation of a notice of completion or notice of cessation.

3116. Each claimant other than an original contractor, in order to enforce a lien, must record his claim of lien after he has ceased furnishing labor, services, equipment, or materials, and before the expiration of (a) 90 days after completion of the work of improvement if no notice of completion or cessation has

been recorded, or (b) 30 days after recordation of a notice of completion or notice of cessation.

3117. Where the work of improvement is not made pursuant to one original contract for the work of improvement but is made in whole or in part pursuant to two or more original contracts, each covering a particular portion of the work of improvement, the owner may, within 10 days after completion of any such contract for a particular portion of the work of improvement, record a notice of completion. If such notice of completion be recorded, notwithstanding the provisions of Sections 3115 and 3116, the original contractor under the contract covered by such notice must, within 60 days after recording of such notice, and any claimant under such contract other than the original contractor must, within 30 days after the recording of such notice of completion, record his claim of lien. If such notice is not recorded, then the period for recording claims of lien shall be as provided for in Sections 3115 and 3116.

3118. Any person who shall willfully include in his claim of lien labor, services, equipment, or materials not furnished for the property described in such claim shall thereby forfeit his lien.

CIVIL CODE SECTIONS 3123-3124

3123. (a) The liens provided for in this chapter shall be direct liens, and shall be for the reasonable value of the labor, services, equipment, or materials furnished or for the price agreed upon by the claimant and the person with whom he or she contracted, whichever is less. The lien shall not be limited in amount by the price stated in the contract as defined in Section 3088, except as provided in Sections 3235 and 3236 and in subdivision (c) of this section.

(b) This section does not preclude the claimant from including in the lien any amount due for labor, services, equipment, or materials furnished based on a written modification of the contract or as a result of the rescission, abandonment, or breach of the contract. However, in the event of rescission, abandonment, or breach of the contract, the amount of the lien may not exceed the reasonable value of the labor, services, equipment, and materials furnished by the claimant.

(c) The owner shall notify the prime contractor and construction lenders of any changes in the contract if the change has the effect of increasing the price stated in the contract by 5 percent or more.

3124. In any case where the claimant was employed by a contractor or subcontractor, his claim of lien shall not extend to any labor, services, equipment, or materials not included in the contract between the owner and original contractor or any modification thereof, if the claimant had actual knowledge or constructive notice of the contract as defined in Section 3088 or any such modification before he furnished such labor, service, equipment, or materials. The filing of a contract for a work of improvement or of a modification of such contract with the county recorder of the county where the property is situated, before the commencement of work, shall be equivalent to the giving of actual notice of the provisions thereof by the owner to all persons performing work or furnishing materials thereunder.

CIVIL CODE SECTIONS 3128-3131

3128. The liens provided for in this chapter shall attach to the work of improvement and the land on which it is situated together with a convenient space about the same or so much as may be required for the convenient use and occupation thereof, if at the commencement of the work or of the furnishing of the materials for the same, the land belonged to the person who caused such work of improvement to be constructed, but if such person owned less than a fee simple estate in such land then only his interest therein is subject to such lien, except as provided in Section 3129.

3129. Every work of improvement constructed upon any land and all work or labor performed or materials furnished in connection therewith with the knowledge of the owner or of any person having or claiming any estate therein shall be held to have been constructed, performed, or furnished at the instance of such owner or person having or claiming any estate therein and such interest shall be subject to any lien recorded under this chapter unless such owner or person having or claiming any estate therein shall give a notice of nonresponsibility pursuant to Section 3094.

3130. In every case in which one claim is filed against two or more buildings or other works of improvement owned or reputed to be owned by the same person or on which the claimant has been employed by the same person to do his work or furnish his materials, whether such works of improvement are owned by one or more owners, the person filing such claim must at the same time designate the amount due to him on each of such works of improvement; otherwise the lien of such claim is postponed to other liens. If such claimant has been employed to furnish labor or materials under a contract providing for a lump sum to be paid to him for his work or materials on such works of improvement as a whole, and such contract does not segregate the amount due for the work done and materials furnished on such works of improvement separately, then such claimant, for the purposes of this section, may estimate an equitable distribution of the sum due him over all of such works of improvement based upon the proportionate amount of work done or materials furnished upon such respective works of improvement. The lien of such claimant does not extend beyond the amount designated as against other creditors having liens, by judgment, mortgage, or otherwise, upon either such works of improvement or upon the land upon which the same are situated.

For all purposes of this section, if there is a single structure on more than one parcel of land owned by one or more different owners, it shall not be the duty of the claimant to segregate the proportion of material or labor entering into the structure on any one of such parcels; but upon the trial thereof the court may, when it deems it equitable so to do, distribute the lien equitably as between the several parcels involved.

3131. If a work of improvement consists in the construction of two or more separate residential units, each such unit shall be considered a separate "work of improvement," and the time for filing claims of lien against each such residential unit shall commence to run upon the completion of each such residential unit. A separate residential unit means one residential structure, including a residential structure containing multiple condominium units, together with any common area, or any garage or other improvements appurtenant thereto. The provisions of this qualification shall not impair any rights conferred under the provisions of Section 3112 and 3130. Materials delivered to or upon any portion of such entire work of improvement or furnished to be used in such entire work of improvement and ultimately used or consumed in one of such separate residential units shall, for all the purposes of this title, be deemed to have been furnished to be used or consumed in the separate residential unit in which the same shall have been actually used or consumed; provided, however, that if the claimant is unable to segregate the amounts used on or consumed in such separate units, he shall be entitled to all the benefits of Section 3130.

For purposes of this section and notwithstanding any other provision of this chapter, the completion of a residential structure containing multiple condominium units, together with any common area, or any garage or other improvements appurtenant thereto, and only such residential structure, shall not operate in any manner to impair the rights of a lien claimant entitled to a lien pursuant to Section 3111, if the claim of lien is recorded in the manner prescribed by this chapter within 120 days of the completion of the residential structure.

CIVIL CODE SECTIONS 3134-3140

3134. The liens provided for in this chapter (other than with respect to site improvements) are, subject to the exception in Section 3138, preferred to any lien, mortgage, deed of trust, or other encumbrance upon the work of improvement and the site, which attaches subsequent to the commencement of the work of improvement, and also to any lien, mortgage, deed of trust, or other encumbrance of which the claimant had no notice and which was unre-

corded at the time of commencement of the work of improvement.

3135. If any site improvement is provided for in a separate contract from any contract with respect to the erection of residential units or other structures, then the site improvement shall be considered a separate work of improvement and the commencement thereof shall not constitute a commencement of the work of improvement consisting of the erection of any residential unit or other structure.

3136. A mortgage or deed of trust which would be prior to the liens provided for in this chapter to the extent of obligatory advances made thereunder in accordance with the commitment of the lender shall also be prior to the liens provided for in this chapter as to any other advances, secured by such mortgage or deed of trust, which are used in payment of any claim of lien which is recorded at the date or dates of such other advances and thereafter in payment of costs of the work of improvement. Such priority shall not, however, exceed the original obligatory commitment of the lender as shown in such mortgage or deed of trust.

3137. The liens provided for in Section 3112 with respect to site improvements are, subject to the exception in Section 3139, preferred to (a) any mortgage, deed of trust, or other encumbrance which attaches subsequent to the commencement of the site improvement work; and (b) any mortgage, deed of trust, or other encumbrance of which the claimant had no notice and which was unrecorded at the time of the commencement of such site improvement; and (c) any mortgage, deed of trust, or other encumbrance recorded before the commencement of the site improvement work which was given for the sole or primary purpose of financing such site improvements, unless the loan proceeds are, in good faith, placed in the control of the lender under a binding agreement with the borrower to the effect that such proceeds are to be applied to the payment of claims of claimants and that no portion of such proceeds will be paid to the borrower in the absence of satisfactory evidence that all such claims have been paid or that the time for recording claims of liens has expired and no such claims have been recorded.

3138. If the holder of any mortgage or deed of trust which is subordinate pursuant to Section 3134 to any lien, shall procure a payment bond as defined in Section 3096 in an amount not less than 75 percent of the principal amount of such mortgage or deed of trust, which bond refers to such mortgage or deed of trust, and shall record such payment bond in the office of the county recorder in the county where the site is located, then such mortgage or deed of trust shall be preferred to all liens for labor, services, equipment, or materials furnished after such recording.

3139. If the owner of the land or holder of any mortgage or deed of trust, which is subordinate pursuant to Section 3137 to any lien, shall procure a payment bond in an amount not less than 50 percent of the principal amount of such mortgage or deed of trust and shall record such payment bond in the office of the county recorder in the county where the site is located before completion of the work of improvement, then such mortgage or deed of trust shall be preferred to all such liens provided in Section 3112.

3140. Any original contractor or subcontractor shall be entitled to recover, upon a claim of lien recorded by him, only such amount as may be due him according to the terms of his contract after deducting all claims of other claimants for labor, services, equipment, or materials furnished and embraced within his contract.

CIVIL CODE SECTIONS 3143-3154

3143. If the owner of property, or the owner of any interest therein, sought to be charged with a claim of lien, or any original contractor or subcontractor disputes the correctness or validity of any claim of lien, he may record in the office of the county recorder in which such claim of lien was recorded, either before or after the commencement of an action to enforce such claim of lien, a bond executed by a corporation authorized to issue surety bonds in the State of California, in a penal sum equal to 1-1/2 times the amount of the claim or 1-1/2 times the amount allocated in the claim of lien to the parcel or parcels of real property sought to be released, which bond shall be conditioned for the payment of any sum which the claimant may recover on the claim together with his cost of suit in the action, if he recovers therein. Upon the recording of such bond the real property described in such bond is released from the lien and from any action brought to foreclose such lien. The principal upon such bond may be either the owner of the property or the owner of any interest therein, or any original contractor, subcontractor, or sub-subcontractor affected by such claim of lien.

3144. (a) No lien provided for in this chapter binds any property for a longer period of time than 90 days after the recording of the claim of lien, unless within that time an action to foreclose the lien is commenced in a proper court, except that, if credit is given and notice of the fact and terms of such credit is recorded in the office of the county recorder subsequent to the recording of such claim of lien and prior to the expiration of such 90-day period, then such lien continues in force until 90 days after the expiration of such credit, but in no case longer than one year from the time of completion of the work of improvement.

(b) If the claimant fails to commence an action to foreclose the lien within the time limitation provided in this section, the lien automatically shall be null and void and of no further force and effect.

3144.5. Any person who obtains a lien release bond which is recorded pursuant to Section 3143 shall give notice of the recording to the lienholder by mailing a copy of the bond to the lienholder at the address appearing on the lien. Service of the notice shall be by certified or registered mail, return receipt requested. Failure to give the notice provided by this section shall not affect the validity of the lien release bond, but the statute of limitations on any action on the bond shall be tolled until the notice is given. Any action on the lien release bond shall be commenced by the claimant within six months of the recording of the lien release bond.

3145. As against any purchaser or encumbrancer for value and in good faith whose rights are acquired subsequent to the expiration of the 90-day period following the recording of the claim of lien, no giving of credit or extension of the lien or of the time to enforce the same shall be effective unless evidenced by a notice or agreement recorded in the office of the county recorder prior to the acquisition of the rights of such purchaser or encumbrancer.

3146. After the filing of the complaint in the proper court, the plaintiff may record in the office of the county recorder of the county, or of the several counties in which the property is situated, a notice of the pendency of such proceedings, as provided in Section 409 of the Code of Civil Procedure. Only from the time of recording such notice shall a purchaser or encumbrancer of the property affected thereby be deemed to have constructive notice of the pendency of the action, and in that event only if its pendency against parties designated by their real names.

3147. If the action to foreclose the lien is not brought to trial within two years after the commencement thereof, the court may in its discretion dismiss the same for want of prosecution.

3148. In all cases the dismissal of an action to foreclose the lien (unless it is expressly stated that the same is without prejudice) or a judgment rendered therein that no lien exists shall be equivalent to the cancellation and removal from the record of such lien.

3149. Any number of persons claiming liens on the same property may join in the same action to foreclose their liens and when separate actions are commenced the court may consolidate them.

3150. In addition to any other costs allowed by law, the court in an action to foreclose a lien must also allow as costs the money paid for verifying and recording the lien, such costs to be allowed each claimant whose lien is established, whether he be plaintiff or defendant.

3151. Whenever on the sale of the property subject to any liens provided for in this chapter, under a judgment of foreclosure of such lien, there is a deficiency of proceeds, judgment for the deficiency may be entered against any party personally liable therefor in like manner and with like effect as in an action for the foreclosure of a mortgage.

3152. Nothing contained in this title affects the right of a claimant to maintain a personal action to recover a debt against the person liable therefor either in a separate action or in the action to foreclose the lien, nor any right the claimant may have to the issuance of a writ of attachment or execution or to enforce a judgment by other means. In an application for a writ of attachment, the claimant shall refer to this section. A lien held by the claimant under this chapter does not affect the right to procure a writ of attachment. The judgment, if any, obtained by the claimant in a personal action, or personal judgment obtained in a mechanic's lien action, does not impair or merge a lien held by the claimant under this chapter, but any money collected on the judgment shall be credited on the amount of the lien.

3153. In all cases where a claim of lien is recorded for labor, services, equipment, or materials furnished to any contractor, he shall defend any action brought thereon at his own expense, and during the pendency of such action the owner may withhold from the original contractor the amount of money for which the claim of lien is recorded. In case of judgment in such action against the owner or his property upon the lien, the owner shall be entitled to deduct from any amount then or thereafter due from him to the original contractor the amount of such judgment and costs. If the amount of such judgment and costs exceeds the amount due from him to the original contractor, or if he has settled with the original contractor in full, he shall be entitled to recover back from the original contractor, or the sureties on any bond given by him for the faithful performance of his contract, any amount of such judgment and costs in excess of the contract price, and for which the original contractor was originally the party liable.

3154. (a) At any time after the expiration of the time period specified by Section 3144 with regard to the period during which property is bound by a lien after recordation of a claim of lien, where no action has been brought to enforce such lien, the owner of the property or the owner of any interest therein may petition the proper court for a decree to release the property from the lien.

(b) The petition shall be verified and shall allege all of the following:

(1) The date of recordation of the claim of lien.

(2) The legal description of the property affected by such claim of lien.

(3) That no action has been filed to foreclose the lien, or that no extension of credit has been recorded, and that the time period during which suit can be brought to foreclose the lien has expired.

(4) That the lien claimant is unable or unwilling to execute a release of the lien or cannot with reasonable diligence be found.

(5) That the owner of the property or interest in the property has not filed for relief under any law governing bankrupts, and that there exists no other restraint to prevent the lien claimant from filing to foreclose his or her lien. A certified copy of the claim of lien shall be attached to the petition. The petition shall be deemed controverted by the lien claimant.

(c) Upon the filing of the petition, and before any further proceedings are had, the clerk, or if there is no clerk, the judge shall set a date for the hearing not more that 30 days following the filing of the petition. The court may continue the hearing beyond the 30-day period, but good cause shall be shown for any continuance.

(d) A copy of the petition and the notice setting the date for the hearing shall be served upon the lien claimant at least 10 days prior to the date set for hearing, in the manner in which a summons is required to be served, or by certified or registered mail, postage prepaid, return receipt requested, addressed to the lien claimant at the claimant's address as shown: (1) on the preliminary 20-day notice served by the claimant pursuant to Section 3097, (2) in the records of the registrar of contractors, (3) on the contract on which the lien is based, or (4) on the claim of lien itself. When service is made by mail as provided in this section, service is complete on the fifth day following the day of the deposit of such mail. No decree shall issue in favor of the petitioner unless the petitioner proves that service of the petition and the order fixing the date for hearing was made in compliance with this subdivision. The issue of compliance with this subdivision shall be deemed controverted by the lien claimant.

(e) In the event judgment is rendered in favor of the petitioner, the decree shall indicate all of the following:

(1) The date the lien was recorded.

(2) The county and city, if any, in which the lien was recorded.

(3) The book and page of the place in the official records where the lien is recorded.

(4) The legal description of the property affected. Upon the recordation of a certified copy of the decree, the property described in the decree shall be released from the lien.

(f) The prevailing party shall be entitled to attorneys' fees not to exceed one thousand dollars ($1,000).

(g) Nothing in this section shall be construed to bar any other cause of action or claim for relief by the owner of the property or an interest in the property, nor shall a decree canceling a claimant's lien bar the lien claimant from bringing any other cause of action or claim for relief, other than an action foreclosing such lien. However, no other action or claim shall be joined with the claim for relief established by this section.

(h) The provisions of Chapter 2.5 (commencing with Section 1141.10) of Title 3 of Part 3 of the Code of Civil Procedure shall not apply to causes commenced pursuant to this section.

CIVIL CODE SECTION 3156

3156. The provisions of this chapter do not apply to any public work.

CIVIL CODE SECTIONS 3158-3159

3158. Any of the persons named in Sections 3110, 3111, and 3112, other than the original contractor, may give to the owner a stop notice. Any person who shall fail to serve such a stop notice after a written demand therefor from the owner shall forfeit his right to a mechanic's lien.

3159. (a) Any of the persons named in Sections 3110, 3111, and 3112 may, prior to the expiration of the period within which his or her claim of lien must be recorded under Chapter 2 (commencing with Section 3109), give to a construction lender a stop notice or a bonded stop notice. The construction lender shall be subject to the following:

(1) The construction lender shall withhold funds pursuant to a bonded stop notice filed by an original contractor, regardless of whether a payment bond has previously been recorded in the office of the county recorder where the site is located in accordance with Section 3235.

(2) The construction lender shall withhold funds pursuant to a bonded stop notice filed by any other person named in Sections 3110, 3111, and 3112, unless a payment bond has previously been recorded in the office of the county recorder where the site is located in accordance with Section 3235. If a payment bond has previously been recorded, the construction lender may, at its option, withhold funds pursuant to the bonded stop notice or stop notice, or may elect not to withhold pursuant to the bonded stop notice or stop notice given by anyone other than an original contractor.

(3) If, when giving the construction lender the stop notice or bonded stop notice, the claimant makes a written request for notice of the election, accompanied by a preaddressed, stamped envelope, the construction lender shall furnish the claimant a copy of the bond within 30 days after making the election. A lender shall not be liable for a failure to furnish a copy of the bond if the failure was not intentional and resulted from a bona fide error, if the lender maintains reasonable procedures to avoid such an error, and if the error was corrected not later than 20 days from the date on which the violation was discovered. The payment bond may be recorded at any time prior to the serving of the first stop notice. The notice may only be given for materials, equipment, or services furnished, or labor performed.

(b) In the case of a stop notice or bonded stop notice filed by the original contractor or by a subcontractor, the original contractor or subcontractor shall only be entitled to recover on his or her stop notice or bonded stop notice the net amount due the original contractor or subcontractor after deducting the stop notice claims of all subcontractors or material suppliers who have filed bonded stop notices on account of work done on behalf of the original contractor or the subcontractor.

(c) In no event shall the construction lender be required to withhold, pursuant to a bonded stop notice, more than the net amount identified in subdivision (b). Notwithstanding any other provision, no construction lender shall have any liability for the failure to withhold more than this net amount upon receipt of a bonded stop notice.

CIVIL CODE SECTIONS 3161-3163

3161. It shall be the duty of the owner upon receipt of a stop notice pursuant to Section 3158 to withhold from the original contractor or from any person acting under his or her authority and to whom labor or materials, or both, have been furnished, or agreed to be furnished, sufficient money due or to become due to such contractor to answer such claim and any claim of lien that may be recorded therefor, unless a payment bond has been recorded pursuant to the provisions of Section 3235, in which case the owner may, but is not obligated to, withhold such money.

If the owner elects not to withhold pursuant to a stop notice by reason of a payment bond having been previously recorded, then the owner shall, within 30 days after receipt of the stop notice, give a written notice to the claimant at the address shown in the stop notice that the bond has been recorded and furnish to the claimant a copy of that bond.

3162. (a) Upon receipt of a stop notice pursuant to Section 3159, the construction lender may, and upon receipt of a bonded stop notice the construction lender shall, except as provided in this section, withhold from the borrower or other person to whom it or the owner may be obligated to make payments or advancement out of the construction fund, sufficient money to answer the claim and any claim of lien that may be recorded therefor. The construction lender shall be subject to the following:

(1) The construction lender shall withhold funds pursuant to a bonded stop notice filed by an original contractor, regardless of whether a payment bond has previously been recorded in the office of the county recorder where the site is located in accordance with Section 3235.

(2) The construction lender shall withhold funds pursuant to a bonded stop notice filed by any other person named in Sections 3110, 3111, and 3112, unless a payment bond has previously been recorded in the office of the county recorder where the site is located in accordance with Section 3235. If a payment bond has previously been recorded, the construction lender may, at its option, withhold funds pursuant to the bonded stop notice or stop notice, or may elect not to withhold pursuant to the bonded stop notice or stop notice given by anyone other than an original contractor.

(3) If, when giving the construction lender the stop notice or bonded stop notice, the claimant makes a written request for notice of the election, accompanied by a preaddressed, stamped envelope, the construction lender shall furnish the claimant a copy of the bond within 30 days after making the election. A lender shall not be liable for a failure to furnish a copy of the bond if the failure was not intentional and resulted from a bona fide error, if the lender maintains reasonable procedures to avoid such an error, and if the error was corrected not later than 20 days from the date on which the violation was discovered. The payment bond may be recorded at any time prior to the serving of the first stop notice.

(b) In the case of a stop notice or bonded stop notice filed by the original contractor or by a subcontractor, the original contractor or subcontractor shall only be entitled to recover on his or her stop notice or bonded stop notice the net amount due the original contractor or subcontractor after deducting the stop notice claims of all subcontractors or material suppliers who have filed bonded stop notices on account of work done on behalf of the original contractor or the subcontractor.

(c) In no event shall the construction lender be required to withhold, pursuant to a bonded stop notice, more than the net amount identified in subdivision (b). Notwithstanding any other provision, no construction lender shall have any liability for the failure to withhold more than this net amount upon receipt of a bonded stop notice.

3163. If the construction lender objects to the sufficiency of the sureties on the bond accompanying the bonded stop notice, he must give notice in writing of such objection to the claimant within 20 days after the service of the bonded stop notice. The claimant may within 10 days after the receipt of such written objection substitute for the initial bond a bond in like amount executed by a corporate surety licensed to write such bonds in the State of California. If the claimant fails to do so, the construction lender may disregard the bonded stop notice and release all funds withheld in response thereto.

CIVIL CODE SECTIONS 3166-3168

3166. No assignment by the owner or contractor of construction loan funds, whether made before or after a stop notice or bonded stop notice is given to a construction lender, shall be held to take priority over the stop notice or bonded stop notice, and such assignment shall have no effect insofar as the rights of claimants who give the stop notice or bonded stop notice are concerned.

3167. (a) If the money withheld or required to be withheld pursuant to any bonded stop notice shall be insufficient to pay in full the valid claims of all persons by whom such notices were given, the same shall be distributed among such persons in the same ratio that their respective claims bear to the aggregate of all such valid claims. Such pro rata distribution shall be made among the persons entitled to share therein without regard to the order of time in which their respective notices may have been given or their respective actions, if any, commenced.

(b) If the money withheld or required to be withheld pursuant to any stop notice shall be insufficient to pay in full the valid claims of all persons by whom such notices were given, the same shall be distributed among such persons in the same ratio that their respective claims bear to the aggregate of all such valid claims. Such pro rata distribution shall be made among the persons entitled to share therein without regard to the order of time in which their respective notices may have been given or their respective actions, if any, commenced.

3168. Any person who willfully gives a false stop notice or bonded stop notice or who willfully includes in his notice labor, services, equipment, or materials not furnished for the property described in such notice forfeits all right to participate in the pro rata distribution of such money and all right to any lien under Chapter 2 (commencing with Section 3109).

CIVIL CODE SECTION 3171

3171. If the owner, construction lender or any original contractor or subcontractor disputes the correctness or validity of any stop notice or bonded stop notice, he may file with the person upon whom such notice was served a bond executed by good and sufficient sureties in a penal sum equal to 1-1/4 times the amount stated in such notice, conditioned for the payment of any sum not exceeding the penal obligation of the bond which the claimant may recover on the claim, together with his costs of suit in the action, if he recovers therein. Upon the filing of such bond, the funds withheld to respond to the stop notice or bonded stop notice shall forthwith be released.

CIVIL CODE SECTIONS 3172-3176.5

3172. An action against the owner or construction lender to enforce payment of the claim stated in the stop notice or bonded stop notice may be commenced at any time after 10 days from the date of the service of the stop notice upon either the owner or construction lender and shall be commenced not later than 90 days following the expiration of the period within which claims of lien must be recorded as prescribed in Chapter 2 (commencing with Section 3109). No such action shall be brought to trial or judgment entered until the expiration of said 90-day period. No money shall be withheld by reason of any such notice longer than the expiration of such 90-day period unless such action is commenced. If no such action is commenced, such notice shall cease to be effective and such moneys shall be paid or delivered to the contractor or other person to whom they are due. Notice of commencement of any such action shall be given within five days after commencement thereof to the same persons and in the same manner as provided for service of a stop notice or bonded stop notice.

3173. In case such action is commenced as provided in Section 3172 but is not brought to trial within two years after the commencement thereof, the court may in its discretion dismiss the action for want of prosecution.

3174. Upon the dismissal of an action to enforce a stop notice or bonded stop notice, unless expressly stated to be without prejudice, or upon a judgment rendered therein against the claimant, the stop notice or bonded stop notice shall cease to be effective and the moneys withheld shall be paid or delivered to the person to whom they are due.

3175. Any number of persons who have given stop notices or bonded stop notices may join in the same action and when separate actions are commenced the court first acquiring jurisdiction may consolidate them. Upon the motion of the owner or construction lender the court shall require all claimants to the moneys withheld pursuant to stop notices and bonded stop notices to be impleaded in one action, to the end that the respective rights of all parties may be adjudicated therein.

3176. In any action against an owner or construction lender to enforce payment of a claim stated in a bonded stop notice, the prevailing party shall be entitled to collect from the party held liable by the court for payment of the claim, reasonable attorney's fees in addition to other costs and in addition to any liability for damages.

The court, upon notice and motion by a party, shall determine who is the prevailing party for purposes of this section, whether or not the suit proceeds to final judgment. Except as otherwise provided by this section, the prevailing party shall be the party who recovered a greater relief in the action. The court may also determine that there is no prevailing party. Where an action has been voluntarily dismissed or dismissed pursuant to a settlement of the case, there shall be no prevailing party for purposes of this section.

Where the defendant alleges in his or her answer that he or she tendered to the plaintiff the full amount to which he or she was entitled, and thereupon deposits in court for the plaintiff, the amount so tendered, and the allegation is found to be true, then the defendant is deemed to be a prevailing party.

3176.5. If the plaintiff is the prevailing party in any action against an owner or construction lender to enforce payment of a claim stated in a bonded stop notice, any amount awarded on the claim shall include interest at the legal rate calculated from the date the bonded stop notice is served upon the owner or construction lender pursuant to Section 3172.

CIVIL CODE SECTIONS 3225-3227

3225. The surety or sureties on any bond given pursuant to any of the provisions of this title shall not be exonerated or released from the obligation of the bond by any change, alteration, or modification in or of any contract, plans, specifications, or agreement pertaining or relating to any scheme or work of im-

provement or pertaining or relating to the furnishing of labor, materials, or equipment therefor, nor by any change or modification of any terms of payment or extension of the time for any payment pertaining or relating to any scheme or work of improvement, nor by any rescission or attempted rescission of the contract, agreement or bond, nor by any conditions precedent or subsequent in the bond attempting to limit the right of recovery of claimants otherwise entitled to recover under any such contract or agreement or under the bond, nor, where the bond is given for the benefit of claimants, by any fraud practiced by any person other than the claimant seeking to recover on the bond.

3226. Any bond given pursuant to the provisions of this title will be construed most strongly against the surety and in favor of all persons for whose benefit such bond is given, and under no circumstances shall a surety be released from liability to those for whose benefit such bond has been given, by reason of any breach of contract between the owner and original contractor or on the part of any obligee named in such bond, but the sole conditions of recovery shall be that claimant is a person described in Section 3110, 3111, or 3112, and has not been paid the full amount of his claim.

3227. (a) The written notice to be given to the surety and the bond principal may be given by personal delivery, or by depositing the notice in the mail, postage prepaid, certified or registered, and addressed in accordance with any of the following that may be applicable:

(1) If to an individual surety, at his or her residence or place of business, if known. If to an individual surety whose residence is unknown, then in care of the clerk of the county in which the bond has been recorded.

(2) If to a corporate surety, at the office of or in care of the agent designated by the surety in the bond as the address to which notice shall be sent.

(3) At the office of or in care of any officer of the surety in this state.

(4) At the office of or in care of the statutory agent of the surety in this state.

(5) To the bond principal at the last known address.

(6) By service in the manner provided by law for the service of a summons in a civil action.

(b) The written notice described in subdivision (a) shall contain all of the following:

(1) The kind of labor, services, equipment, or materials furnished or agreed to be furnished by the claimant.

(2) The name of the person to or for whom the labor, services, equipment, or materials were furnished.

(3) The amount in value, as near as may be determined, of any labor, services, equipment, or materials already furnished or to be furnished.

CIVIL CODE SECTIONS 3235-3237

3235. In case the original contract for a private work of improvement is filed in the office of the county recorder of the county where the property is situated before the work is commenced, and the payment bond of the original contractor in an amount not less than 50 percent of the contract price named in such contract is recorded in such office, then the court must, where it would be equitable so to do, restrict the recovery under lien claims to an aggregate amount equal to the amount found to be due from the owner to the original contractor and render judgment against the original contractor and his sureties on such bond for any deficiency or difference there may remain between such amount so found to be due to the original contractor and the whole amount found to be due to claimants.

3236. It is the intent and purpose of Section 3235 to limit the owner's liability, in all cases, to the measure of the contract price where he shall have filed or caused to be filed in good faith his original contract and recorded a payment bond as therein provided. It shall be lawful for the owner to protect himself against any failure of the original contractor to perform his contract and make full payment for all work done and materials furnished thereunder by exacting such bond or other security as he may deem necessary.

3237. When a lending institution requires that a payment bond be furnished as a condition of lending money to finance a private work of improvement, and accepts in writing as sufficient a payment bond posted in fulfillment of this requirement, it may thereafter object to the borrower as to the validity of that payment bond or refuse to make the loan based upon any objection to the payment bond only if the bond underwriter was licensed by the Department of Insurance.

As used in this section, "lending institution" includes commercial banks, savings and loan institutions, credit unions, and any other organizations or persons that are engaged in the business of financing loans.

CIVIL CODE SECTIONS 3239-3242

3239. No provision in any payment bond given pursuant to any of the provisions of this chapter attempting by contract to shorten the period prescribed in Section 337 of the Code of Civil Procedure for the commencement of an action thereon shall be valid if such provision attempts to limit the time for commencement of action thereon to a shorter period than six months from the completion of any work of improvement, nor shall any provision in any of such bonds attempting to limit the period for the commencement of actions thereon be valid insofar as actions brought by claimants are concerned, unless such bond is recorded, before the work of improvement is commenced, with the county recorder of the county in which the property referred to therein is situated.

3240. Notwithstanding Section 3239, if a surety on any payment bond given pursuant to this chapter records the payment bond in the office of the county recorder of the county in which the property is situated before the work of improvement is completed, then any action against the surety or sureties shall be commenced not later than six months after the completion of the work of improvement.

3242. (a) With regard to a contract entered into on or after January 1, 1995, in order to enforce a claim upon any payment bond given in connection with a private work, a claimant shall give the 20-day private work preliminary notice provided in Section 3097.

(b) If the 20-day private work preliminary notice was not given as provided in Section 3097, a claimant may enforce a claim by giving written notice to the surety and the bond principal as provided in Section 3227 within 15 days after recordation of a notice of completion. If no notice of completion has been recorded, the time for giving written notice to the surety and the bond principal is extended to 75 days after completion of the work of improvement.

CIVIL CODE SECTIONS 3258-3267

3258. The county recorder shall number, index, and preserve all contracts, plans, and other papers presented to him for filing pursuant to this title, and shall number, index, and transcribe into the official records in his office in the same manner as a conveyance of land, all notices, claims of lien, payment bonds, and other papers recorded pursuant to this title. He shall receive therefor the fees prescribed in Article 5 (commencing with Section 27360), Chapter 6, Part 3, Division 2, Title 3 of the Government Code.

3259. Except as otherwise provided in this title, the provisions of Part 2 (commencing with Section 307) of the Code of Civil Procedure are applicable to, and constitute the rules of practice in, the proceedings mentioned in this title. The provisions of Part 2 (commencing with Section 307) of the Code of Civil Procedure, relative to new trials and appeals, except insofar as they are inconsistent with the provisions of this title or with rules adopted by the Judicial Council, apply to the proceedings mentioned in this title.

3260. (a) This section is applicable with respect to all contracts entered into on or after July 1, 1991, relating to the construction of any private work of improvement. However, the amendments made to this section during the 1992 portion of the 1991-92 Regular Session of the Legislature are applicable only with respect to contracts entered into on or after January 1, 1993, relating to the construction of any private work of improvement. Moreover, the amendments made to this section during the 1993 portion of the 1993-94 Regular Session of the Legislature are applicable only with respect to contracts entered into on or after January 1, 1994, relating to the construction of any private work of improvement.

(b) The retention proceeds withheld from any payment by the owner from the original contractor, or by the original contractor from any subcontractor, shall be subject to this section.

(c) Within 45 days after the date of completion, the retention withheld by the owner shall be released. "Date of completion," for purposes of this section, means any of the following:

(1) The date of issuance of any certificate of occupancy covering the work by the public agency issuing the building permit.

(2) The date of completion indicated on a valid notice of completion recorded pursuant to Section 3093.

(3) The date of completion as defined in Section 3086.

However, release of retentions withheld for any portion of the work of improvement which ultimately will become the property of a public agency, may be conditioned upon the acceptance of the work by the public agency. In the event of a dispute between the owner and the original contractor, the owner may withhold from the final payment an amount not to exceed 150 percent of the disputed amount.

(d) Subject to subdivision (e), within 10 days from the time that all or any portion of the retention proceeds are received by the original contractor, the original contractor shall pay each of its subcontractors from whom retention has been withheld, each subcontractor's share of the retention received. However, if a retention payment received by the original contractor is specifically designated for a particular subcontractor, payment of the retention shall be made to the designated subcontractor, if the payment is consistent with the terms of the subcontract.

(e) If a bona fide dispute exists between a subcontractor and the original contractor, the original contractor may withhold from that subcontractor with whom the dispute exists its portion of the retention proceeds. The amount withheld from the retention payment shall not exceed 150 percent of the estimated value of the disputed amount.

(f) Within 10 days of receipt of written notice by the owner from the original contractor or by the original contractor from the subcontractor, as the case may be, that any work in dispute has been completed in accordance with the terms of the contract, the owner or original contractor shall advise the notifying party of the acceptance or rejection of the disputed work. Within 10 days of acceptance of the disputed work, the owner or original contractor, as the case may be, shall release the retained portion of the retention proceeds.

(g) In the event that retention payments are not made within the time periods required by this section, the owner or original contractor withholding the unpaid amounts shall be subject to a charge of 2 percent per month on the improperly withheld amount, in lieu of any interest otherwise due. Additionally, in any action for the collection of funds wrongfully withheld, the prevailing party shall be entitled to his or her attorney's fees and costs.

(h) It shall be against public policy for any party to require any other party to waive any provision of this section.

(i) This section shall not be construed to apply to retentions withheld by a lender in accordance with the construction loan agreement.

3260.1. (a) This section is applicable with respect to all contracts entered into on or after January 1, 1992, relating to the construction of any private work of improvement.

(b) Except as otherwise agreed in writing, the owner shall pay to the contractor, within 30 days following receipt of a demand for payment in accordance with the contract, any progress payment due thereunder as to which there is no good faith dispute between the parties. In the event of a dispute between the owner and the contractor, the owner may

withhold from the progress payment an amount not to exceed 150 percent of the disputed amount. If any amount is wrongfully withheld in violation of this subdivision, the contractor shall be entitled to the penalty specified in subdivision (f) of Section 3260.

(c) Nothing in this section shall be deemed to supersede any requirement of Section 3260 respecting the withholding of retention proceeds.

3261. No mistake or errors in the statement of the demand, or of the amount of credits and offsets allowed, or of the balance asserted to be due the claimant, or in the description of the property against which the lien is recorded, shall invalidate the lien, unless the court finds that such mistake or error in the statement of the demand, credits and offsets, or of the balance due, was made with the intent to defraud, or that an innocent third party, without notice, direct or constructive, has since the claim was recorded become the bona fide owner of the property, and that the notice of claim was so deficient that it did not put the party on further inquiry in any manner.

3262. (a) Neither the owner nor original contractor by any term of their contract, or otherwise, shall waive, affect, or impair the claims and liens of other persons whether with or without notice except by their written consent, and any term of the contract to that effect shall be null and void. Any written consent given by any claimant pursuant to this subdivision shall be null, void, and unenforceable unless and until the claimant executes and delivers a waiver and release. Such a waiver and release shall be binding and effective to release the owner, construction lender, and surety on a payment bond from claims and liens only if the waiver and release follows substantially one of the forms set forth in this section and is signed by the claimant or his or her authorized agent, and, in the case of a conditional release, there is evidence of payment to the claimant. Evidence of payment may be by the claimant's endorsement on a single or joint payee check which has been paid by the bank upon which it was drawn or by written acknowledgment of payment given by the claimant.

(b) No oral or written statement purporting to waive, release, impair or otherwise adversely affect a claim is enforceable or creates any estoppel or impairment of a claim unless (1) it is pursuant to a waiver and release prescribed herein, or (2) the claimant had actually received payment in full for the claim.

(c) This section does not affect the enforceability of either an accord and satisfaction regarding a bona fide dispute or any agreement made in settlement of an action pending in any court provided the accord and satisfaction or agreement and settlement make specific reference to the mechanic's lien, stop notice, or bond claims.

(d) The waiver and release given by any claimant hereunder shall be null, void, and unenforceable unless it follows substantially the following forms in the following circumstances:

(1) Where the claimant is required to execute a waiver and release in exchange for, or in order to induce the payment of, a progress payment and the claimant is not, in fact, paid in exchange for the waiver and release or a single payee check or joint payee check is given in exchange for the waiver and release, the waiver and release shall follow substantially the following form:

CONDITIONAL WAIVER AND RELEASE
UPON PROGRESS PAYMENT

Upon receipt by the undersigned of a check from _(Maker of Check)_ in the sum of $_(Amount of Check)_ payable to _(Payee or Payees of Check)_ and when the check has been properly endorsed and has been paid by the bank upon which it is drawn, this document shall become effective to release any mechanic's lien, stop notice, or bond right the undersigned has on the job of _(Owner)_ located at _(Job Description)_ to the following extent. This release covers a progress payment for labor, services, equipment, or material furnished to _(Your Customer)_ through _(Date)_ only and does not cover any retentions retained before or after the release date; extras furnished before the release date for which payment has not been received ; extras or items furnished after the release date.

Rights based upon work performed or items furnished under a written change order which has been fully executed by the parties prior to the release date are covered by this release unless specifically reserved by the claimant in this release. This release of any mechanic's lien, stop notice, or bond right shall not otherwise affect the contract rights, including rights between parties to the contract based upon a rescission, abandonment, or breach of the contract, or the right of the undersigned to recover compensation for furnished labor, services, equipment, or material covered by this release if that furnished labor, services, equipment, or material was not compensated by the progress payment. Before any recipient of this document relies on it, said party should verify evidence of payment to the undersigned.

Dated: _____   _____(Company Name)_____
                        By _____(Title)_____

(2) Where the claimant is required to execute a waiver and release in exchange for, or in order to induce payment of, a progress payment and the claimant asserts in the waiver it has, in fact, been paid the progress payment, the waiver and release shall follow substantially the following form:

UNCONDITIONAL WAIVER AND RELEASE
UPON PROGRESS PAYMENT

The undersigned has been paid and has received a progress payment in the sum of $_(Amount of Check)_ for labor, services, equipment, or material furnished to _(Your Customer)_ on the job of _(Owner)_ located at _(Job Description)_ and does hereby release any mechanic's lien, stop notice, or bond right that the undersigned has on the above referenced job to the following extent. This release covers a progress payment for labor, services, equipment, or materials furnished to _(Your Customer)_ through _(Date)_ only and does not cover any retentions retained before or after the release date; extras furnished before the release date for which payment has not been received ; extras or items furnished after the release date. Rights based upon work performed or items furnished under a written change order which has been fully executed by the parties prior to the release date are covered by this release unless specifically reserved by the claimant in this release. This release of any mechanic's lien, stop notice, or bond right shall not otherwise affect the contract rights, including rights between parties to the contract based upon a rescission, abandonment, or breach of the contract, or the right of the undersigned to recover compensation for furnished labor, services, equipment, or material covered by this release if that furnished labor, services, equipment, or material was not compensated by the progress payment.

Dated: _____ _____(Company Name)_____

By _____(Title)_____

Each unconditional waiver in this provision shall contain the following language, in at least as large a type as the largest type otherwise on the document:

"NOTICE: THIS DOCUMENT WAIVES RIGHTS UNCONDITIONALLY AND STATES THAT YOU HAVE BEEN PAID FOR GIVING UP THOSE RIGHTS. THIS DOCUMENT IS ENFORCEABLE AGAINST YOU IF YOU SIGN IT, EVEN IF YOU HAVE NOT BEEN PAID. IF YOU HAVE NOT BEEN PAID, USE A CONDITIONAL RELEASE FORM."

(3) Where the claimant is required to execute a waiver and release in exchange for, or in order to induce the payment of, a final payment and the claimant is not, in fact, paid in exchange for the waiver and release or a single payee check or joint payee check is given in exchange for the waiver and release, the waiver and release shall follow substantially the following form:....[See Conditional Waiver and Release Upon Final Payment form in Appendix B.]

(4) Where the claimant is required to execute a waiver and release in exchange for, or in order to induce payment of, a final payment and the claimant asserts in the waiver it has, in fact, been paid the final payment, the waiver and release shall follow substantially the following form: [See Unconditional Waiver and Release Upon Final Payment form in Appendix B.]

3262.5. (a) Any person or corporation which has contracted to do business with a public utility, hereafter referred to in this section as a contractor, shall pay any subcontractors within 15 working days of receipt of each progress payment from the public utility, unless otherwise agreed in writing by the parties, the respective amounts allowed the contractor on account of the work performed by the subcontractors, to the extent of each of the subcontractors' interest in that work. In the event that there is a good faith dispute over all or any portion of the amount due on a progress payment from a contractor to a subcontractor, then the contractor may withhold no more than 150 percent of the disputed amount.

(b) Any contractor who violates this section shall pay to the subcontractor a penalty of 2 percent of the disputed amount due per month for every month that payment is not made. In any action for the collection of funds wrongfully withheld, the prevailing party shall be entitled to his or her attorney's fees and costs.

(c) This section shall not be construed to limit or impair any contractual, administrative, or judicial remedies otherwise available to a contractor or a subcontractor in the event of a dispute involving late payment or nonpayment by a contractor, or deficient performance or nonperformance by a subcontractor.

3263. No act done by an owner in good faith and in compliance with any of the provisions of this title shall be held to be a prevention of the performance of any contract between the owner and an original contractor by an original contractor, or to exonerate the sureties on any bond given for faithful performance or for the payment of claimants.

3264. The rights of all persons furnishing labor, services, equipment, or materials for any work of improvement, with respect to any fund for payment of construction costs, are governed exclusively by Chapters 3 (commencing with Section 3156) and 4 (commencing with Section 3179) of this title, and no person may assert any legal or equitable right with respect to such fund, other than a right created by direct written contract between such person and the person holding the fund, except pursuant to the provisions of such chapters.

3265. The claim filing procedures set forth in Part 3 (commencing with Section 900) of Division 3.6 of Title 1 of the Government Code do not apply to actions commenced pursuant to Section 3210 of this code.

3266. (a) This title does not supersede the Oil and Gas Lien Act, Chapter 2.5 (commencing with Section 1203.50), Title 4, Part 3, of the Code of Civil Procedure, and the provisions of that act shall govern those transactions to which it applies rather than the provisions of this title.

(b) This title does not supersede Chapter 12 (commencing with Section 5290), Part 3, Division 7, of the Streets and Highways Code, and the provisions of that chapter shall govern those transactions to which it applies rather than the provisions of this title.

3267. Nothing contained in this title shall be construed to give to any person any right of action on any original contractor's private or public work payment bond described in Chapter 6 (commencing with Section 3235) or Chapter 7 (commencing with Section 3247), unless the work forming the basis for his claim was performed by such person for the principal on such payment bond, or one of his subcontractors, pursuant to the contract between the original contractor and the owner.

Nothing in this section shall affect the stop notice rights of, and relative priorities among, architects, registered engineers, or licensed land surveyors and holders of secured interests on the land.

CIVIL CODE SECTION 3268

3268. Except where it is otherwise declared, the provisions of the foregoing titles of this part, in respect to the rights and obligations of parties to contracts, are subordinate to the intention of the parties, when ascertained in the manner prescribed by the chapter on the interpretation of contracts; and the benefit

thereof may be waived by any party entitled thereto, unless such waiver would be against public policy.

BUSINESS AND PROFESSIONS CODE SECTIONS 7000-7020

7000. This chapter constitutes, and may be cited as, the Contractors' State License Law.

7000.2. Nothing in this code shall be interpreted to prohibit cities, counties, and cities and counties from requiring contractors to show proof that they are in compliance with local business tax requirements of the entity prior to issuing any city, county, or city and county permit. Nothing in this code shall be interpreted to prohibit cities, counties, and cities and counties from denying the issuance of a permit to a licensed contractor who is not in compliance with local business tax requirements.

Any business tax required or collected as part of this process shall not exceed the amount of the license tax or license fee authorized by Section 37101 of the Government Code or Section 16000 of the Business and Professions Code.

7000.5. (a) There is in the Department of Consumer Affairs a Contractors' State License Board, which consists of 13 members.

(b) The repeal of this section renders the board subject to the review required by Division 1.2 (commencing with Section 473). However, the review of this board by the department shall be limited to only those unresolved issues identified by the Joint Legislative Sunset Review Committee.

(c) This section shall become inoperative on July 1, 2000, and, as of January 1, 2001, is repealed, unless a later enacted statute, which becomes effective on or before January 1, 2001, deletes or extends the dates on which it becomes inoperative and is repealed.

7001. All members of the board, except the public members, shall be contractors actively engaged in the contracting business, have been so engaged for a period of not less than five years preceding the date of their appointment and shall so continue in the contracting business during the term of their office.

No one, except a public member, shall be eligible for appointment who does not at the time hold an unexpired license to operate as a contractor.

The public members shall not be licentiates of the board.

7002. One member of the board shall be a general engineering contractor, two members shall be general building contractors, two members shall be specialty contractors, one member shall be a member of a labor organization representing the building trades, and seven members shall be public members, one of whom shall be an active local building official.

For the purposes of construing this article, the terms "general engineering contractor," "general building contractor," and "specialty contractor" shall have the meanings given in Article 4 (commencing with Section 7055) of this chapter.

Each contractor member of the board shall be of recognized standing in his or her branch of the contracting business. Each member of the board shall be at least 30 years of age and of good character.

Each member of the board shall have been a citizen and resident of the State of California for at least five years next preceding his or her appointment.

7003. Except as otherwise provided, an appointment to fill a vacancy caused by the expiration of the term of office shall be for a term of four years and shall be filled, except for a vacancy in the term of a public member, by a member from the same branch of the contracting business as was the branch of the member whose term has expired. A vacancy in the term of a public member shall be filled by another public member. Each member shall hold office until the appointment and qualification of his or her successor or until one year shall have elapsed since the expiration of the term for which he or she was appointed, whichever first occurs.

Vacancies occurring in the membership of the board for any cause shall be filled by appointment for the balance of the unexpired term.

No person shall serve as a member of the board for more than two consecutive terms.

The Governor shall appoint five of the public members, including the local building official, and the six members qualified as provided in Section 7002. The Senate Rules Committee and the Speaker of the Assembly shall each appoint a public member.

7005. The Governor may remove any member of the board for misconduct, incompetency or neglect of duty.

7006. The board shall hold not less than four regular meetings each fiscal year, once in July, once in October, once in January and once in April, for the purpose of transacting such business as may properly come before it. At the July meeting of each year the board shall elect officers.

Special meetings of the board may be held at such times as the board may provide in its bylaws. Four members of the board may call a special meeting at any time.

7007. Seven members constitute a quorum at a board meeting.

Due notice of each meeting and the time and place thereof shall be given each member in the manner provided by the bylaws.

7008. The board may appoint such committees and make such rules and regulations as are reasonably necessary to carry out the provisions of this chapter. Such rules and regulations shall be adopted in accordance with the provisions of the Administrative Procedure Act.

7009. Any member or committee of the board may administer oaths and may take testimony and proofs concerning all matters within the jurisdiction of the board.

7010. The board is vested with all functions and duties relating to the administration of this chapter, except those functions and duties vested in the director under the provisions of Division I of this code.

7011. The board by and with the approval of the director shall appoint a registrar of contractors and fix his or her compensation.

The registrar shall be the executive officer and secretary of the board and shall carry out all of the administrative duties as provided in this chapter and as delegated to him or her by the board.

For the purpose of administration of this chapter, there may be appointed a deputy registrar, a chief reviewing and hearing officer and, subject to Section 159.5, other assistants and subordinates as may be necessary.

Appointments shall be made in accordance with the provisions of civil service laws. This section shall become inoperative on July 1, 2000, and, as of January 1, 2001, is repealed, unless a later enacted statute, which becomes effective on or before January 1, 2001, deletes or extends the dates on which it becomes inoperative and is repealed.

7011.3. The registrar shall not assess a civil penalty against a licensed contractor who has been assessed a specified civil penalty by the Labor Commissioner under Section 1020 or 1022 of the Labor Code for the same offense.

7011.4. (a) Notwithstanding Section 7011, there is in the Contractors' State License Board, a separate enforcement unit which shall rigorously enforce this chapter prohibiting all forms of unlicensed activity.

(b) Persons employed as deputy registrars in this unit and designated by the Director of Consumer Affairs are not peace officers and are not entitled to safety member retirement benefits. They do not have the power of arrest. However, they may issue a written notice to appear in court pursuant to Chapter 5c (commencing with Section 853.5) of Title 3 of Part 2 of the Penal Code.

7011.5. Persons employed as investigators of the Special Investigations Unit of the Contractors' State License Board and designated by the Director of Consumer Affairs have the authority of peace officers while engaged in exercising the powers granted or performing the duties imposed upon them in investigating the laws administered by the Contractors' State License Board or commencing directly or indirectly any criminal prosecution arising from any investigation conducted under these laws. All persons herein referred to shall be deemed to be acting within the scope of employment with respect to all acts and matters in this section set forth.

7011.7. The registrar shall review and investigate complaints filed in a manner consistent with this chapter and the Budget Act. It is the intent of the Legislature that complaints be reviewed and investigated as promptly as resources allow.

7011.8. (a) Any person who reports to, or causes a complaint to be filed with, the Contractors' State License Board that a person licensed by that entity has engaged in professional misconduct, knowing the report or complaint to be false, is guilty of an infraction punishable by a fine not to exceed one thousand dollars ($1,000).

(b) The board may notify the appropriate district attorney or city attorney that a person has made or filed what the entity believes to be a false report or complaint against a licensee.

(c) The board shall report to the appropriate policy committees of each house of the Legislature the number of false complaints the board has received against licensed contractors for the last three fiscal years and the number of false complaints the board has referred to the appropriate district attorney or city attorney pursuant to subdivision (b). The report shall be completed and forwarded to the Legislature no later than July 1 of each year.

7012. The registrar, with the approval of the board and the director, may, when funds are available, cooperate in the enforcement of governmental legislation relating to the construction industry, and, except as provided by Section 159.5, shall appoint such assistants as may be necessary therefor.

7013. The board may in its discretion review and sustain or reverse by a majority vote any action or decision of the registrar.

This section shall apply to any action, decision, order, or proceeding of the registrar conducted in accordance with the provisions of Chapter 5 (commencing with Section 11500) of Part 1 of Division 3 of Title 2 of the Government Code.

7014. The board may procure equipment and records necessary to carry out the provisions of this chapter.

7015. The board shall adopt a seal for its own use. The seal shall have the words "Contractors' State License Board, State of California, Department of Consumer Affairs," and the care and custody thereof shall be in the hands of the registrar.

7016. Each member of the board shall receive a per diem and expenses as provided in Section 103.

7017. The board, in addition to the usual periodic reports, shall within 30 days prior to the meeting of the general session of the Legislature submit to the Governor a full and true report of its transactions during the preceding biennium including a complete statement of the receipts and expenditures of the board during the period.

A copy of the report shall be filed with the Secretary of State.

7018.5. (a) The board shall prescribe a form entitled "Notice to Owner" which shall state:

"Under the California Mechanics' Lien Law, any contractor, subcontractor, laborer, supplier, or other person or entity who helps to improve your property, but is not paid for his or her work or supplies, has a right to place a lien on your home, land, or property where the work was performed and to sue you in court to obtain payment.

This means that after a court hearing, your home, land, and property could be sold by a court officer and the proceeds of the sale used to satisfy what you owe. This can happen even if you have paid your contractor in full if the contractor's subcontractors, laborers, or suppliers remain unpaid.

To preserve their rights to file a claim or lien against your property, certain claimants such as subcontractors or material suppliers are each required to provide you with a document called a "Preliminary Notice." Contractors and laborers who contract with owners directly do not have to provide such notice since you are aware of their existence as an owner. A preliminary notice is not a lien against your property. Its purpose is to notify you of persons or enti-

ties that may have a right to file a lien against your property if they are not paid. In order to perfect their lien rights, a contractor, subcontractor, supplier, or laborer must file a mechanics' lien with the county recorder which then becomes a recorded lien against your property. Generally, the maximum time allowed for filing a mechanics' lien against your property is 90 days after substantial completion of your project.

TO INSURE EXTRA PROTECTION FOR YOURSELF AND YOUR PROPERTY, YOU MAY WISH TO TAKE ONE OR MORE OF THE FOLLOWING STEPS:

(1) Require that your contractor supply you with a payment and performance bond (not a license bond), which provides that the bonding company will either complete the project or pay damages up to the amount of the bond. This payment and performance bond as well as a copy of the construction contract should be filed with the county recorder for your further protection. The payment and performance bond will usually cost from 1 to 5 percent of the contract amount depending on the contractor's bonding ability. If a contractor cannot obtain such bonding, it may indicate his or her financial incapacity.

(2) Require that payments be made directly to subcontractors and material suppliers through a joint control. Funding services may be available, for a fee, in your area which will establish voucher or other means of payment to your contractor. These services may also provide you with lien waivers and other forms of protection. Any joint control agreement should include the addendum approved by the registrar.

(3) Issue joint checks for payment, made out to both your contractor and subcontractors or material suppliers involved in the project. The joint checks should be made payable to the persons or entities which send preliminary notices to you. Those persons or entities have indicated that they may have lien rights on your property, therefore you need to protect yourself. This will help to insure that all persons due payment are actually paid.

(4) Upon making payment on any completed phase of the project, and before making any further payments, require your contractor to provide you with unconditional "Waiver and Release" forms signed by each material supplier, subcontractor, and laborer involved in that portion of the work for which payment was made. The statutory lien releases are set forth in exact language in Section 3262 of the Civil Code. Most stationery stores will sell the "Waiver and Release" forms if your contractor does not have them. The material suppliers, subcontractors, and laborers that you obtain releases from are those persons or entities who have filed preliminary notices with you. If you are not certain of the material suppliers, subcontractors, and laborers working on your project, you may obtain a list from your contractor. On projects involving improvements to a single-family residence or a duplex owned by individuals, the persons signing these releases lose the right to file a mechanics' lien claim against your property. In other types of construction, this protection may still be important, but may not be as complete.

To protect yourself under this option, you must be certain that all material suppliers, subcontractors, and laborers have signed the "Waiver and Release" form. If a mechanics' lien has been filed against your property, it can only be voluntarily released by a recorded "Release of Mechanics' Lien" signed by the person or entity that filed the mechanics' lien against your property unless the lawsuit to enforce the lien was not timely filed. You should not make any final payments until any and all such liens are removed. You should consult an attorney if a lien is filed against your property."

(b) Each contractor licensed under this chapter, prior to entering into a contract with an owner for work specified as home improvement or swimming pool construction pursuant to Section 7159, shall give a copy of this "Notice to Owner" to the owner, the owner's agent, or the payer. The failure to provide this notice as required shall constitute grounds for disciplinary action.

7019. (a) If funding is made available for that purpose, the board may contract with licensed professionals, as appropriate, for the site investigation of consumer complaints. The registrar shall determine the rate of reimbursement for licensed professionals performing inspections on behalf of the board. All reports shall be completed on a form prescribed by the registrar.

(b) As used in this section, "licensed professionals" means, but is not limited to, engineers, architects, landscape architects, and geologists licensed, certificated, or registered pursuant to this division.

7019.1. (a) On and after July 1, 1998, the board shall furnish a copy of any opinion prepared by the licensed professional, including any contractor, retained pursuant to Section 7019, to the complainant, to the licensee against whom the complaint has been made, and, upon request, to the successors, receivers, trustees, executors, administrators, assignees, or guarantors of either party, if directly or collaterally interested under this chapter or otherwise as provided by law.

(b) The opinion specified in subdivision (a) shall include all of the following:

(1) An identification of the nature of the condition that produced the complaint and the cause or basis or contributing cause of that condition.

(2) Whether the cause or basis of the condition complained of constituted a departure from plans, codes, or accepted trade standards.

(3) What the code provisions or trade standards specified in paragraph (2) are.

(4) The cost to correct each item identified under paragraph (2) as being the result of a departure from plans, specifications, codes, or accepted trade standards.

(5) The cost to correct the damages specified in paragraph (4) was established on the following basis:

☐ Time and Materials

☐ Unit Cost

☐ Other (identify) _____

and was calculated from standards provided by

    ☐ Means Data Systems

    ☐ Dodge Data Systems

☐ National Construction Estimator
☐ Marshall-Swift
☐ Software Program (identify) _____
☐ Other (identify) _____

(c) The opinion shall also provide the name, identification, address, license number, and license classification or classifications of the professional who prepared the opinion, and a statement of any other qualifications that the professional asserts he or she relied upon as stated in the industry expert report submitted to the board. The license and other information required to be furnished under this subdivision may be provided on a form prescribed by the registrar.

The opinion shall also state the date or dates of any inspection of the site or other investigation and the date of the report. The board shall endeavor to assure that all items in subdivision (b) that are subject to the pertinent cause of action are completed on the report.

(d) The board shall make the opinion available on, or promptly following, the earliest date upon which the opinion or the information from it is available for the purpose of mediation or the purpose of preparing a citation pursuant to Section 7099, or to any arbitrator or arbitration panel, or the date of service of any accusation pursuant to Section 11505 of the Government Code on any matter upon which the opinion relates.

(e) The board may impose a charge for furnishing a copy of an opinion pursuant to this section to any person except the complainant or the licensee against whom the complaint has been made. The charge shall be reasonably related to the cost of preparing and transmitting that copy and of processing the request.

(f) This section shall become inoperative on July 1, 2000, and, as of January 1, 2001, is repealed, unless a later enacted statute, that becomes operative on or before January 1, 2001, deletes or extends the dates on which it becomes inoperative and is repealed.

7019.5. The board shall contract for a feasibility study relating to the development of a system for joint enforcement actions with respect to contractors by the board, the Department of Industrial Relations, the Employment Development Department, and the Franchise Tax Board. The study should include, but not be limited to, the means of accomplishing the following:

(a) Establishment of a common identification number which may be utilized by all those agencies.

(b) Assessment of the current state of technology in the affected departments.

(c) Assessment of the ability, and any impediments, of the affected departments to share information.

(d) Comparison of the standards of proof in the issuance of citations and other administrative enforcement actions.

(e) Ways to consolidate enforcement actions and procedures among the departments.

7020. The board shall maintain a computerized enforcement tracking system for consumer complaints.

BUSINESS AND PROFESSIONS CODE SECTIONS 7025-7034

7025. "Person" as used in this chapter includes an individual, a firm, copartnership, corporation, association or other organization, or any combination of any thereof.

7026. The term contractor for the purposes of this chapter is synonymous with the term "builder" and, within the meaning of this chapter, a contractor is any person, who undertakes to or offers to undertake to or purports to have the capacity to undertake to or submits a bid to, or does himself or by or through others, construct, alter, repair, add to, subtract from, improve, move, wreck or demolish any building, highway, road, parking facility, railroad, excavation or other structure, project, development or improvement, or to do any part thereof, including the erection of scaffolding or other structures or works in connection therewith, or the cleaning of grounds or structures in connection therewith, and whether or not the performance of work herein described involves the addition to or fabrication into any structure, project, development or improvement herein described of any material or article of merchandise. The term contractor includes subcontractor and specialty contractor.

7026.1.   The term "contractor" includes:

(a) Any person not exempt under Section 7053 who maintains or services air-conditioning, heating, or refrigeration equipment that is a fixed part of the structure to which it is attached.

(b) Any person, consultant to an owner-builder, firm, association, organization, partnership, business trust, corporation, or company, who or which undertakes, offers to undertake, purports to have the capacity to undertake, or submits a bid, to construct any building or home improvement project, or part thereof.

(c) Any person not otherwise exempt by this chapter, who performs tree removal, tree pruning, stump removal, or engages in tree or limb cabling or guying. The term contractor does not include a person performing the activities of a nurseryman who in the normal course of routine work performs incidental pruning of trees, or guying of planted trees and their limbs. The term contractor does not include a gardener who in the normal course of routine work performs incidental pruning of trees measuring less than 15 feet in height after planting.

(d) Any person engaged in the business of drilling, digging, boring, or otherwise constructing, deepening, repairing, reperforating, or abandoning any water well, cathodic protection well, or monitoring well.

7026.2.   (a) For the purposes of this chapter, "contractor" includes any person engaged in the business of the construction, installation, alteration, repair, or preparation for moving of a mobilehome or mobilehome accessory buildings and structures upon a site for the purpose of occupancy as a dwelling.

(b) "Contractor" does not include the manufacturer of the mobilehome or mobilehome accessory building or structure if it is constructed at a place other than the site upon which it is installed for the purpose of occupancy as a dwelling, and does not include the manufacturer when the manufacturer is solely performing work in compliance with the manufacturer's warranty. "Contractor" includes the manufacturer if the manufacturer is engaged in onsite construction, alteration, or repair of a mobilehome or mobilehome accessory buildings and structures pursuant to specialized plans, specifications, or models, or any work other than in compliance with the manufacturer's warranty.

(c) "Contractor" does not include a seller of a manufactured home or mobilehome who holds a retail manufactured home or mobilehome dealer's license under Chapter 7 (commencing with Section 18045) of Part 2 of Division 13 of the Health and Safety Code, if the installation of the manufactured home or mobilehome is to be performed by a licensed contractor and the seller certifies that fact in writing to the buyer prior to the performance of the installation. The certification shall include the name, business address, and contractor's license number of the licensed contractor by whom the installation will be performed.

(d) For the purposes of this chapter, the following terms have the following meanings:

(1) "Mobilehome" means a vehicle defined in Section 18008 of the Health and Safety Code.

(2) "Mobilehome accessory building or structure" means a building or structure defined in Section 18008.5 of the Health and Safety Code.

(3) "Manufactured home" means a structure defined in Section 18007 of the Health and Safety Code.

7026.3. For the purpose of this chapter, "contractor" includes any person who installs or contracts for the installation of carpet wherein the carpet is attached to the structure by any conventional method as determined by custom and usage in the trade; except that a seller of installed carpet who holds a retail furniture dealer's license under Chapter 3 (commencing with Section 19000) of Division 8 shall not be required to have a contractor's license if the installation of the carpet is performed by a licensed contractor and the seller so certifies in writing to the buyer prior to the performance of the installation, which certification shall include the name, business address, and contractor's license number of the licensed contractor by whom the installation will be performed.

7026.12. The installation of a fire protection system, excluding an electrical alarm system, shall be performed only by a contractor holding a fire protection contractor classification as defined in the regulations of the board or by an owner-builder of an owner-occupied, single-family dwelling, if not more than two single-family dwellings on the same parcel are constructed within one year, plans are submitted to and approved by the city, county, or city and county authority, and the city, county, or city and county authority inspects and approves the installation.

7027. Any person who advertises or puts out any sign or card or other device after the effective date of this section which would indicate to the public that he or she is a contractor, or who causes his or her name or business name to be included in a classified advertisement or directory after the effective date of this section under a classification for construction or work of improvement covered by this chapter is subject to the provisions of this chapter regardless of whether his or her operations as a builder are otherwise exempted.

7027.1. (a) It is a misdemeanor for any person to advertise for construction or work of improvement covered by this chapter unless that person holds a valid license under this chapter in the classification so advertised, except that a licensed building or engineering contractor may advertise as a general contractor.

(b) "Advertise," as used in this section, includes, but not by way of limitation, the issuance of any card, sign, or device to any person, the causing, permitting, or allowing of any sign or marking on or in any building or structure, or in any newspaper, magazine, or by airwave transmission, or in any directory under a listing for construction or work of improvement covered by this chapter, with or without any limiting qualifications.

(c) A violation of this section is punishable by a fine of not less than seven hundred dollars ($700) and not more than one thousand dollars ($1,000), which fine shall be in addition to any other punishment imposed for a violation of this section.

(d) If upon investigation, the registrar has probable cause to believe that an unlicensed individual is in violation of this section, the registrar may issue a citation pursuant to Section 7028.7 or 7099.10.

7027.2. Notwithstanding any other provision of this chapter, any person not licensed pursuant to this chapter may advertise for construction work or work of improvement covered by this chapter, provided that he or she shall state in the advertisement that he or she is not licensed under this chapter.

7027.3. Any person, licensed or unlicensed, who willfully and intentionally uses, with intent to defraud, a contractor's license number which does not correspond to the number on a currently valid contractor's license held by that person, is punishable by a fine not exceeding ten thousand dollars ($10,000), or by imprisonment in state prison, or in county jail for not more than one year, or by both the fine and imprisonment. The penalty provided by this section is cumulative to the penalties available under all other laws of this state.

7027.5. A landscape contractor working within the classification for which the license is issued may design systems or facilities for work to be performed and supervised by that contractor.

7028. (a) It is a misdemeanor for any person to engage in the business or act in the capacity of a contractor within this state without having a license therefor, unless such person is particularly exempted from the provisions of this chapter.

(b) If such a person has been previously convicted of the offense described in this section, the court shall impose a fine of 20 percent of the price of the contract under which the unlicensed person performed contracting work, or four thousand five hundred dollars ($4,500), whichever is greater, or imprisonment in the county jail for not less than 10 days nor more than six months, or both.

(c) In the event the person performing the contracting work has agreed to furnish materials and labor on an hourly basis, "the price of the contract" for the purposes of this section means the aggregate sum of the cost of materials and labor furnished and the cost of completing the work to be performed.

(d) Notwithstanding any other provision of law to the contrary, an indictment for any violation of this section by the unlicensed contractor shall be found or an information or complaint filed within four years from the date of the contract proposal, contract, completion, or abandonment of the work, whichever occurs last.

7028.1. It is a misdemeanor for any contractor to perform or engage in asbestos-related work, as defined in Section 6501.8 of the Labor Code, without certification pursuant to Section 7058.5 of this code, or to perform or engage in a removal or remedial action, as defined in subdivision (d) of Section 7058.7, or, unless otherwise exempted by this chapter, to bid for the installation or removal of, or to install or remove, an underground storage tank, without certification pursuant to Section 7058.7. A contractor in violation of this section is subject to one of the following penalties:

(a) Conviction of a first offense is punishable by a fine of not less than one thousand dollars ($1,000) or more than three thousand dollars ($3,000), and by possible revocation or suspension of any contractor's license.

(b) Conviction of a subsequent offense requires a fine of not less than three thousand dollars ($3,000) or more than five thousand dollars ($5,000), or imprisonment in the county jail not exceeding one year, or both the fine and imprisonment, and a mandatory action to suspend or revoke any contractor's license.

7028.2. A criminal complaint pursuant to this chapter may be brought by the Attorney General or by the district attorney or prosecuting attorney of any city, in the municipal court of any county in the state with jurisdiction over the contractor or employer, by reason of the contractor's or employer's act, or failure to act, within that jurisdiction. Any penalty assessed by the court shall be paid to the office of the prosecutor bringing the complaint.

7028.3. In addition to all other remedies, when it appears to the registrar, either upon complaint or otherwise, that a licensee has engaged in, or is engaging in, any act, practice, or transaction which constitutes a violation of this chapter whereby another person may be substantially injured, or that any person, who does not hold a state contractor's license in any classification, has engaged in, or is engaging in, any act, practice, or transaction which constitutes a violation of this chapter, whether or not there is substantial injury, the registrar may, either through the Attorney General or through the district attorney of the county in which the act, practice, or transaction is alleged to have been committed, apply to the superior court of that county or any other county in which such person maintains a place of business or resides, for an injunction restraining such person from acting in the capacity of a contractor without a license in violation of this chapter, or from acting in violation of this chapter when another person may be substantially injured, and, upon a proper showing, a temporary restraining order, a preliminary injunction, or a permanent injunction shall be granted.

7028.4. In addition to the remedies set forth in Section 7028.3, on proper showing by (1) a licensed contractor, or an association of contractors, (2) a consumer affected by the violation, (3) a district attorney, or (4) the Attorney General, of a continuing violation of this chapter by a person who does not hold a state contractor's license in any classification, an injunction shall issue by a court specified in Section 7028.3 at the request of any such party, prohibiting such violation. The plaintiff in any such action shall not be required to prove irreparable injury.

7028.5. It is unlawful for any person who is or has been a member, officer, director or responsible managing officer of a licensed copartnership, corporation, firm, association or other organization to individually engage in the business or individually act in the capacity of a contractor within this State without having a license in good standing to so engage or act.

7028.6. The Registrar of Contractors is hereby empowered to issue citations containing orders of abatement and civil penalties against persons acting in the capacity of or engaging in the business of a contractor within this state without having a license in good standing to so act or engage.

7028.7. If upon inspection or investigation, either upon complaint or otherwise, the registrar has probable cause to believe that a person is acting in the capacity of or engaging in the business of a contractor within this state without having a license in good standing to so act or engage, and the person is not otherwise exempted from this chapter, the registrar shall issue a citation to that person. Within 72 hours of receiving notice that a public entity is intending to award, or has awarded, a contract to an unlicensed contractor, the registrar shall give written notice to the public entity that a citation may be issued if a contract is awarded to an unlicensed contractor. If after receiving the written notice from the registrar the public entity has awarded or awards the contract to an unlicensed contractor the registrar may issue a citation to the responsible officer or employee of the public entity as specified in Section 7028.15. Each citation shall be in writing and shall describe with particularity the basis of the citation. Each citation shall contain an order of abatement and an assessment of a civil penalty in an amount not less than two hundred dollars ($200) nor more than fifteen thousand dollars ($15,000). With the approval of the Contractors' State License Board the registrar shall prescribe procedures for the issuance of a citation under this section. The Contractors' State License Board shall adopt regulations covering the assessment of a civil penalty which shall give due consideration to the gravity of the violation, and any history of previous violations. The sanctions authorized under this section shall be separate from, and in addition to, all other remedies either civil or criminal.

7028.8. Service of a citation issued under Section 7028.7 may be made by certified mail at the last known business address or residence address of the person cited.

7028.9. A citation under Section 7028.7 shall be issued by the registrar within four years after the act or omission that is the basis for the citation.

7028.10. Any person served with a citation under Section 7028.7 may appeal to the registrar within 15 working days after service of the citation with respect to violations alleged, scope of the order of abatement, or amount of civil penalty assessed.

7028.11. If within 15 working days after service of the citation, the person cited fails to notify the registrar that he or she intends to appeal the citation, the citation shall be deemed a final order of the registrar and not subject to review by any court or agency. The 15-day period may be extended by the registrar for good cause.

7028.12. If the person cited under Section 7028.7 timely notifies the registrar that he or she intends to contest the citation, the registrar shall afford an opportunity for a hearing. The registrar shall thereafter issue a decision, based on findings of fact, affirming, modifying, or vacating the citation or directing other appropriate relief. The proceedings under this section shall be conducted in accordance with the provisions of Chapter 5 (commencing with Section 11500) of Part 1 of Division 3 of Title 2 of the Government Code, and the registrar shall have all the powers granted therein.

7028.13. After the exhaustion of the review procedures provided for in Sections 7028.10 to 7028.12, inclusive, the registrar may apply to the appropriate superior court for a judgment in the amount of the civil penalty and an order compelling the cited person to comply with the order of abatement. The application, which shall include a certified copy of the final order of the registrar, shall constitute a sufficient showing to warrant the issuance of the judgment and order.

7028.14. Notwithstanding any other provision of the law, the registrar may waive part of the civil penalty if the person against whom the civil penalty is assessed satisfactorily completes all the requirements for, and is issued, a contractor's license. Any outstanding injury to the public shall be satisfactorily settled prior to issuance of the license.

7028.15. (a) It is a misdemeanor for any person to submit a bid to a public agency in order to engage in the business or act in the capacity of a contractor within this state without having a license therefor, except in any of the following cases:

(1) The person is particularly exempted from this chapter.

(2) The bid is submitted on a state project governed by Section 10164 of the Public Contract Code or on any local agency project governed by Section 20103.5 of the Public Contract Code.

(b) If a person has been previously convicted of the offense described in this section, the court shall impose a fine of 20 percent of the price of the contract under which the unlicensed person performed contracting work, or four thousand five hundred dollars ($4,500), whichever is greater, or imprisonment in the county jail for not less than 10 days nor more than six months, or both.

In the event the person performing the contracting work has agreed to furnish materials and labor on an hourly basis, "the price of the contract" for the purposes of this subdivision means the aggregate sum of the cost of materials and labor furnished and the cost of completing the work to be performed.

(c) This section shall not apply to a joint venture license, as required by Section 7029.1. However, at the time of making a bid as a joint venture, each person submitting the bid shall be subject to this section with respect to his or her individual licensure.

(d) This section shall not affect the right or ability of a licensed architect, land surveyor, or registered professional engineer to form joint ventures with licensed contractors to render services within the scope of their respective practices.

(e) Unless one of the foregoing exceptions applies, a bid submitted to a public agency by a contractor who is not licensed in accordance with this chapter shall be considered nonresponsive and shall be rejected by the public agency. Unless one of the foregoing exceptions applies, a local public agency shall, before awarding a contract or issuing a purchase order, verify that the contractor was properly licensed when the contractor submitted the bid. Notwithstanding any other provision of law, unless one of the foregoing exceptions applies, the registrar may issue a citation to any public officer or employee of a public entity who knowingly awards a contract or issues a purchase order to a contractor who is not licensed pursuant to this chapter. The amount of civil penalties, appeal, and finality of such citations shall be subject to Sections 7028.7 to 7028.13, inclusive. Any contract awarded to, or any purchase order issued to, a contractor who is not licensed pursuant to this chapter is void.

(f) Any compliance or noncompliance with subdivision (e) of this section, as added by Chapter 863 of the Statutes of 1989, shall not invalidate any contract or bid awarded by a public agency during which time that subdivision was in effect.

(g) A public employee or officer shall not be subject to a citation pursuant to this section if the public employee, officer, or employing agency made an inquiry to the board for the purposes of verifying the license status of any person or contractor and the board failed to respond to the inquiry within three business days. For purposes of this section, a telephone response by the board shall be deemed sufficient.

7028.16. Any person who engages in the business or acts in the capacity of a contractor, without having a license therefor, in connection with the offer or performance of repairs to a residential or nonresidential structure for damage caused by a natural disaster for which a state of emergency is proclaimed by the Governor pursuant to Section 8625 of the Government Code, or for which an emergency or major disaster is declared by the President of the United States, shall be punished by a fine up to ten thousand dollars ($10,000), or by imprisonment in the state prison for 16 months, or for two or three years, or by both the fine and imprisonment, or by a fine up to one thousand dollars ($1,000), or by imprisonment in the county jail not exceeding one year, or by both the fine and imprisonment.

7028.17. (a) The failure of an unlicensed individual to comply with a citation after it is final is a misdemeanor.

(b) Notwithstanding Section 1462.5 or 1463 of the Penal Code or any other provision of law, any fine collected upon conviction in a criminal action brought under this section shall be distributed as follows:

(1) If the action is brought by a district attorney, any fine collected shall be paid to the treasurer of the county in which the judgment was entered to be designated for use by the district attorney.

(2) If the action is brought by a city attorney or city prosecutor, any fine collected shall be paid to the treasurer of the city in which the judgment was entered, to be designated for use by the city attorney.

7029. A joint venture license is a license issued to any combination of individuals, corporations, partnerships, or other joint ventures, each of which holds a current, active license in good standing. A joint venture license may be issued in any classification in which at least one of the entities is licensed. An active joint venture license shall be automatically suspended by operation of law during any period in which any member of the entity does not hold a current, active license in good standing.

7029.1. It is unlawful for any two or more licensees, each of whom has been issued a license to act separately in the capacity of a contractor within this state, to be awarded a contract jointly or otherwise act as a contractor without first having secured a joint venture license in accordance with the provisions of this chapter as provided for an individual, partnership or corporation. Any violation of this section shall also constitute a cause for disciplinary action. If a combination of licensees submit a bid for the performance of work for which a joint venture license is required, a failure to obtain that license shall not prevent the imposition of any penalty specified by law for the failure of a contractor who submits a bid to enter into a contract pursuant to the bid.

7029.5. Every plumbing contractor, electrical sign contractor, and well-drilling contractor licensed under this chapter shall have displayed on each side of each motor vehicle used in his or her business, for which a commercial vehicle registration fee has been paid pursuant to Article 3 (commencing with Section 9400) of Chapter 6 of Division 3 of the Vehicle Code, his or her name, permanent business address, and contractor's license number, all in letters and numerals not less than 1 1/2 inches high.

The identification requirements of this section shall also apply to any drill rig used for the drilling of water wells.

Failure to comply with this section constitutes a cause for disciplinary action.

7030. (a) Every person licensed pursuant to this chapter shall include the following statement in at least 10-point type on all written contracts with respect to which the person is a prime contractor:

"Contractors are required by law to be licensed and regulated by the Contractors' State License Board which has jurisdiction to investigate complaints against contractors if a complaint regarding a patent act or omission is filed within four years of the date of the alleged violation. A complaint regarding a latent act or omission pertaining to structural defects must be filed within 10 years of the date of the alleged violation. Any questions concerning a contractor may be referred to the Registrar, Contractors' State License Board, P.O. Box 26000, Sacramento, California 95826."

(b) At the time of making a bid or prior to entering into a contract to perform work on residential property with four or fewer units, whichever occurs first, a contractor shall provide the following notice in capital letters in at least 10-point roman boldface type or in contrasting red print in at least 8-point roman boldface type:

"STATE LAW REQUIRES ANYONE WHO CON-TRACTS TO DO CONSTRUCTION WORK TO BE LICENSED BY THE CONTRACTORS' STATE LI-CENSE BOARD IN THE LICENSE CATEGORY IN WHICH THE CONTRACTOR IS GOING TO BE WORKING—IF THE TOTAL PRICE OF THE JOB IS $300 OR MORE (INCLUDING LABOR AND MATE-RIALS). LICENSED CONTRACTORS ARE REGU-LATED BY LAWS DESIGNED TO PROTECT THE PUBLIC. IF YOU CONTRACT WITH SOMEONE WHO DOES NOT HAVE A LICENSE, THE CON-TRACTORS' STATE LICENSE BOARD MAY BE UN-ABLE TO ASSIST YOU WITH A COMPLAINT. YOUR ONLY REMEDY AGAINST AN UNLICENSED CONTRACTOR MAY BE IN CIVIL COURT, AND YOU MAY BE LIABLE FOR DAMAGES ARISING OUT OF ANY INJURIES TO THE CONTRACTOR OR HIS OR HER EMPLOYEES. YOU MAY CON-TACT THE CONTRACTORS' STATE LICENSE BOARD TO FIND OUT IF THIS CONTRACTOR HAS A VALID LICENSE. THE BOARD HAS COM-PLETE INFORMATION ON THE HISTORY OF LI-CENSED CONTRACTORS, INCLUDING ANY POSSIBLE SUSPENSIONS, REVOCATIONS, JUDG-MENTS, AND CITATIONS. THE BOARD HAS OF-FICES THROUGHOUT CALIFORNIA. PLEASE CHECK THE GOVERNMENT PAGES OF THE WHITE PAGES FOR THE OFFICE NEAREST YOU OR CALL 1-800-321-CSLB FOR MORE INFORMA-TION."

(c) Failure to comply with the notice require-ments set forth in subdivision (a) or (b) of this sec-tion is cause for disciplinary action.

7030.1. (a) A contractor, who has his or her license suspended or revoked two or more times within an eight-year period, shall disclose either in capital let-ters in 10-point roman boldface type or in contrast-ing red print in at least 8-point roman boldface type, in a document provided prior to entering into a con-tract to perform work on residential property with four or fewer units, any disciplinary license suspen-sion, or license revocation during the last eight years resulting from any violation of this chapter by the contractor, whether or not the suspension or revoca-tion was stayed.

(b) The disclosure notice required by this section may be provided in a bid, estimate, or other docu-ment prior to entering into a contract.

(c) A violation of this section is subject to the fol-lowing penalties:

(1) A penalty of one thousand dollars ($1,000) shall be assessed for the first violation.

(2) A penalty of two thousand five hundred dol-lars ($2,500) shall be assessed for the second viola-tion.

(3) A penalty of five thousand dollars ($5,000) shall be assessed for a third violation in addition to a one-year suspension of license by operation of law.

(4) A fourth violation shall result in the revoca-tion of license in accordance with this chapter.

7030.5. Every person licensed pursuant to this chapter shall include his license number in: (a) all construc-tion contracts; (b) subcontracts and calls for bid; and (c) all forms of advertising, as prescribed by the reg-istrar of contractors, used by such a person.

7031. (a) Except as provided in subdivision (d), no person engaged in the business or acting in the ca-pacity of a contractor, may bring or maintain any ac-tion, or recover in law or equity in any action, in any court of this state for the collection of compensation for the performance of any act or contract for which a license is required by this chapter without alleging that he or she was a duly licensed contractor at all times during the performance of that act or contract, regardless of the merits of the cause of action brought by the person, except that this prohibition shall not apply to contractors who are each individu-ally licensed under this chapter but who fail to com-ply with Section 7029.

(b) A security interest taken to secure any pay-ment for the performance of any act or contract for which a license is required by this chapter is unen-forceable if the person performing the act or contract was not a duly licensed contractor at all times during the performance of the act or contract.

(c) If licensure or proper licensure is controverted, then proof of licensure pursuant to this section shall be made by production of a verified certificate of licensure from the Contractors' State License Board which establishes that the individual or entity bringing the action was duly licensed in the proper classification of contractors at all times during the performance of any act or contract covered by the action. Nothing herein shall require any person or entity controverting licensure or proper licensure to produce a verified certificate. When licensure or proper licensure is controverted, the burden of proof to establish licensure or proper licensure shall be on the licensee.

(d) The judicial doctrine of substantial compliance shall not apply under this section where the person who engaged in the business or acted in the capacity of a contractor has never been a duly licensed contractor in this state. However, the court may determine that there has been substantial compliance with licensure requirements under this section if it is shown at an evidentiary hearing that the person who engaged in the business or acted in the capacity of a contractor (1) had been duly licensed as a contractor in this state prior to the performance of the act or contract, (2) acted reasonably and in good faith to maintain proper licensure, and (3) did not know or reasonably should not have known that he or she was not duly licensed. Subdivision (b) of Section 143 does not apply to contractors subject to this subdivision.

(e) The exceptions to the prohibition against the application of the judicial doctrine of substantial compliance found in subdivision (d) shall apply to all contracts entered into on or after January 1, 1992, and to all actions or arbitrations arising therefrom, except that the amendments to subdivisions (d) and (e) enacted during the 1994 portion of the 1993-94 Regular Session of the Legislature shall not apply to either of the following:

(1) Any legal action or arbitration commenced prior to January 1, 1995, regardless of the date on which the parties entered into the contract.

(2) Any legal action or arbitration commenced on or after January 1, 1995, if the legal action or arbitra-

tion was commenced prior to January 1, 1995, and was subsequently dismissed.

7031.5. Each county or city which requires the issuance of a permit as a condition precedent to the construction, alteration, improvement, demolition or repair of any building or structure shall also require that each applicant for such a permit file as a condition precedent to the issuance of a permit a statement which he has prepared and signed stating that the applicant is licensed under the provisions of this chapter, giving the number of the license and stating that it is in full force and effect, or, if the applicant is exempt from the provisions of this chapter, the basis for the alleged exemption.

Any violation of this section by any applicant for a permit shall be subject to a civil penalty of not more than five hundred dollars ($500).

7032. Nothing in this chapter shall limit the power of a city or county to regulate the quality and character of installations made by contractors through a system of permits and inspections which are designed to secure compliance with and aid in the enforcement of applicable state and local building laws, or to enforce other local laws necessary for the protection of the public health and safety. Nothing in this chapter shall limit the power of a city or county to adopt any system of permits requiring submission to and approval by the city or county of plans and specifications for an installation prior to the commencement of construction of the installation.

Cities or counties may direct complaints to the registrar against licensees based upon determinations by city or county enforcement officers of violations by such licensees of codes the enforcement of which is the responsibility of the complaining city or county. Such complaints shall to the extent determined to be necessary by the registrar be given priority in processing over other complaints.

Nothing contained in this section shall be construed as authorizing a city or county to enact regulations relating to the qualifications necessary to engage in the business of contracting.

7033. Every city or city and county which requires the issuance of a business license as a condition precedent to engaging, within the city or city and county, in a business which is subject to regulation under this chapter, shall require that each licensee and each applicant for issuance or renewal of such license shall file, or have on file, with such city or city and county, a signed statement that such licensee or applicant is licensed under the provisions of this chapter and stating that the license is in full force and effect, or, if such licensee or applicant is exempt from the provisions of this chapter, he shall furnish proof of the facts which entitle him to such exemption.

7034. (a) No contractor who is required to be licensed under this chapter shall insert in any contract, or be a party, with a subcontractor who is licensed under this chapter to any contract which contains, a provision, clause, covenant, or agreement which is void or unenforceable under Section 2782 of the Civil Code.

(b) No contractor who is required to be licensed under this chapter shall require a waiver of lien rights from any subcontractor, employee, or supplier in violation of Section 3262 of the Civil Code. ■

Tear-Out Forms

The tear-out forms in this Appendix, with the exception of the Summons and Civil Case Cover Sheet, are also on the disk that accompanies this book. The forms with asterisks may have to be prepared on numbered paper. Check with your court clerk. This paper is available at most stationery stores.

Form	File Name	Chapter/Section
Preliminary Notice	PRELIM	2E
Proof of Service of Preliminary Notice	PRFPREL	2G
Mechanics' Lien Claim Worksheet	MLCWKSHT	3B3
Demand Letter	DEMLTR	3B3
Claim of Mechanics' Lien	MECHCLM	3D
Interest Calculation Worksheet	INTCALC	3D3
Design Professional's Demand Letter	DEPLTR	3H5
Notice of Design Professionals' Lien	PROLIEN	3H6
Partial Release of Lien	PARTREL	3H8
Full Release of Lien	FULLREL	3H8
Stop Notice for Private Works	STOPNOT	4C,5F
Proof of Service of Stop Notice	PRSTOP	4E,5H
Request Notice of Election	REQELECT	5I
Notice to Surety on Payment Bond (also called Notice of Action)	NOTACTN	7F1
Complaint*	COMPLNT	8F
Summons	Form not on disk	8G
Civil Case Cover Sheet	Form not on disk	8G
Notice of Lis Pendens (Pending Action)*	LISPEND	8L
Notice of Completion	NOTCMPLT	9B3
Notice of Cessation	NOTCESS	9B3
Notice of Non-Responsibility	NOTNORES	9B4
Request Letter for Release of Lien	LNRELREQ	11B
Release of Lien	RELIEN	11B
Petition for Release of Lien*	PETITION	11C
Notice of Hearing*	HEARNOT	11D
Decree Releasing Lien*	DECREE	11E
Settlement Letters	SETLTRS	12C
Notice of Credit	CREDIT	12H
Conditional Waiver and Release	CONWVR	12I
Unconditional Waiver and Release	UNCONWVR	12I

California Preliminary Notice

NOTICE TO PROPERTY OWNER

IF BILLS ARE NOT PAID IN FULL FOR THE LABOR, SERVICES, EQUIPMENT OR MATERIALS FURNISHED OR TO BE FURNISHED, A MECHANICS' LIEN LEADING TO THE LOSS, THROUGH COURT FORECLOSURE PROCEEDINGS, OF ALL OR PART OF YOUR PROPERTY BEING SO IMPROVED MAY BE PLACED AGAINST THE PROPERTY EVEN THOUGH YOU HAVE PAID YOUR CONTRACTOR IN FULL. YOU MAY WISH TO PROTECT YOURSELF AGAINST THIS CONSEQUENCE BY (1) REQUIRING YOUR CONTRACTOR TO FURNISH A SIGNED RELEASE BY THE PERSON OR FIRM GIVING YOU THIS NOTICE BEFORE MAKING PAYMENT TO YOUR CONTRACTOR OR (2) ANY OTHER METHOD OR DEVICE THAT IS APPROPRIATE UNDER THE CIRCUMSTANCES. (THIS STATEMENT IS APPLICABLE TO PRIVATE WORKS ONLY.)

Please take notice that _____ ,whose address is at
_____ ,
has furnished or will furnish labor, services, equipment or materials to the work of improvement located at _____
_____ , as
follows:_____
_____
_____ .
_____

Signature   Title   Date

The name and address of the person or business who contracted for the labor, services, equipment or supplies described earlier is _____
_____ .

This preliminary notice is being served on the following persons and businesses at the indicated addresses

☐ Owner

_____
_____ .

☐ Original Contractor

_____
_____ .

[Continued on back]

☐ Construction Lender

_____

_____.

☐ Insurer

_____

_____.

☐ Trust

_____

_____.

☐ Subcontractor

_____

_____.

Estimated price of the labor, services, equipment or materials described above is

$_____.

Proof of Service of Preliminary Notice

I,_____ , declare that I served copies of the
above Preliminary Notice as follows:

☐ On the Owner

    ☐ by personally delivering a copy to _____
        at _____ .

    ☐ by First Class Certified or Registered Mail service, postage prepaid,
        addressed to _____
        at _____
        on _____ .

☐ On the Original (General) Contractor

    ☐ by personally delivering a copy to _____
        at _____ .

    ☐ by First Class Certified or Registered Mail service, postage prepaid,
        addressed to _____
        at _____
        on _____ .

☐ On the Construction Lender or Insurer

    ☐ by personally delivering a copy to _____
        at _____ .

    ☐ by First Class Certified or Registered Mail service, postage prepaid,
        addressed to _____
        at _____
        on _____ .

☐ On the Subcontractor

    ☐ by personally delivering a copy to _____
        at _____ .

    ☐ by First Class Certified or Registered Mail service, postage prepaid,
        addressed to _____
        at _____
        on _____ .

[Continued on back]

☐ On the Express Trust

    ☐ by personally delivering a copy to _____

        at _____.

    ☐ by First Class Certified or Registered Mail service, postage prepaid,
        addressed to _____

        at _____

        on _____.

VERIFICATION [CCP § 446]

I declare under penalty of perjury under the laws of the State of California that the

foregoing is true and correct, this _____ day of _____

at _____, California.

_____

Signature

Mechanics' Lien Claim Worksheet

	Unit 1	Unit 2	Unit 3	Unit 4	Unit 5	Unit 6	Unit 7
Materials	$	$	$	$	$	$	$
Labor	$	$	$	$	$	$	$
Services	$	$	$	$	$	$	$
Equipment	$	$	$	$	$	$	$
Less credits	$	$	$	$	$	$	$
Less offsets	$	$	$	$	$	$	$
Total Due	$	$	$	$	$	$	$

Demand Letter

_____

_____

_____

[name and address of sender]

Date: _____

Re: _____

Dear Owner:

On _____ I served you with a preliminary notice explaining that I had or would be furnishing ☐ labor ☐ services ☐ equipment ☐ materials towards the work of improvement located at

_____

and owned by you. I have in fact furnished such items but have not yet received payment for them. I am currently entitled to receive $_____.

As you know, under the California mechanics' lien law, the property being improved is ultimately responsible for payment of those who contribute to the improvement. I am therefore requesting that you, the owner of the improved property, pay me the amount stated above or agree to meet with me to explore other ways to resolve this issue.

Unfortunately, if I am to preserve my mechanics' lien remedy, time is of the essence. I therefore request that you get back to me within five days of receiving this letter. Otherwise, I will be forced to record a Claim of Mechanics' Lien in the _____ County Recorder's Office against your property. Please understand that even if I have to take that step, I will still be open to settlement discussions.

Sincerely,

_____

Signature

Recording requested by

and when recorded mail
this document to

For recorder's use

_____

Claim of Mechanics' Lien

Name of Claimant: _____

Legal Description of Property Where Work of Improvement Occurred:

_____

_____

_____.

Claimant hereby claims a lien in the real property described above in the following amounts:

☐ Total claim after offsets and credits _____

☐ Total claim of $_____ , allocated after credits and offsets among two or more units as follows: Unit 1 _____ Unit 2 _____ Unit 3 _____ Unit 4 _____.

This claim includes the principal due from _____ , plus interest at the rate of %_____ per annum.

Description of ☐ labor ☐ services ☐ equipment ☐ supplies furnished to be used and actually used in the Work of Improvement: _____

_____

_____

_____.

General Description of Work of Improvement:_____

_____

_____

_____.

[Continued on back]

Name of Party Who Contracted for or Requested Claimant's labor, services, equipment or materials: _____.

Name and Address of Owner of Work of Improvement:

_____

_____

_____.

_____
Signature

VERIFICATION

I, _____, the undersigned, say I am the _____ of the claimant of the foregoing Claim of Mechanics' Lien. I have read said Claim of Mechanics' Lien and know the contents thereof; the same is true of my own knowledge.

I declare under penalty of perjury that the foregoing is true and correct. Executed on _____, at _____, California.

_____
Signature

Interest Calculation Worksheet

A Starting Date	B Ending Date	C No. of Days	D Balance (F from line above)	E Payment	F New Balance (D – E)	G Interest Due (D x ___% x C/360)
						(Sub)total

Design Professional's Demand Letter

_____

_____

_____

[name and address of sender]

Date: _____

Re: _____

Dear Owner,

As you may know, I have contributed ☐ architectural ☐ surveying ☐ engineering services for a planned work of improvement located at

_____

under a written contract dated _____. My services were contributed between the dates of _____ and _____. I have not been paid for these services as required by the contract and you are therefore in default. I hereby demand that you pay me this amount within 10 days, plus interest at 10% per annum. Otherwise I will be forced to record a Design Professionals' Lien against your property.

Sincerely,

_____

Signature

Recording requested by

_____

and when recorded mail
this document to

For recorder's use

_____

Notice of Design Professionals' Lien

_____, Claimant, hereby records a Design
Professionals' Lien against the following property in regard to which Claimant
contributed professional services:

_____

_____

_____.

Amount of claim and lien: $_____, including the principal due from

_____, plus interest at the rate of _____% per annum.

Description of Services:

_____

_____

_____.

Building Permit Information:

_____

_____

_____.

Name and Address of Owner of Property:

_____

_____

_____.

_____

Signature

[Continued on back]

VERIFICATION

I, _____, the undersigned, say I am the

_____ of the claimant of the foregoing Notice of

Design Professionals' Lien. I have read said Notice of Design Professionals' Lien and

know the contents thereof; the same is true of my own knowledge.

I declare under penalty of perjury that the foregoing is true and correct. Executed on

_____ at _____,

California.

_____

Signature

Partial Release of Lien

The Claim of Mechanics' Lien recorded on _____, in

Book ____ of Official Records, page _____, records of _____

County, California, against _____

is hereby partially satisfied and is therefore partially released and discharged

as follows:

_____

_____

_____.

State of _____

County of _____

On _____ , before me, a notary public in and for

said state, personally appeared _____,

personally known to me (or proved to me on the basis of satisfactory evidence)

to be the person(s) whose name(s) is/are subscribed to the within instrument,

and acknowledged to me that he/she/they executed the same in his/her/their

authorized capacity(ies) and that by his/her/their signature(s) on the

instrument the person(s), or the entity upon behalf of which the person(s) acted,

executed the instrument.

_____
Signature of Notary

Full Release of Lien

The Claim of Mechanics' Lien recorded on _____, in

Book _____ of Official Records, page _____, records of _____

County, California, against _____

is hereby fully satisfied and is therefore fully released and discharged.

The property affected by this release is described as follows:

_____

_____

_____.

State of _____

County of _____

On _____ , before me, a notary public in and for said

state, personally appeared _____,

personally known to me (or proved to me on the basis of satisfactory evidence)

to be the person(s) whose name(s) is/are subscribed to the within instrument,

and acknowledged to me that he/she/they executed the same in his/her/their

authorized capacity(ies) and that by his/her/their signature(s) on the

instrument the person(s), or the entity upon behalf of which the person(s) acted,

executed the instrument.

_____

Signature of Notary

Stop Notice for Private Works

☐ To Owner: _____

☐ To Lending Institution: _____

YOU ARE HEREBY NOTIFIED that:

Claimant: _____, who is located at _____

_____,

has contributed ☐ labor ☐ services ☐ equipment ☐ materials

in the amount of $_____

under contract with _____

for the contract price of $_____

to be used and actually used in the work of improvement consisting of

_____

_____

_____

located on the property described as

_____

_____

_____

owned by _____.

Claimant hereby demands that, under Section ☐ 3158 ☐ 3159 of the California Civil Code, you withhold from construction funds under your possession or control the amount of $_____, which amount is due and owning Claimant as of the date of this stop notice.

Dated: _____   Signed: _____

VERIFICATION [CCP § 446]

I declare under penalty of perjury under the laws of the State of California that the foregoing is true and correct, this _____day of _____ at _____

_____, California.

_____

Signature

Proof of Service of Stop Notice

I, _____, declare that I served copies of the above Stop Notice on:

☐ (Owner)

_____

_____

☐ (Lender)

_____

_____

   ☐ by personally delivering a copy to ☐ Owner at _____

_____

   ☐ Lender at _____

_____

   ☐ by First Class Certified or Registered Mail service, postage prepaid, addressed to

      ☐ Owner at _____

      on _____.

      ☐ Lender at _____

      on _____.

VERIFICATION [CCP § 446]

I declare under penalty of perjury under the laws of the State of California that the foregoing is true and correct, this _____day of _____ at _____
_____, California.

_____
Signature

Request Notice of Election

_____

_____

_____

[name and address of sender]

Date: _____

Re: _____

To:_____

Please notify me within 30 days as to whether you intend to withhold the amount claimed in my stop notice served on you on _____, or whether you elect instead to not withhold because of a payment bond taken out by the beneficiary of the construction funds. If you do elect not to withhold, please furnish me with a copy of the payment bond.

Sincerely,

_____
Signature

Notice to Surety on Payment Bond

To: _____

YOU ARE HEREBY NOTIFIED UNDER CIVIL CODE SECTIONS 3240 AND

3241 that _____ (Claimant)

furnished ☐ labor ☐ services ☐ equipment or ☐ materials consisting of

_____

_____

_____

to _____ , to be used and

actually used in the work of improvement consisting of

_____

_____,

located at _____.

The labor, services, equipment or materials described above were to be

furnished for the contractual amount of $_____. The value of the

labor, services, equipment or materials actually furnished ☐ is equal to the

contractual amount ☐ is $_____.

Dated: _____

Signed by Claimant: _____

_____ COURT OF CALIFORNIA, COUNTY OF

STREET ADDRESS:
MAILING ADDRESS:
CITY AND ZIP CODE:
BRANCH NAME:

PETITIONER/PLAINTIFF:

RESPONDENT/DEFENDANT:

COMPLAINT

CASE NUMBER:

Complaint

1. The Plaintiff(s) in This Action Are:

_____

2. Plaintiff(s) License Qualifications

a. ☐ At all relevant times, Plaintiff(s) was duly licensed by the California State Contractor's Licensing Board under the laws of the State of California as

_____.

b. ☐ Plaintiff(s) was not required to be licensed as a condition of providing services or supplying materials to the work of improvement.

3. Defendant(s)

a. ☐ The following persons or entities owe Plaintiff(s) money under a contract for goods or services more completely described in paragraph 5:

_____

_____

_____.

In addition, I name DOES 1 through 5 as Defendant(s) whose identities are currently unknown to me. If Plaintiff(s) later discovers their identity, Plaintiff(s) asks leave to amend this complaint accordingly.

[Continued on back]

b. ☐ The following persons or entities own, reputedly own or have an ownership interest in the real property described in paragraph 5:

_____

_____

_____.

Plaintiff(s) also names Does One through Fifty as Defendant(s) having an interest
in the Property. Plaintiff(s) is ignorant of the true name(s) of Defendant(s) Doe One
to Doe Fifty, inclusive, and is informed and believes that each of said Defendant(s)
claims an interest in the property. Plaintiff(s) therefore asks that when their true
name(s) are discovered this complaint may be amended by inserting their true
name(s) in lieu of said fictitious name(s).

c. ☐ The following persons or entities were served with stop notices under Civil
Code § 3160:

_____

_____

_____.

d. ☐ The following persons or entities, as the Principal and the Surety, are
liable to me for the amount of payment bond $_____:

_____

_____

_____.

4. Agency Relationship

At all times mentioned in this complaint, Defendant(s) other than the owner(s) of
the Property described in Paragraph ____ were the agent(s) and employee(s) of
said owner(s).

5. The Property

The property being improved by the work of improvement relevant to this lawsuit
(Property) is located in the City of _____, County of
_____, California, and legally described as follows:

_____

_____

_____.

[Continued on next page]

6. The Contract

On or about _____, Plaintiff(s) and Defendant(s) entered into an ☐ oral ☐ written agreement in which Plaintiff(s) agreed to ☐ act as general contractor ☐ furnish labor/services/equipment/materials for a work of improvement on the real property described in paragraph 3 for an agreed contract price of $_____, which Defendant(s) _____ _____ agreed to pay. The whole of the real property and the entire estate of Defendant(s) in the real property are required for the convenient use and occupation of the work of improvement.

7. Performance by Plaintiff(s) of Obligations Under the Contract

Between _____ and _____, at the special instance and request of _____, Plaintiff(s) furnished the following services, labor or materials used and intended to be used in a work of improvement on the Property:

_____

_____

_____

☐ Plaintiff(s) has performed all required obligations to be performed under the contract.

☐ Except to the extent prevented and excused by the following actions of Defendant(s), Plaintiff(s) has performed all required obligations to be performed under the contract:

_____

_____

_____.

☐ The contribution to the work of improvement described earlier in this paragraph was in addition to that specified in the contract described in paragraph _____ because of the following change orders:

_____

_____

_____.

[Continued on back]

8. Value of Contribution

The contribution by Plaintiff(s) to the work of improvement described in paragraph 7 was furnished at the reasonable and current market rate of $_____, which Defendant(s) agreed ☐ orally ☐ in writing to pay.

9. Breach of Contract: Non-payment

Defendant(s) described in paragraph 3a have breached the contract described in paragraph 6 in that said Defendant(s) have paid Plaintiff(s) $_____ and no more, and there is due, owing and unpaid since _____, a balance of $_____ plus interest at the legal rate.

10. Attorney Fees

☐ The contract described in paragraph 6 does not provide for the payment of attorney fees.

☐ The contract described in paragraph 6 provides that attorney fees shall be paid in any action brought on the agreement. Plaintiff(s) is entitled to recover reasonable attorney fees incurred in bringing and prosecuting this action, as determined by the court.

☐ 11. First Cause of Action—Breach of Contract

If the above box is checked, as a first cause of action, Plaintiff(s) realleges and incorporates by reference all allegations contained in paragraphs 1 through 10, and further alleges that the Defendant(s) described in paragraph 3a owe Plaintiff(s) the sum of $_____ because of the breach of contract described in paragraph 9.

☐ 12. Second Cause of Action—Enforcement of Mechanics' Lien

If the above box is checked, as a second cause of action, Plaintiff(s) realleges and incorporates by reference all allegations contained in paragraphs 1 through 10 and further alleges as follows:

_____

_____

_____

_____

_____.

[Continued on next page]

13. Preliminary Notices

On or about _____, Plaintiff(s) served the following Defendant(s) with a preliminary 20-day notice (private works) within the time required by law:

_____

_____

_____

Copies of the preliminary notices and proofs of service are attached to this complaint as Exhibit _____.

14. Recording of Claim of Mechanics' Lien

☐ **a. Prime Contractor**

Plaintiff(s) recorded a valid Claim of Mechanics' Lien on _____, in the office of the county recorder of _____ County:

☐ after Plaintiff(s) completed ☐ his ☐ her ☐ their contribution and before the expiration of 90 days after the work of improvement was completed, no notice of completion or cessation having been recorded.

☐ after Plaintiff(s) ceased furnishing ☐ his ☐ her ☐ their contribution to the work of improvement as alleged above, and before the expiration of 60 days after the notice of completion or cessation was recorded.

☐ **b. Other Lien Claimant**

Plaintiff(s) recorded a valid Claim of Mechanics' Lien on _____, in the office of the country recorder of _____ County:

☐ after Plaintiff(s) completed ☐ his ☐ her ☐ their contribution and before the expiration of 90 days after the work of improvement was completed, no notice of completion or cessation having been recorded.

☐ after Plaintiff(s) ceased furnishing ☐ his ☐ her ☐ their contribution to the work of improvement as alleged above and before the expiration of 30 days after the notice of completion or cessation was recorded.

A copy of the recorded Claim of Mechanics' Lien is attached to this complaint as Exhibit ___ and incorporated by reference.

[Continued on back]

15. Costs and Amount Due

At the time Plaintiff(s) recorded the Claim of Mechanics' Lien as described in paragraph 14, the amount shown unpaid on the Claim of Mechanics' Lien was due, owing and unpaid. The cost of verifying and recording the lien claim was $_____, no part of which has been repaid.

☐ 16. Third Cause of Action—Stop Notice

If the above box is checked, as a third cause of action, Plaintiff(s) realleges and incorporates by reference all allegations contained in paragraphs 1 through 13 and further alleges as follows: _____

_____

_____.

17. Service of Stop Notice

On or about _____, at which time there remained due, owing and unpaid to Plaintiff(s) $_____ for ☐ his ☐ her ☐ their contribution furnished to the work of improvement on the Property described in paragraph 5, Plaintiff(s) served on the Defendant(s) described in paragraph 3c a stop notice signed and verified by Plaintiff(s).

☐ The stop notice was accompanied by a bond with good and sufficient sureties conforming to the requirements of Civil Code § 3083. Plaintiff(s) expended $_____ as an annual premium on the bond.

A copy of the stop notice and proof of service is attached to this Complaint as Exhibit ___ and is incorporated by reference.

18. Funds Due or to Become Due

At the time the stop notice was served, on information and belief, the Defendant(s) described in paragraph 3c had in their possession or in their control funds earmarked to pay construction costs on the work of improvement and therefore due or to become due to the Plaintiff(s) in an amount unknown to Plaintiff(s) but known to Defendant(s).

[Continued on next page]

☐ **19. Fourth Cause of Action—Payment Bond**

If the above box is checked, as a fourth cause of action, Plaintiff(s) realleges and incorporates by reference all allegations contained in paragraphs 1 through 13 and further alleges as follows:

_____

_____

_____

_____

_____

_____.

Plaintiff(s) is informed and believes and on the basis of such information and belief alleges that the Defendant(s) described in paragraph 3d, as principals and sureties, executed a payment bond in connection with the work of improvement on the Property described in paragraph 5. The bond provides for payment in full of the claims of all claimants and is by its terms made to inure to the benefit of all claimants to give them a right of action to recover on the bond in this action.

20. Prerequisites to Action on Payment Bond

Plaintiff(s):

☐ has recorded a Claim of Mechanics' Lien as described in the Second Cause of Action of this Complaint.

☐ gave written notice to _____ before expiration of the time for recording a Claim of Mechanics' Lien, a copy of which is attached to this Complaint as Exhibit _____ and incorporated by reference.

WHEREFORE, Plaintiff(s) demands judgment as follows:

☐ For Breach of Contract:

Judgment against the Defendant(s), and each of them, described in paragraph 3a for $_____ in favor of Plaintiff(s), together with interest provided by law from _____ until paid, plus costs and ☐ reasonable attorneys fees.

[Continued on back]

☐ For Foreclosure of Mechanics' Lien

That the sum of $_____, together with interest provided by law until paid and the further sum of $_____ for verifying and recording the Claim of Mechanics' Lien and Plaintiff(s)'s costs in bringing this action, be adjudged and decreed to be a lien on the real property described in paragraph _____ of this Complaint.

That the demands of Plaintiff(s) and all persons having claims of lien, or any interest in the Property described in paragraph 5 of this complaint, be ascertained and adjudged, and that the interests of Defendant(s) described in paragraph 3b and any persons claiming under these Defendant(s) be sold under the decree of this court to satisfy the amount of the liens ascertained and adjudged in favor of Plaintiff(s).

That, if any deficiency results from the sale of the real property under this court's decree, the Plaintiff(s) have judgment for such deficiency against the Defendant(s)

_____.

That the court clerk be directed to docket and enter the personal judgment for breach of contract demanded in this prayer independently of any deficiency judgment that may be entered after sale of the real property under the court's decree.

☐ For Enforcement of Stop Notice

That Plaintiff's stop notice claim in the amount of $_____, ☐ including the premium on Plaintiff's stop notice bond, together with Plaintiff(s)'s costs incurred in bringing this action, be decreed to be an equitable garnishment and lien on the funds that Defendant(s) described in paragraph 3c had in ☐ his ☐ her ☐ its ☐ their possession at the time of service of the stop notice alleged in paragraph 17 of this Complaint, and that a trust be imposed on such funds for the benefit of Plaintiff(s), and that Plaintiff(s) have judgment against Defendant(s) for the amount so adjudged, and if it is determined that Defendant(s) improperly disbursed any part of such funds, and that there now are inadequate funds because of such disbursement to satisfy Plaintiff(s)'s claim in full, that Plaintiff(s) have a personal judgment against Defendant(s) for whatever amount has been improperly disbursed.

[Continued on next page]

☐ For Recovery under Payment Bond

Judgment under Payment Bond #_____against Defendant(s)
_____ for $_____ in favor of
Plaintiff(s), together with interest provided by law from _____
until paid, plus costs and ☐ reasonable attorneys fees.

For such other relief as the court considers just and proper.

Dated: _____   Signed: _____

SUMMONS
(CITACION JUDICIAL)

NOTICE TO DEFENDANT: *(Aviso a Acusado)*

FOR COURT USE ONLY
(SOLO PARA USO DE LA CORTE)

YOU ARE BEING SUED BY PLAINTIFF:
(A Ud. le está demandando)

You have *30 CALENDAR DAYS* after this summons is served on you to file a typewritten response at this court.	*Después de que le entreguen esta citación judicial usted tiene un plazo de 30 DIAS CALENDARIOS para presentar una respuesta escrita a máquina en esta corte.*
A letter or phone call will not protect you; your typewritten response must be in proper legal form if you want the court to hear your case.	*Una carta o una llamada telefónica no le ofrecerá protección; su respuesta escrita a máquina tiene que cumplir con las formalidades legales apropiadas si usted quiere que la corte escuche su caso.*
If you do not file your response on time, you may lose the case, and your wages, money and property may be taken without further warning from the court.	*Si usted no presenta su respuesta a tiempo, puede perder el caso, y le pueden quitar su salario, su dinero y otras cosas de su propiedad sin aviso adicional por parte de la corte.*
There are other legal requirements. You may want to call an attorney right away. If you do not know an attorney, you may call an attorney referral service or a legal aid office (listed in the phone book).	*Existen otros requisitos legales. Puede que usted quiera llamar a un abogado inmediatamente. Si no conoce a un abogado, puede llamar a un servicio de referencia de abogados o a una oficina de ayuda legal (vea el directorio telefónico).*

CASE NUMBER: *(Número del Caso)*

The name and address of the court is: *(El nombre y dirección de la corte es)*

The name, address, and telephone number of plaintiff's attorney, or plaintiff without an attorney, is:
(El nombre, la dirección y el número de teléfono del abogado del demandante, o del demandante que no tiene abogado, es)

DATE: Clerk, by _____ , Deputy
(Fecha)   *(Actuario)*   *(Delegado)*

[SEAL]

NOTICE TO THE PERSON SERVED: You are served
1. ☐ as an individual defendant.
2. ☐ as the person sued under the fictitious name of *(specify)*:

3. ☐ on behalf of *(specify)*:

under: ☐ CCP 416.10 (corporation)   ☐ CCP 416.60 (minor)
       ☐ CCP 416.20 (defunct corporation)   ☐ CCP 416.70 (conservatee)
       ☐ CCP 416.40 (association or partnership) ☐ CCP 416.90 (individual)
       ☐ other:
4. ☐ by personal delivery on *(date)*:

Form Adopted by Rule 982
Judicial Council of California
982(a)(9) [Rev. January 1, 1984]

(See reverse for Proof of Service)
SUMMONS

CCP 412.20

[Continued on back]

PROOF OF SERVICE — SUMMONS
(Use separate proof of service for each person served)

1. I served the
   a. ☐ summons ☐ complaint ☐ amended summons ☐ amended complaint
      ☐ completed and blank Case Questionnaires ☐ Other *(specify)*:
   b. on defendant *(name)*:

   c. by serving ☐ defendant ☐ other *(name and title or relationship to person served)*:

   d. ☐ by delivery ☐ at home ☐ at business
      (1) date:
      (2) time:
      (3) address:

   e. ☐ by mailing
      (1) date:
      (2) place:

2. Manner of service *(check proper box)*:
   a. ☐ **Personal service.** By personally delivering copies. (CCP 415.10)
   b. ☐ **Substituted service on corporation, unincorporated association (including partnership), or public entity.** By leaving, during usual office hours, copies in the office of the person served with the person who apparently was in charge and thereafter mailing (by first-class mail, postage prepaid) copies to the person served at the place where the copies were left. (CCP 415.20(a))
   c. ☐ **Substituted service on natural person, minor, conservatee, or candidate.** By leaving copies at the dwelling house, usual place of abode, or usual place of business of the person served in the presence of a competent member of the household or a person apparently in charge of the office or place of business, at least 18 years of age, who was informed of the general nature of the papers, and thereafter mailing (by first-class mail, postage prepaid) copies to the person served at the place where the copies were left. (CCP 415.20(b)) *(Attach separate declaration or affidavit stating acts relied on to establish reasonable diligence in first attempting personal service.)*
   d. ☐ **Mail and acknowledgment service.** By mailing (by first-class mail or airmail, postage prepaid) copies to the person served, together with two copies of the form of notice and acknowledgment and a return envelope, postage prepaid, addressed to the sender. (CCP 415.30) *(Attach completed acknowledgment of receipt.)*
   e. ☐ **Certified or registered mail service.** By mailing to an address outside California (by first-class mail, postage prepaid, requiring a return receipt) copies to the person served. (CCP 415.40) *(Attach signed return receipt or other evidence of actual delivery to the person served.)*
   f. ☐ Other *(specify code section)*:
      ☐ additional page is attached.

3. The "Notice to the Person Served" (on the summons) was completed as follows (CCP 412.30, 415.10, and 474):
   a. ☐ as an individual defendant.
   b. ☐ as the person sued under the fictitious name of *(specify)*:
   c. ☐ on behalf of *(specify)*:
      under: ☐ CCP 416.10 (corporation)   ☐ CCP 416.60 (minor)   ☐ other:
             ☐ CCP 416.20 (defunct corporation) ☐ CCP 416.70 (conservatee)
             ☐ CCP 416.40 (association or partnership) ☐ CCP 416.90 (individual)
   d. ☐ by personal delivery on *(date)*:

4. At the time of service I was at least 18 years of age and not a party to this action.

5. Fee for service: $

6. Person serving:
   a. ☐ California sheriff, marshal, or constable.
   b. ☐ Registered California process server.
   c. ☐ Employee or independent contractor of a registered California process server.
   d. ☐ Not a registered California process server.
   e. ☐ Exempt from registration under Bus. & Prof. Code 22350(b).

   f. Name, address and telephone number and, if applicable, county of registration and number:

I declare under penalty of perjury under the laws of the State of California that the foregoing is true and correct.

(For California sheriff, marshal, or constable use only)
I certify that the foregoing is true and correct.

Date:

Date:

▶ _____
(SIGNATURE)

▶ _____
(SIGNATURE)

982(a)(9) [Rev. January 1, 1984]

ATTORNEY OR PARTY WITHOUT ATTORNEY (Name and Address):	TELEPHONE NO.:	FOR COURT USE ONLY

ATTORNEY FOR (Name):

INSERT NAME OF COURT, JUDICIAL DISTRICT, AND BRANCH COURT, IF ANY:

CASE NAME:

CIVIL CASE COVER SHEET (Case Cover Sheets)	CASE NUMBER:

1. ☐ Case category (Insert code from list below for the ONE case type that best describes the case):

01 Abuse of Process
02 Administrative Agency Review
03 Antitrust/Unfair Business Practices
04 Asbestos
05 Asset Forfeiture
06 Breach of Contract/Warranty
07 Business Tort
08 Civil Rights (Discrimination, False Arrest)
09 Collections (Money Owed, Open Book Accounts)
10 Construction Defect
11 Contractual Arbitration
12 Declaratory Relief
13 Defamation (Slander, Libel)
14 Eminent Domain/Inverse Condemnation
15 Employment (Labor Commissioner Appeals, EDD Actions, Wrongful Termination)
16 Fraud
17 Injunctive Relief

18 Insurance Coverage/Subrogation
19 Intellectual Property
20 Enforcement of Judgment (Sister State, Foreign, Out-of-Country Abstracts)
21 Partnership and Corporate Governance
22 PI/PD/WD—Auto (Personal Injury/Property Damage/ Wrongful Death)
23 PI/PD/WD—Nonauto
24 Product Liability
25 Professional Negligence (Medical or Legal Malpractice, etc.)
26 Real Property (Quiet Title)
27 RICO
28 Securities Litigation
29 Tax Judgment
30 Toxic Tort/Environmental
31 Unlawful Detainer—Commercial
32 Unlawful Detainer—Residential
33 Wrongful Eviction
34 Other: _____

2. Type of remedies sought (check all that apply): a. ☐ Monetary b. ☐ Nonmonetary c. ☐ Punitive
3. Number of causes of action:
4. Is this a class action suit? ☐ Yes ☐ No

Date:

▶

....
(TYPE OR PRINT NAME)

_____
(SIGNATURE OF PARTY OR ATTORNEY FOR PARTY)

NOTE TO PLAINTIFF

- This cover sheet shall accompany each civil action or proceeding, except those filed in small claims court or filed under the Probate Code, Family Law Code, or Welfare and Institutions Code.
- File this cover sheet in addition to any cover sheet required by local court rule.
- Do not serve this cover sheet with the complaint.
- This cover sheet shall be used for statistical purposes only and shall have no effect on the assignment of the case.

Form Adopted by Rule 982.2
Judicial Council of California
982.2(b)(1) [New July 1, 1996]

CIVIL CASE COVER SHEET
(Case Cover Sheets)

Notice of Pending Action, CCP § 409

NOTICE IS HEREBY GIVEN that the above-entitled action concerning and affecting real property as described below was commenced on _____, in the above-named Court by Plaintiff(s) _____ against the Defendant(s) _____ and Does 1 through 5 inclusive. The action is now pending in the _____ *[name of court and county]*, State of California.

The action affects title to real property situated in _____ *[name of county]*, State of California, and is legally described as follows:

_____

_____

_____.

The object of this action is to enforce the Claim of Mechanics' Lien by Plaintiff(s) against the property described above.

Dated:_____   Signature:_____

VERIFICATION [CCP § 446]

I declare under penalty of perjury under the laws of the State of California that the foregoing is true and correct, this _____ day of _____ at _____, California.

_____

Signature

Notice of Completion

State of California

County of _____

NOTICE IS HEREBY GIVEN THAT:

1. I am ☐ the owner of a fee simple interest ☐ the purchaser under contract ☐ the lessee of real property (Property) described in paragraph 5.

2. The full names and addresses of the owner or co-owners of Property are:

a. _____

_____

b. _____

_____

c. _____

_____.

3. On the day of _____ a work of improvement on Property was completed as follows: _____

_____

_____.

4. The name of the original (prime, general) contractor for the work of improvement as a whole was: _____.

5. The Property is situated in the City of _____, County of _____, State of California and described as follows: _____

_____

_____

_____.

6. The street address of Property is: _____

_____.

By: _____

VERIFICATION [CCP § 446]
I declare under penalty of perjury under the laws of the State of California that the foregoing is true and correct, this _____day of _____ at _____, California.

_____
Signature

Notice of Cessation

State of California

County of _____

NOTICE IS HEREBY GIVEN THAT:

1. I am ☐ the owner of a fee simple interest ☐ the purchaser under contract ☐ the lessee of real property (Property) described in Paragraph 5.

2. The full names and addresses of the owner or co-owners of Property are:

a. _____

_____

b. _____

_____

c. _____

_____.

3. A cessation from labor on a work of improvement on Property commenced on or about the _____ day of _____, and the cessation from labor has continued for a period of more than 30 days and until the date of this notice.

4. The name of the original (prime, general) contractor for the work of improvement as a whole was: _____.

5. The Property is situated in the City of _____, County of _____, State of California and described as follows:

_____

_____

_____.

6. The street address of Property is: _____

_____.

By: _____

VERIFICATION [CCP § 446]

I declare under penalty of perjury under the laws of the State of California that the foregoing is true and correct, this _____ day of _____ at _____, California.

_____

Signature

Notice of Non-Responsibility

TO WHOM IT MAY CONCERN:

NOTICE IS HEREBY GIVEN that _____ is the

owner ☐ in fee simple ☐ _____ (other type of

ownership) of real property (Property) situated in _____,

_____ County, described as follows: _____

_____

_____

_____.

The name of the ☐ contract purchaser ☐ lessee of Property is _____

_____.

Within the previous 10 days I obtained knowledge that a work of improvement best

described as _____

has been commenced (is being made) upon Property.

The Provider of Notice will not be responsible for this work of improvement, nor for the

payment of any labor, services or materials used or to be used in connection with this

work of improvement.

_____

Signature of Owner or Other Provider of Notice

VERIFICATION

I, _____, say that this notice is a true copy of a

notice posted at _____ in

the City of _____, County of _____, State of California,

on the day of _____, by _____

and that the facts stated in this notice are true of my own knowledge.

I declare under penalty of perjury that the foregoing is true and correct and that this

document was executed at _____, California, on

_____.

_____

Signature

Request Letter for Release of Lien

_____

_____

_____

[name and address of sender]

Date: _____

Re: Mechanics' lien on my property

Dear _____,

On _____ you recorded a Claim of Mechanics' Lien
against my property at the _____ County
Recorder's Office. It is now _____, more than 90 days
since that recording date. Because you have not filed an action to enforce the
mechanics' lien within the 90-day period set by law (Civil Code § 3144), your
lien is null and void. I would now like to have the lien removed from my
property record.

The easiest way for this to happen is for you to sign the enclosed Release of
Lien before a notary public and return it to me. I'll then record the Release, and
the lien will be removed from my property record.

If you are unwilling to sign the enclosed Release of Lien before a notary and
return it to me, I'll be forced to petition the court to order the lien released.
Please be aware that the law allows me to collect attorney fees up to $1,000
from you if I am successful in that action.

I hope we can resolve this without involving the court. Please let me know your
intentions no later than 10 days from the date of this letter.

Sincerely,

_____

Release of Lien

That certain Claim of Mechanics' Lien recorded _____, in Book _____ of Official Records, page _____, records of _____ County, California, against _____ is hereby fully satisfied, released and discharged.

The property affected by this release is described as follows: *(Same description that is on the recorded Claim of Mechanics' Lien)*

_____

_____

_____

_____.

Date:_____   Signature: _____

VERIFICATION [CCP § 446]

I declare under penalty of perjury under the laws of the State of California that the foregoing is true and correct, this _____day of _____ at _____, California.

_____

Signature

PARTY WITHOUT ATTORNEY (Name and Address):	MY TELEPHONE NO:	FOR COURT USE ONLY

_____ **COURT OF CALIFORNIA, COUNTY OF**

STREET ADDRESS:

MAILING ADDRESS:

CITY AND ZIP CODE:

BRANCH NAME:

PETITIONER/PLAINTIFF:

RESPONDENT/DEFENDANT:

PETITION FOR RELEASE OF LIEN	CASE NUMBER:

Petition for Release of Lien

I. Petitioner and Respondent

Petitioner _____ is the ☐ owner ☐ owner of an interest in the property described in paragraph II. Respondent (Lien Claimant) is, and at all times herein mentioned was, a:

    ☐ corporation organized and existing under the laws of _____.

    ☐ limited liability company organized and existing under the laws of

    _____.

    ☐ partnership existing under the laws of _____.

    ☐ sole proprietor or individual residing in the county of _____.

II. The Property

The property that is the subject of this petition is described as follows:

_____

_____

_____.

III. The Claim of Mechanics' Lien

On or about _____, Lien Claimant caused to be recorded in the Official Records of the County of _____, Book____, page_____, a duly verified Claim of Mechanics' Lien against the Property. A copy of the Claim of Mechanics' Lien is attached hereto as Exhibit A and made a part hereof.

IV. No Foreclosure Action Filed nor Extension of Credit Granted

No action has been filed to foreclose the lien, no extension of credit has been recorded and the time period during which suit can be brought to foreclose the lien has expired.

[Continued on back]

V. Lien Claimant's Non-Cooperation

Lien Claimant _____ is ☐ unable ☐ unwilling to
execute a release of the lien in that _____
_____
_____,
or ☐ Lien Claimant cannot with reasonable diligence be found in that _____
_____
_____.

VI. No Bankruptcy or Restraint

Petitioner has not filed for relief under any law governing bankrupts, and Petitioner
knows of no other restraint that exists to prevent the lien claimant from filing to foreclose
his or her lien.

VII. Attorney Fees

Petitioner ☐ has not ☐ has incurred attorney's fees in bringing and
prosecuting this petition.

VERIFICATION [CCP §§ 446, 2015.5]
I, _____, am the petitioner in this proceeding. I have read
the foregoing petition and know the contents thereof. The same is true of my own
knowledge, except as to those matters which are therein alleged on information and
belief, and, as to those matters, I believe it to be true.

I declare under penalty of perjury under the laws of the State of California that the
foregoing is true and correct, this _____ day of _____ at
_____, California.

_____
Signature

To Respondent _____

Please take notice that on _____, Petitioner _____

_____ will appear at the time and place noticed earlier and request that the honorable court order the release of the Mechanics' Lien on property located at _____.

This request will be based on the Petition to Release Property From Mechanics' Lien attached to this Notice of Hearing, and on the evidence and arguments to be introduced in the hearing.

Dated: _____   Signed:_____

PARTY WITHOUT ATTORNEY (Name and Address): MY TELEPHONE NO:	FOR COURT USE ONLY
_____ **COURT OF CALIFORNIA, COUNTY OF** STREET ADDRESS: MAILING ADDRESS: CITY AND ZIP CODE: BRANCH NAME: PETITIONER/PLAINTIFF: RESPONDENT/DEFENDANT:	
DECREE RELEASING LIEN [§ 3154]	CASE NUMBER:

Decree Releasing Lien [§ 3154]

This proceeding came on for hearing before the court on _____,
the Honorable _____ presiding. Petitioner appeared
☐ in pro persona ☐ by counsel _____, and
Respondent appeared ☐ in pro persona ☐ by counsel _____.

Having considered the evidence introduced and the argument of ☐ the parties ☐
counsel, the Court finds as follows:

1. A copy of the petition and of the order fixing this hearing were served on
respondent in compliance with law;

2. On _____, a claim of lien was recorded in the office of
the Recorder of _____County, California, in Book _____ of
Official Records, against the following described property: _____
_____
_____; and

3. No action has been filed to foreclose the lien, no extension of credit has been
recorded and the time period during which suit can be brought to foreclose the lien has
expired.

WHEREFORE, IT IS ADJUDGED AND DECREED that, on recordation of a certified copy
of this decree, the above-described property is released from the claim of lien of
respondent herein.

IT IS FURTHER ADJUDGED AND DECREED that petitioner have and recover from
respondent the sum of $_____ as attorney's fees incurred in this proceeding.

Dated:_____   JUDGE_____

Settlement Letter:
From General Contractor to Owner

_____

_____

_____

[name and address of sender]

Date: _____

Re: _____

Dear Owner:

When it recently became clear that our bill was not getting paid, we felt it prudent to record a mechanics' lien against your property. To keep the mechanics' lien alive we will have to file an enforcement action in court no later than _____, unless, of course, we are able to settle this matter among ourselves.

Certainly there have been some serious misunderstandings along the way. To get negotiations started, we would like to briefly describe how we understood our agreements when we first decided to work together on this project, and how things changed as we got into the job. Then we would like to know how you see the situation. Would you be willing to review the following factual chronology of key events and make notes on where you think we are not seeing things clearly? It's important to us to understand your perspective on this.

_____

_____

_____

_____

_____

_____.

We want to work something out that feels fair to you. At this stage we still control the outcome of this ourselves and have a common interest in avoiding a legal fight with an unknown ending handed down by a court (or arbitrator). I'm convinced that we can work out something we can all live with. We look forward to hearing from you in the next week.

Sincerely,

_____

Signature

Settlement Letter:
From Subcontractor or Materials Supplier to Owner

_____

_____

_____

[name and address of sender]

Date: _____

Re: _____

Dear Owner:

When it recently became clear that our bill was not getting paid we felt it prudent to record a mechanics' lien against your property. To keep the mechanics' lien alive we will have to file an enforcement action in court no later than _____, unless, of course, we are able to settle this matter among ourselves.

Towards that end, we would like to briefly describe our view of the situation:

_____

_____

_____

_____

_____

_____.

At this stage we still control the outcome of this dispute ourselves and have a common interest in avoiding a legal fight with an unknown ending handed down by a court (or arbitrator). I'm convinced that we can work out something we can both live with. We look forward to hearing from you in the next week.

Sincerely,

_____

Signature

Settlement Letter:
From Owner to General Contractor

_____

_____

_____

[name and address of sender]

Date: _____

Re: _____

Dear General Contractor:

We recently learned that you have recorded a mechanics' lien against our property. In the hope that we can settle this matter without further legal proceedings, we would welcome an opportunity to meet with you.

To get negotiations started, we would like to briefly describe how we understood our agreements when we first decided to work together on this project, and how things changed as we got into the job. Then we would like to know how you see the situation. Would you be willing to review the following chronology of key events and make notes on where you think we are not seeing things clearly? It's important to us to understand your perspective on this.

_____

_____

_____

_____

_____

_____

We want to work something out that feels fair to you. At this stage we still control the outcome of this ourselves and have a common interest in avoiding a legal fight with an unknown ending handed down by a court (or arbitrator). I'm convinced that we can work out something we can all live with. We look forward to hearing from you in the next week.

Sincerely,

_____

Signature

Settlement Letter:
From Subcontractor or Materials Supplier to General Contractor or Subcontractor

_____

_____

_____

[name and address of sender]

Date: _____

Re: _____

Dear _____,

As you know, I have not been paid for my _____,
contributed to the work of improvement on the property located at:

_____

on _____.

Unless we can settle this matter I will be forced to file a lawsuit in the near future to enforce my remedies, which would include a breach of contract claim against you.

As a first step to settlement, I would like to briefly describe how I interpret our contract and how things changed as we got into the job. Then I would like to know how you see the situation. Would you be willing to review the following chronology of key events and make notes on where you think I am not seeing things clearly? It's important to me to understand your perspective on this.

_____

_____

_____

_____

_____

_____

I want to work something out that feels fair to you. Because I would also be proceeding against the owner's property in any lawsuit that I file, I think the best approach would be for you, the owner and me to sit down and reach a solution that is satisfactory to all of us.

[Continued on back]

At this stage we still control the outcome of this dispute ourselves and have a common interest in avoiding a legal fight with an unknown ending handed down by a court (or arbitrator). I'm convinced that we can work out something we can all live with. We look forward to hearing from you in the next week.

Sincerely,

_____

Signature

cc: Owner

Extension of Time to Enforce Lien
and Notice of Credit

_____ (Claimant) and _____
(Owner) agree as follows:

1. On _____ , Claimant recorded a Claim of Mechanics' Lien
for $_____ in Book _____ , Page _____ of Official Records in the Office
of the County Recorder of _____ County, State of California
against the following property:

_____

_____

_____ .

2. To preserve his/her Claim of Mechanics' Lien, Claimant must file a lawsuit to
enforce Claimant's Claim of Mechanics' Lien in the near future unless Owner is willing
to extend the time for filing such lawsuit by agreeing to a credit in the manner
permitted in Section 3144 of the California Civil Code.

3. Owner and Claimant agree that a credit of _____ days from and after the
date this agreement is signed shall be given, and Claimant's Claim of Mechanics' Lien
shall be extended for a period of 90 days after the credit period expires.

4. Owner waives any and all right to object to a lawsuit brought by Claimant to
foreclose on Claimant's Claim of Mechanics' Lien if the lawsuit is filed within the period
of time permitted by this Notice of Credit.

5. Owner waives the right to raise any statute of limitations defense against an action
brought by Claimant to foreclose Claimant's Claim of Mechanics' Lien.

Dated: _____   Signed: _____

Conditional Waiver and Release
Upon Final Payment

Upon receipt by the undersigned of a check from _____

in the sum of $_____ payable to _____,

and when the check has been properly endorsed and has been paid by the

bank upon which it is drawn, this document shall become effective to release

any mechanics' lien, stop notice or bond right the undersigned has on the job

of _____ located at _____

_____.

This release covers the final payment to the undersigned for all labor, services,

equipment or materials furnished on the job, except for disputed claims for

additional work in the amount of $_____. Before any recipient of

this document relies on it, the party should verify evidence of payment to the

undersigned.

Dated: _____

_____

[Company Name]

By: _____

[Title]

Unconditional Waiver and Release
Upon Final Payment

The undersigned has been paid in full for all labor, services, equipment or materials furnished to _____ on the job of

_____ located at _____

_____ and does hereby waive and release any right to a mechanics' lien, stop notice or any right against a labor and material bond on the job, except for disputed claims for extra work in the amount of $_____.

Dated: _____

_____

[Company Name]

By: _____
[Title]

NOTICE: THIS DOCUMENT WAIVES RIGHTS UNCONDITIONALLY AND STATES THAT YOU HAVE BEEN PAID FOR GIVING UP THOSE RIGHTS. THIS DOCUMENT IS ENFORCEABLE AGAINST YOU IF YOU SIGN IT, EVEN IF YOU HAVE NOT BEEN PAID. IF YOU HAVE NOT BEEN PAID, USE A CONDITIONAL RELEASE FORM.

Using the Forms Disk

The forms on the accompanying disk are the same as in Appendix B. Sections A and B below tell you how to copy the forms onto your computer and how to use them to create your documents.

The disk does not contain software, and you do not need to install any files. The forms disk contains only files that can be opened and edited using a word processor. This is not a software program. See below and the README.TXT file included on the disk for additional instructions on how to use these files.

How to View the README File

If you do not know how to view the file README.TXT, insert the forms disk into your computer's floppy disk drive and follow these instructions:

- Windows 95: (1) On your PC's desktop, double-click the My Computer icon; (2) double-click the icon for the floppy disk drive into which the forms disk was inserted; (3) double-click the file README.TXT.

- Windows 3.1: (1) Open File Manager; (2) double-click the icon for the floppy disk drive into which the forms disk was inserted; (3) double-click the file README.TXT.

- Macintosh: (1) On your Mac desktop, double-click the icon for the floppy disk that you inserted; (2) double-click the file README.TXT.

- DOS: At the DOS prompt, type EDIT A:README.TXT and press the Enter key.

While the README file is open, print it out by using the Print command in the File menu.

A. COPYING THE DISK FILES ONTO YOUR COMPUTER

Before you do anything else, copy the files from the forms disk onto your hard disk. Then work on these copies only. This way the original files and instructions will be untouched and can be used again. Instructions on how to copy files are provided below. In accordance with U.S. copyright laws, remember that copies of the disk and its files are for your personal use only.

Insert the forms disk and do the following:

1. Windows 95 Users

(These instructions assume that the A: drive is the source you want to copy from and that the C: drive is the location you want to copy the files to.)

Step 1.   Double-click the My Computer icon to open the My Computer window.

Step 2.   Double-click the A: drive icon in the My Computer window to open the drive window.

Step 3.   First, choose Select All from the Edit menu (Ctrl+A). Then choose Copy from the Edit menu (Ctrl+C). Then close the drive window.

Step 4.   Double-click the My Computer icon to open the My Computer window.

Step 5.   Double-click the C: drive icon in the My Computer window to open the drive window.

Step 6.   Choose New... from the File menu, then choose Folder to create a new, untitled folder on the C: drive.

Step 7.   Type "Mechanics Liens" to rename the
            untitled folder.
Step 8.   Double-click on the "Mechanics Liens"
            folder icon to open that folder.
Step 9.   Choose Paste from the Edit menu (Ctrl+V).

2. Windows 3.1 Users

(These instructions assume that the A: drive is the
source you want to copy from and that the C: drive is
the location you want to copy the files to.)

Step 1.   Open File Manager.
Step 2.   Double-click the A: drive icon at the top of
            the File Manager window.
Step 3.   Choose Select Files... from the File menu to
            open the Select Files dialog box.
Step 4.   First, click the Select button to select all the
            files on the floppy disk. Then click the
            Close button to close the Select Files dialog
            box.
Step 5.   Choose Copy... from the File menu to open
            the Copy dialog box.
Step 6.   In the TO box, type C:\ML_FORMS and
            click OK. Click OK again when you're
            asked if you want to copy the selected files
            to the C:\ML_FORMS directory.

3. Macintosh Users

Step 1.   If the ML_FORMS folder is open, close it.
Step 2.   Click on the ML_FORMS disk icon and
            drag it onto the icon of your hard disk.
Step 3.   Read the message to make sure you want to
            go ahead, then click OK.

4. DOS Users

(These instructions assume that the A: drive is the
source you want to copy from and that the C: drive is
the location you want to copy the files to.)

Step 1.   To create a directory named "ML_FORMS"
            on your C: hard disk drive, type the
            following at the DOS prompt:
            C: <ENTER>

CD\ <ENTER>
MD ML_FORMS <ENTER>

Step 2.   To change to the ML_FORMS directory you
            just created, type:
            CD ML_FORMS <ENTER>
Step 3.   To copy all the files from the floppy disk (in
            your A: drive) to the current directory, at
            the C:\ML_FORMS> prompt, type:
            XCOPY A:*.* /s <ENTER>

All of the files in all directories on the floppy disk
will be copied to the ML_FORMS directory on your C:
drive.

B. CREATING YOUR DOCUMENTS WITH THE FORMS DISK FILES

This disk contains all forms in two file types (or
formats):

- the standard ASCII text format (TXT), and
- rich text format (RTF).

For example, the form for the General Agreement
for Independent Contractors discussed in Chapter 4 is
on the files GEN2.RTF and GEN2.TXT.

ASCII text files can be read by every word processor
or text editor including DOS Edit, all flavors of MS
Word and WordPerfect (including Macintosh), Windows Notepad, Write and WordPad and Macintosh
SimpleText and TeachText.

RTF files have the same text as the ASCII files, but
have additional formatting. They can be read by most
recent word processing programs including all versions
of MS Word for Windows and Macintosh WordPad for
Windows 95 and recent versions of WordPerfect for
Windows and Macintosh.

To use a form on the disk to create your documents
you must: (1) open a file in your word processor or text
editor; (2) edit the form by filling in the required
information; (3) print it out; (4) save your revised file.

The following are general instructions on how to do
this. However, each word processor uses different
commands to open, format, save and print documents.

Please read your word processor's manual for specific instructions on performing these tasks.

DO NOT CALL NOLO'S TECHNICAL SUPPORT IF YOU HAVE QUESTIONS ON HOW TO USE YOUR WORD PROCESSOR.

Step 1: Opening a File

To open a file in your word processor, you need to start your word processing program and open the file from within the program. This process usually entails going to the File menu and choosing the Open command. This opens a dialog box where you will tell the program (1) the type of file you want to open (either *.TXT or *.RTF) and (2) the location and name of the file (you will need to navigate through the directory tree to get to the folder/directory on your hard disk that you created and copied the disk's files to). If these directions are unclear you will need to look through the manual for your word processing program—Nolo's technical support department will NOT be able to help you with the use of your word processing program.

WHICH FILE FORMAT SHOULD YOU USE?

If you are not sure which file format to use with your word processor, try opening the RTF files first. Rich text files (RTF) contain most of the formatting included in the sample forms found in this book and in Appendix B. Most current Windows and Macintosh word processing programs, such as Microsoft Word or WordPerfect, can read RTF files.

If you are unable to open the RTF file in your word processor, or a bunch of "garbage" characters appear on screen when you do, then use the TXT files instead. All word processors and text editors can read TXT files, which contain only text, tabs and carriage returns; all other formatting and special characters have been stripped.

Windows and Mac users can also open a file more directly by double-clicking on it. Use File Manager (Windows 3.1), My Computer or Windows Explorer (Windows 95) or the Finder (Macintosh) to go to the folder/directory you created and copied the disk's files to. Then, double-click on the specific file you want to open. If you click on an RTF file and you have a program installed that "understands" RTF, your word processor should launch and load the file that you double-clicked on. If the file isn't loaded, or if it contains a bunch of garbage characters, use your word processor's Open command, as described above, to open the TXT file instead. If you directly double-click on a TXT file, it will load into a basic text editor like Notepad or SimpleText rather than your word processor.

Step 2: Editing Your Document

Fill in the appropriate information according to the instructions and sample agreements in the book. Underlines are used to indicate where you need to enter your information, frequently followed by instructions in brackets. Be sure to delete the underlines and instructions from your edited document and, if necessary, renumber the clauses. If you do not know how to use your word processor to edit a document, you will need to look through the manual for your word processing program—Nolo's technical support department will NOT be able to help you with the use of your word processing program.

EDITING FORMS THAT HAVE OPTIONAL OR ALTERNATIVE TEXT

Some of the forms have check boxes before text. The check boxes indicate:

- optional text, which you choose whether to include or exclude

- alternative text, where you select one alternative to include and exclude the other alternatives.

If you are using the tear-out forms in the Appendix, you simply mark the appropriate box to make your choice.

If you are using the forms disk, however, we recommend that instead of marking the check boxes, you do the following:

Optional text

If you **don't want** to include optional text, just delete it from your document.

If you **do want** to include optional text, just leave it in your document.

In either case, delete the check box itself as well as the italicized instructions that the text is optional.

Alternative text

First delete all the alternatives that you do not want to include.

Then delete the remaining check box, as well as the italicized instructions that you need to select one of the alternatives provided.

Step 3: Printing Out the Document

Use your word processor's or text editor's Print command to print out your document. If you do not know how to use your word processor to print a document, you will need to look through the manual for your word processing program—Nolo's technical support department will NOT be able to help you with the use of your word processing program.

Step 4: Saving Your Document

After filling in the form, use the "Save As" command to save and rename the file. Because all the files are "read-only," you will not be able to use the "Save" command. This is for your protection.

IF YOU SAVE THE FILE WITHOUT RENAMING IT, THE UNDERLINES THAT INDICATE WHERE YOU NEED TO ENTER YOUR INFORMATION WILL BE LOST AND YOU WILL NOT BE ABLE TO CREATE A NEW DOCUMENT WITH THIS FILE WITHOUT RECOPYING THE ORIGINAL FILE FROM THE FLOPPY DISK. MAKE SURE NEVER TO EDIT THE ORIGINAL FILE ON YOUR FLOPPY.

If you do not know how to use your word processor to save a document, you will need to look through the manual for your word processing program—Nolo's technical support department will NOT be able to help you with the use of your word processing program. ■

Index

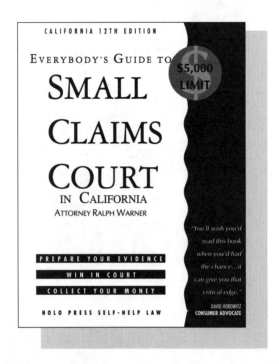

Take a minute & Get a 1-year
Nolo *News* subscription free!*

With our quarterly magazine, the **NOLO** *News*, you'll

- **Learn** about important legal changes that affect you
- **Find out first** about new Nolo products
- **Keep current** with practical articles on everyday law
- **Get answers** to your legal questions in *Ask Auntie Nolo's* advice column
- **Save money** with special Subscriber Only discounts
- **Tickle your funny bone** with our famous *Lawyer Joke* column.

It only takes a minute to reserve your free 1-year subscription or to extend your **NOLO** *News* subscription.

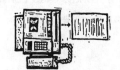

CALL	FAX	E-MAIL	OR MAIL US THIS REGISTRATION CARD
1-800-992-6656	1-800-645-0895	NOLOSUB@NOLOPRESS.com	

 *U.S. ADDRESSES ONLY. ONE YEAR INTERNATIONAL SUBSCRIPTIONS: CANADA & MEXICO $10.00; ALL OTHER FOREIGN ADDRESSES $20.00.

fold here

- -

NOLO
PRESS

REGISTRATION CARD

NAME _____ DATE _____

ADDRESS _____

CITY _____ STATE _____ ZIP _____

PHONE _____ E-MAIL _____

WHERE DID YOU HEAR ABOUT THIS PRODUCT? _____

WHERE DID YOU PURCHASE THIS PRODUCT? _____

DID YOU CONSULT A LAWYER? (PLEASE CIRCLE ONE)   YES   NO   NOT APPLICABLE

DID YOU FIND THIS BOOK HELPFUL?   (VERY)   5   4   3   2   1   (NOT AT ALL)

COMMENTS _____

_____

_____

_____

WAS IT EASY TO USE?   (VERY EASY)   5   4   3   2   1   (VERY DIFFICULT)

DO YOU OWN A COMPUTER? IF SO, WHICH FORMAT? (PLEASE CIRCLE ONE)   WINDOWS   DOS   MAC

❑ If you do not wish to receive mailings from these companies, please check this box.

❑ You can quote me in future Nolo Press promotional materials. Daytime phone number _____.

MIEN 1.0

NOLO IN THE NEWS

"**N**olo helps lay people perform legal tasks without the aid—or fees—of lawyers."

—USA TODAY

Nolo books are ..."written in plain language, free of legal mumbo jumbo, and spiced with witty personal observations."

—ASSOCIATED PRESS

"...Nolo publications...guide people simply through the how, when, where and why of law."

—WASHINGTON POST

"Increasingly, people who are not lawyers are performing tasks usually regarded as legal work... And consumers, using books like Nolo's, do routine legal work themselves."

—NEW YORK TIMES

"...All of [Nolo's] books are easy-to-understand, are updated regularly, provide pull-out forms...and are often quite moving in their sense of compassion for the struggles of the lay reader."

—SAN FRANCISCO CHRONICLE

fold here

- -

NOLO PRESS
950 Parker Street
Berkeley, CA 94710-9867

Attn: | **MIEN 1.0** |